THE SPY WHO HELPED THE SOVIETS WIN STALINGRAD & KURSK

THE SPY WHO HELPED THE SOVIETS WIN STALINGRAD & KURSK

ALEXANDER FOOTE AND THE LUCY SPY RING

CHRIS JONES

Pen & Sword
MILITARY

AN IMPRINT OF PEN & SWORD BOOKS LTD.
YORKSHIRE – PHILADELPHIA

First published in Great Britain in 2025 by
Pen & Sword Military
An imprint of
Pen & Sword Books Ltd
Yorkshire - Philadelphia

Copyright © Chris Jones, 2025

ISBN 978 1 03611 572 2

The right of Chris Jones to be identified as the Author of this work has been asserted by him in accordance with the Copyright, Designs and Patents Act 1988.

A CIP catalogue record for this book is available from the British Library.

All rights reserved. No part of this book may be reproduced or transmitted in any form or by any means, electronic or mechanical, including photocopying, recording or by any information storage and retrieval system, without permission from the Publisher in writing.

Typeset in INDIA by IMPEC eSolutions
Printed and bound in the United States of America by
Integrated Books International.

Pen & Sword Books Limited incorporates the imprints of Archaeology, Atlas, Aviation, Battleground, Digital, Discovery, Family History, Fiction, History, Local, Local History, Maritime, Military, Military Classics, Politics, Select, Transport, True Crime, After the Battle, Air World, Claymore Press, Frontline Publishing, Leo Cooper, Remember When, Seaforth Publishing, The Praetorian Press, Wharncliffe Books, Wharncliffe Local History, Wharncliffe Transport, Wharncliffe True Crime and White Owl.

For a complete list of Pen & Sword titles please contact

PEN & SWORD BOOKS LIMITED
47 Church Street, Barnsley, South Yorkshire, S70 2AS, England
E-mail: enquiries@pen-and-sword.co.uk
Website: www.pen-and-sword.co.uk

or

PEN AND SWORD BOOKS
1950 Lawrence Rd, Havertown, PA 19083, USA
E-mail: uspen-and-sword@casematepublishers.com
Website: www.penandswordbooks.com

Contents

A Note on the Images — viii

Foreword: Trust nobody. Doubt everything. Everybody is lying. — ix

Chapter One   Early life and personal qualities — 1
A knock on the door in the middle of the night — 1
The boy born in Kirkdale, Liverpool — 2
The character of Alexander Foote — 5
The politics of Alexander Foote — 9

Chapter Two   Spain — 12
Spain and the International Brigade — 12

Chapter Three   London — 17
Recruitment to Soviet intelligence — 17
The Agnes Zimmerman affair — 21

Chapter Four   Germany — 25
Agent Sonya: Superspy — 25
The Franz Obermanns affair — 25
The arrival of Len Beurton — 27

Chapter Five   Switzerland — 36
Sándor Radó (Codename Dora): Resident Director, Geneva — 36

	Structure of the *Rote Drei*	42
	Codename Lucy	46
Chapter Six	Lausanne	51
	Radio Station Foote, Apartment 45, Chemin de Longeraie 2, Lausanne	51
	Foote's network in Lausanne	59
	Political pressure on the Swiss	63
	Foote and the financing of the *Rote Drei*	67
	The Rachel Dübendorfer affair	71
	Lorenz and Laura	73
	Foote's attempted abduction by the Abwehr	74
	Foote and the rounding up of the Radó network	75
Chapter Seven	Paris	90
	Arrival: 7 November 1944	90
Chapter Eight	Moscow	94
	Arrival: 16 January 1945	94
	Interrogation One: Moscow	96
Chapter Nine	Berlin	105
	Alone in Berlin: 7 March 1947	105
Chapter Ten	Hanover – The MI5 files	108
	Interrogation One: Saturday morning, 19 July 1947	114
	Interrogation Two: Saturday afternoon, 19 July 1947	116

	Interrogation Three: Sunday morning, 20 July 1947	118
	Interrogation Four: Sunday afternoon, 20 July 1947	122
	Interrogation Five: Monday morning, 21 July 1947	126
Chapter Eleven	London	128
	Arrival: 7 August 1947	128
	British attitudes to Foote	131
	Foote's prospects	134
	Handbook For Spies	140
	Responses to *Handbook for Spies*	144
	The reception of *Handbook for Spies* in Switzerland	146
Chapter Twelve	Controversies	150
	Foote, Agent Sonya and Roger Hollis	150
	The background of Roger Hollis	151
	Was Foote a double agent for the British?	160
	A double agent theory of my own	176
Chapter Thirteen	Decline and Fall	181

Epilogue: And in the end, a personal view   184

Bibliography   190

Endnotes   192

Index   200

A Note on the Images

Every attempt has been made to track down the sources of the images used in this work. The people who took the photographs, like their subjects, are frequently long dead. But still, I would like to acknowledge the kindness of the following people and organisations for the use of images in this book.

The archive of Drago Arsenijevic. Several photographs from this archive were published in his book *Genève Appelle Moscou* published by Robert Lafont, Paris 1969.

The screenshot of the article 'Un Parfait Gentleman' was reproduced with the kind permission of Monique GRABER at *Le Temps* newspaper publishers, Geneva.

Der Spiegel were endlessly supportive in providing a high quality print of their 1954 cover featuring Alexander Foote.

I would also like to thank Jessica Brändli of the Archiv für Zeitgeschicte ETH Zürich for her assistance in providing high definition images.

A further source of images was Werner Ring's 1974 book *Schweiz am Krieg* published by Ex Libris books, Zürich.

I would also like to express my appreciation for the work of The National Archives; an incredible resource.

Foreword: Trust nobody. Doubt everything. Everybody is lying.

At the risk of running ahead of the story of Alexander Foote, the boy from Kirkdale in Liverpool, it would be well to reflect on the quality of the information on which this history is based. Reading about the life and times of Alexander Foote is a confusing and disorientating experience. It is hard to distinguish truth from clever deceit. Nobody – nobody at all – can be entirely trusted when talking about this period. The political sensitivities of the actors or their masters must always be taken into account when consulting sources. What is one to make of an account of Foote's spying activities published by the CIA at the height of the 'Reds Under The Beds' panic in the USA of the 1950s? Can an autobiography published by a state publishing house in a country behind the Iron Curtain ever be trusted to be clear of political interference? The accounts offered by the people who lived through the events about to be described all differ in mutually contradictory ways and none of them, as we shall see, are entirely free from lies, omissions and self aggrandising overstatement. Even the dates they give for events do not match. All of the main actors cast doubt on the motives driving their former comrades to put pen to paper, and possibly because he was the first person to write about their spy ring, Alexander Foote was subject to the most criticism.

Foote's memoir, *Handbook for Spies*, is an excellent example of how hard it is to trust the words one is reading. In time, Foote came to be highly critical of it himself and described his story as being 'mangled' by the man paid to write it, though he must surely have seen the final draft before it went to the printers, right? According to Roger Hollis of MI5, the book was ghost-written for him at 'four shillings a line' by a man called Courtenay Young, a career MI5 officer. This was not the name Young gave to Foote however; that was Bernard Willis, a codename. According to Young, he was well qualified for the job because as a secret service man he could give MI5 control over Foote's narrative. He said this quite explicitly when he volunteered for the job. At one point in Foote's MI5 file, Young even mentioned that Foote's book had been discussed with the CIA when they visited London.[1] As engaging and entertaining as Foote's book is, the thought that one is actually reading the words of one of his MI5 handlers tends to compromise trust in his account. Foote was told in no uncertain terms about what he was and was not allowed to talk about. Michael Serpell, who had first interrogated him in Hanover, laid down the law when he said:

> We had no objection to him publishing the story of his life providing the story ended with him leaving the Russian zone of Berlin. It is essential that he should make no reference whatsoever to his connections with British intelligence. I went on to emphasise that this was a general reservation and that Foote's relations with British intelligence were not to be mentioned to anyone.[2]

Foote, as we shall see, was adept at conveying to his interrogators a version of events, and of his beliefs, that he felt suited the demands of his interrogators. This ability probably saved him from a long sentence in one of Stalin's prison camps, which was the fate of many of his less flexible comrades. When he presented himself to the British authorities, it is entirely possible that he tailored the account he gave of his life to what he felt they would like to hear.

In this history every effort has been made to follow a hierarchy of evidence. Eye witness accounts have been given top priority, even though they disagree one with another on occasions – sometimes vehemently. Sometimes they may also be demonstrably untruthful. The unity of purpose and regard for each other's interests evaporated quickly as the war was ending. Comradely regard for each other broke down into mutual recrimination and denunciation. Foote saw the sale of his somewhat romanticised version of events as his chance for a comfortable post-war existence, particularly if Hollywood took up the option of turning his life into a movie. Of the eye witness accounts of the period, that of Sándor Radó convinces the reader the most, certainly this reader. This is because he seeks to deduct from the story any of the exaggeration that started to glamourise the wartime events in Switzerland from the 1960s onward. Radó's autobiography seeks to de-glorify his own role in the events and he displays a laudable modesty. On the other hand, it has been revealed that his book was subject to both Hungarian and Soviet 'editorial assistance' with approximately 10 per cent of its original content censored.[3] Radó also neglected to mention the fact that his reward for his vital, risky and unrelenting assistance to Soviet intelligence was a ten-year sentence in a labour camp. This is how he described the period in which he was in hiding from the Swiss police and German intelligence, the Abwehr, stuck in a tiny room with his wife Hélène:

> I think it was perhaps the hardest period of my whole life except the post-war years that were the lot I shared with many others as a result of false accusations made at a time when socialist justice was in abeyance.[4]

'When socialist justice was in abeyance' is Stalinist speak for 'when I was banged up for ten years for nothing'. Nobody in these sources is entirely to be trusted, not even the noble Radó, who was described by Arthur Koestler as 'one of the most remarkable personalities I have met ... short, rather fattish, with a round gentle scholarly face. He was kind and warm-hearted by nature.'[5]

Ursula Kuczynski, Agent Sonya, is not above this sort of talk either. Berating Foote for his exposure of the Swiss network to British intelligence she said:

> In contrast to such wretched characters as Jim [Foote], there are comrades like Gabo, Rolf and hundreds of others who experienced harder times than he did in this period of deviations and mistakes – and never wavered. As soon as they were free, they worked on as communists.

Deviations and mistakes is one way of describing a ten-year stretch in Siberia, which was the fate of her first husband, also a Soviet spy. And if only this was the fate of mere 'hundreds'! How many thousands of the other unfortunate victims of these 'mistakes' never came home?

When it comes to second-hand accounts of the events in Switzerland the reader must be even more careful. It is a minefield. In *Operation Lucy* by Read and Fisher, to take one example, some very great claims are made with some very tenuous evidence to support them. Claims made that Foote was a British agent from the outset of the war in Spain are made without any reference to the sources these claims are based on. It is not possible therefore to assess the strength of their evidence when reading their admittedly enjoyable and novelistic history of events. For instance, they report a conversation with Fred Copeman, Foote's International Brigade commander, without any hint of the context or content of the conversation that can be independently evaluated. Copeman is acknowledged in the foreword and thanked as a contact but it is never absolutely clear that their play-like account of Copeman's words was not a case of 'scene added for dramatic effect'. Anthony Read was after all a writer of TV dramas. The only written evidence Read and Fisher present is a bibliography at the end of their book, and if readers wish to check their sources they must read all the books in their list with no guarantee that any reliable evidence will be forthcoming. There are no page references to guide the reader to relevant sections of the books they used.

Foote's name itself requires some caution. On his birth certificate he was registered as Alexander Allan Foote. Biographical references to him almost universally use the forename Alexander. Anybody intimate with him used the name Allan. He is referred to by his comrades and by Moscow Centre as 'Jim', his codename. He had at least four other names, some of which went with a passport. This study will use the name Alexander.

In fact names are quite a problem when following the subject of the *Rote Drei* (Red Three), as Foote's team came to be known. Between real names, codenames, anglicised German names and pseudonyms used in the histories of the period by authors who, for their own reasons, did not wish to identify the real actors in this drama, it can be a hard subject to follow.

In referencing the MI5 files from The National Archives (released in 2004) page numbers have been added as they are annotated by the Adobe PDF reader, and in addition an indication of where references are situated in the overall file, that is (page) 31/80 (pages in total).

Finally, I have used some software to calculate the value of 1930s and 1940s money into modern Sterling. This was trickier than I thought it would be. Inflation, devaluations and currency market instability will affect any such calculations. Please regard all equivalents as highly approximated.

Chapter One

Early life and personal qualities

A knock on the door in the middle of the night

At 01.00 on 20 November 1943, Alexander Allan Foote was sitting in his flat on the top floor of an apartment block in Lausanne. Chain smoking at his Morse code key, he was tapping away some of the most guarded secrets of the German high command. In the USSR the radio operators of Soviet military intelligence sat at their receivers twenty-four hours a day waiting for Foote's call sign 'FRX…FRX…FRX'. For the previous two years Comrade Jim, Foote's codename, had been informing the Russians of the most intimate details of German troop movements, arms supplies and morale. Generals of the Red Army had planned much of their strategy in the battles of Stalingrad and Kursk around the information coming from Foote and the transmitters of two of his comrades based in Geneva.

But tonight was different. At 01.15 Comrade Jim heard the rumble of men's boots approaching his front door. This was a moment he had been dreading. He had read in the Swiss press that arrests had been made in Geneva of people with illegal shortwave radio transmitters. He had heard the call signs of his Geneva comrades coming from Russia and not being replied to. The question for Foote was this: who was approaching his door? Was it the Swiss police? Or was it German military intelligence? This meant the difference between the relative comfort of a Swiss prison cell or a Gestapo cellar, as German intelligence officers sought to uncover the sources of his information. After all, he knew that the Germans were on to him. German agents had been asking questions about him in his neighbourhood and he had been the subject

2 The Spy Who Helped the Soviets Win Stalingrad and Kursk

of an abduction attempt, thought later to have been the work of Klaus Barbie the 'Butcher of Lyon'. So, who was it now beating on his door?

Foote had collected items on his desk for this moment. There was lighter fluid and a hammer. The hammer was depicted on the cover of a book written about Foote's espionage network in 1966. As he heard his door being broken open, he collected his messages and his code book and dropped them into a large brass ash tray. Then he squirted them with lighter fluid and set them on fire. With whoever it was now beating their way in through the heavy doors of his flat, he smashed the delicate mechanism of his radio with his hammer.

By now the intruders were inside so that Foote came to know his captors: two senior Swiss police officers and a Swiss code breaker. His relief must have been enormous. With his ashtray in flames and the wreckage of his radio on his desk, he turned to his uninvited guests and said 'Good evening, gentlemen. Would anyone care for a glass of Scotch?'

Thus ended the radio career of one of the most successful Soviet spies of the Second World War. This is the story of how a boy from Kirkdale in Liverpool came to change the course of the war against Nazism.

The boy born in Kirkdale, Liverpool

> 'In my opinion the bizarre character of the late Alexander Foote, with whom I became briefly acquainted, rates a biographical study on his own account.'
>
> Paraphrased from Malcolm Muggeridge, 1980

On the wall of 'The Casa', a bar owned by ex-dockers on Hope Street in Liverpool, there hangs a long list of names. It contains the names of all the men from Liverpool who went to fight in support of the Spanish Republican government in the late 1930s. The list sits among an impressive collection of memorabilia from the Spanish Civil War. One of the columns includes the name of 'Foote Alec A'. This is a reference to Alexander Allan Foote, born at 7 Rockley Street on 14 April 1905. His parents were William and May Foote, and they lived in the working-class district of Kirkdale. They were of Scottish and English heritage, respectively.

William Foote was described on the birth certificate as a 'poultry farm manager'.[6] Alexander had two sisters. The most that has been published about the early life of Alexander Allan Foote is in the book *Operation Lucy* by Read and Fisher.[7] They conjure a picture of an unhappy family in which the patriarch, fleeing from professional failure to professional failure, was permanently brutish to his wife and his only son. He mocked his wife for her accent and took against his son from his earliest days.[8] It is impossible to evaluate the truth of this assessment because the authors give no reference for the reader to check their interpretation of events. Foote's sister Margaret is thanked in the foreword of the book for her assistance but it is left to the reader to infer that these insights derive from an interview with her. No information is given about how or where such an interview took place. In a post-war interview with British intelligence, Foote described his father as being 'queer like me', and being one-track-minded about poultry farming. His father does not appear to have been responsible for the affable ease which so many people commented on in Foote's later life.

It is something of a stretch to describe Foote as being a Liverpool volunteer. Certainly he was born in Liverpool, but by 1910 he was registered in a school in Brodsworth, Yorkshire. His family were registered there in the 1911 census. Later addresses placed him in Manchester in 1920, where he would eventually be trained as an apprentice motor mechanic and later on as a salesman at the Forder and Dodge engineering works. He went back to live with his parents in Northenden in Manchester, where he worked for a time as a corn merchant, selling chicken food.[9] In a post-war interview with MI5 he also stated that he had lived for a time at 313A Winslow Road, Fallowfield, Manchester, with 'an artist' called Charles Barber, who he described as being 'leftish' but not Marxist.[10]

Foote's connection with Liverpool was never revived and there is no evidence that he had any relatives in the city. He is also claimed as an ex-International Brigadier by other regions in the country, where he may have lived for a longer period.[11] His peripatetic life would make it hard for any city or region to claim Foote as a citizen, even if they wanted to. But Liverpool was his birthplace, and his birthplace was within walking distance of Scottie Road. Liverpool has a strong claim to him.

Foote said this of his early life:

> A psychoanalyst would be hard put to find anything in my early life which would indicate that one day I would be running a portion of a Soviet network. My upbringing was as ordinary as that of any child of middle-class parentage brought up between the wars. On leaving school I tried my hands at many jobs, ranging from managing a small business to running a garage, but never found anything which satisfied me for any length of time. I moved from job to job hoping that I would one day find something which suited me.[12]

This was not the recollection of his sister Margaret. At least, of all the people that Read and Fisher interviewed for their book *Operation Lucy*, she is the likeliest unreferenced source of this insight into Foote's early years:

> Allan's best friend as a boy was the local vicar's son. Growing up during the First World War naturally influenced them. Perhaps this was the reason why Allan Foote's favourite boyhood game was pretending to be a spy, and why he always said his ambition was to become one![13]

In 1935 Foote, now 30, signed up with the Royal Air Force for a six-year term, describing his religion as 'free thinker' on his enlistment forms. Recruited in Manchester, he was subsequently stationed in Gosport on the Hampshire coast where he was employed as a fitter. He became an aircraftman first class, but on 23 December 1936 he was declared illegally absent from his post. He had left the country on that date and he next surfaced in Albacete in Spain, having signed up for the British section of the 15th International Brigade.

Alexander Foote had an extraordinary life that led to him being a transmitter by radio of some of Germany's most closely guarded military secrets at the height of the war against the USSR. Foote's career as a spy concluded in him returning ten years later to Britain, through the British section of Berlin in 1947. He emerged from the Russian sector of that devastated city requesting that he be put in touch with British intelligence. When he was introduced to an appropriate officer he made them an offer: he wanted repatriation to Britain and the renewal of his British passport in return for chapter and verse information about the Russian Intelligence Services (RIS) as seen from the inside. From this point on, every aspect of Foote's life was enquired into by the security services, just as it had recently been in Moscow.

The files relating to his numerous interrogations and the correspondence about him amounted to five volumes in the end, held by MI5. They are all now declassified and sit in The National Archives. They are downloadable as PDF files free of charge to holders of a reader's card. Their catalogue numbers are KV 2_1611 to KV 2_1616, inclusive. These files are broken down into smaller packages and are numbered with a suffix _1, _2, _3 etc. Collectively, they are a window into some of the most sensitive espionage operations conducted by Soviet intelligence at a crucial time in the Second World War. And they lay bare the invaluable role played on behalf of Soviet intelligence by the boy from Liverpool. It is no exaggeration to say that the activities of Alexander Allan Foote ('Jim') may have altered the course of the war on the Eastern Front, in favour of our ally at the time, the USSR.

The character of Alexander Foote

> 'Alexander Allan Foote is one of the most important, but also one of the most enduringly mysterious, figures in modern espionage history.'[14]
> Ben Macintyre in *Agent Sonya* (2020)

6 The Spy Who Helped the Soviets Win Stalingrad and Kursk

As with so much of Foote's history, an analysis of his character rather depends on the opinion of the person who is conveying the impression. He was tall and well-built but, according to the director of his espionage network Sándor Radó, he had the sort of pallor that suggested an underlying long-term medical problem. He was affable and humorous but with a sense of humour that suggested a cynical view of the world. He had an eye for the ladies but was also popular with his female friends. He gave his communist friends cause for believing that he may have been a little too fond of the good things in life.

Ursula Kuczynski, the famous Agent Sonya who was his first contact with Soviet intelligence in Switzerland, recalled her first meeting with Foote:

> He grasped things quickly and asked sensible questions. He seemed resourceful and shrewd; that was an advantage in our work; in new and unaccustomed situations, Jim would react quickly … Jim made a good impression on me and, with a few minor exceptions, so it remained for the whole period of our work together … from the beginning I had noticed his taste for the good life and the gourmet approach to food and drink. During our first conversations he also showed a tendency towards cynicism … He was tall and a bit overweight. His appearance was very acceptable and he knew how to behave.[15]

It is perhaps a measure of Foote's character that he recalled his first meeting with Sonya quite differently. He described his new comrade as having 'a good figure and even better legs'.[16] In Munich and Switzerland, Foote played the part of the eccentric Englishman with a private income. His northern accent might have suggested something else to a fellow Briton, but this was convincingly disguised when speaking in another language. Sándor Radó said that he spoke German poorly but French better.

Quick wit and intelligence is not the impression that comes across in Foote's interrogation by MI5 after the war. Here he was described as being a half-witted semi-illiterate with a catastrophic overestimation of his own abilities. Perhaps this can be explained, at least in part, by the snobbishness which pervaded the secret services in the 1940s. The fact that Foote did not come with a public school accent and an Oxbridge degree in itself may have condemned him in the eyes of his interrogators.

The television intellectual and public moralist Malcolm Muggeridge, himself a grammar school boy, gave a different account of Foote's character than his erstwhile intelligence colleagues. Muggeridge too had been a British spy during the war:

> Foote was a burly, genial and humorous Englishman whom I got to know in his last years. His political sympathies were and remained leftish but ... I never had the feeling that he was capable of revolutionary fanaticism or especially interested in revolutionary doctrine. He was just a nice, easy going man who was caught up momentarily in the gale and whirlwind of our time.

When it came out in Switzerland that Foote had been spying, the news came as a shock to his friends in Lausanne. One of them was quoted in the *Gazette de Lausanne* and her comments were reprinted by Tarrant in *The Red Orchestra*:[17]

> He was stout and placid with small porcelain like eyes and thin blond hair. He once made an appearance in our group and nobody gave him a second thought. He was the least mysterious fellow in the world! His face was so completely unexpressive that he never aroused curiosity on the part of his friends. Foote pretended to be in Switzerland for reasons of health. We made fun of his imaginary ills, which we suspected were a cover for his innate laziness. However, his paleness and slight cough, which he exhibited at the right moment, made these reasons plausible. He used to drink a lot, but never too much. He enjoyed eating immensely; he gave

the impression that if the restaurant and the whole town collapsed completely he would not let himself be disturbed. He was a perfect listener. Every little story made him laugh heartily, but noiselessly; even when his pale eyes brightened during conversations on military matters, nobody became suspicious. Everybody liked him very much.

The American historian David Dallin, who had met Foote on visits to Britain while researching for his book on Soviet intelligence, was impressed by what he found:

Foote had the personal traits which are prerequisites for a successful spy. His capacity for work was astounding. He performed duties which would normally require a team, and often slept without undressing. He worked at night and spent his days with his non-communist friends. Moderately tall, quiet in demeanour, somewhat heavy, he had unusual composure and could not easily be embarrassed by a question. To the police he appeared a well to do, politically innocent Englishman with enough funds to permit him to live in leisure in Lausanne far from the commotion of war.[18]

Accoce and Quet published a different vision of Foote, without having had any recorded meetings with him:

Foote's life had been a chaotic one – he seemed fated to become a secret agent. He was an anxious, insecure man. He belonged to that category of human beings that is perpetually unsatisfied. They love money but abhor work. They are possessed by a lust for power but paralysed by timidity. They rage constantly at their own failure, but do nothing to escape from it. The profession of espionage provides them with that escape.[19]

The politics of Alexander Foote

> 'Foote is most insistent that he has never been a party member, that he is a Marxist and not a communist.'[20]
>
> Interview with Michael Serpell of MI5 in 1947

It is not clear what politics Alexander Foote had before he emerged as an International Brigadier. There are few landmarks to define his political outlook. It is not uncommon to read statements that he originally had conservative views but these are usually from secondary, unverifiable sources. According to Foote he was not a member of the Communist Party and never had been. This was not everyone's opinion, as we shall see.

His motivation in becoming a spy puzzled Foote as much as anyone else:

> It is difficult for anyone, including myself, to look back dispassionately and objectively at those times and try to analyse the feelings one had and the motives for one's actions. It was not really political sense or political education, leading me from the industrial Midlands to Switzerland, to post-war Russia and ultimately back to England again. From a restless sales manager to a Russian spy is a difficult game of consequences.[21]

Agent Sonya (writing under the nom de plume Ruth Werner) contended that he joined the Spanish Communist Party and joined the British Communist Party when he arrived back from Spain, but in this I think she may have been mistaken – or worse, propagandising.[22] She may have been seeking to present the anti-Nazi struggle in Europe as being exclusively communist in inspiration, because she said that Len Beurton was in the Communist Party too. Whatever his politics in the post-war period, Beurton was not in the Communist Party in 1938.

It is true that Foote attended the national congress of the Communist Party in Birmingham when he arrived back from Spain, but it was with a visitor's pass and not as a member.

After the war, Foote described himself as a mere 'fellow traveller' and struck his MI5 interrogators in 1947 as being ignorant of the basics of Marxist theory and of the communist view of the world. One of his MI5 interviewers pretty much hit the nail on the head when he wrote that Foote 'eschewed the wordy side of Bolshevik life'. In these interviews Foote described himself as a 'bit of a bolshie' and as a 'true socialist', and said that he thought Britain would become a socialist state one day. But he worried that the headlong rush to socialism under Attlee would land Britain with the sort of over-centralised system which afflicted Russia, as he put it.[23]

His lack of any firm political background would presumably have made him an ideal clean skin recruit for any intelligence service. A background full of letters to communist newspapers, office holding in communist organisations and family connections to well known party activists would be easily discoverable by a hostile service.

In a meeting with his sister, Margaret Powell, after the war, which was bugged by MI5, Foote came out with some highly pro-German, anti-socialist and anti-Semitic remarks. It is not clear whether he was playing to the gallery and seeking to impress his MI5 eavesdroppers that he was now one of them, but the views that he expressed to Mrs Powell were a long way from the ones that took him to Spain. He said that the Russian state was more Nazi than the one he saw in Germany. He said that he foresaw the far right coming to power in Britain and in Germany and continuing the extermination of the Jews. He said that the German occupation of countries had been gentlemanly and disciplined compared to the occupation of Germany by the British and the Americans. His journey from International Brigade leftist to pro-German reactionary was apparently complete. After saying that, this impression can hardly be squared with that of Muggeridge, published in 1967. This conveyed the image of a man of mild left-wing attitude.

In Foote's autobiographical book, ghost-written it should be remembered by an MI5 officer, he does not drift into discussions of politics much, if at all. He seemed to regard himself as a sort of civil servant in the struggle against Nazism; a man preoccupied with operationalising the practicalities of the war without paying too much attention to its political aspects.

Chapter Two

Spain

Spain and the International Brigade

However vague Foote's political ideas were, it was to be Spain which condensed them into something like an ideology:

> The outbreak of the Spanish Civil War crystallised my somewhat inchoate thoughts on the whole matter. Until that time I had been convinced that something was wrong but had found precise analysis difficult. The Civil War in Spain seemed to show everything in neat black and white, and I was convinced that the Rebels were inspired and supported by the German-Italian Fascists ... Ranged against these enemies of democracy were the Spanish Republican government, almost alone ... Rallying to their aid were only the freedom loving individuals of the world and the Soviet Union.

Foote had been recommended for recruitment in the International Brigade by a leading member of the Communist Party in Portsmouth, Archie Campbell Williams. When he was in the RAF, Foote was put in contact with Williams by a friend called Corporal Barnes. Barnes knew Williams' wife, who was an active Communist Party member in Gosport. Williams was already known to the secret services and it was he who first accompanied Foote to 16 King Street in Covent Garden, the headquarters of the Communist Party of Great Britain. There, he vouched for him as a possible recruit for the International Brigade at the same time as he himself volunteered. They went to Paris on a weekend ticket, thereby getting around the need for a passport. Williams and Foote went to Spain in the same group of sixteen men and were stationed at Albacete. Barnes was supposed to travel with them too, but never volunteered.

His motivation for travelling to Spain was as strong in 1949 as it was in 1936: 'I myself ... departed to fight for my clear cut ideals; to fight to prevent Fascism from overrunning Europe.' Looking back on his time in Spain the personal cost for Foote, for good and ill, was clear:

> Too many of my comrades have died to make it easy for me to write about it at all. It was for me merely a halting place on my way. The fact that I did not realise that it was only a halting place and regarded it as the be-all-and-end-all of my existence at the time is neither here nor there. For me the war was a struggle where my friends fought and died.[24]

Foote was quickly given the rank of sergeant in the transport section of the battalion. Written after his defection from the Soviet service, Foote looked back on his time in the International Brigade with a somewhat jaundiced eye:

> Ranks at this time bore little relation to fact. I was not 'politically reliable' and as such ranked lower in the political hierarchy than the fellow comrade who had sold the Daily Worker with distinction in North Shields. Though I never achieved commissioned rank, I performed all the duties for my battalion which would have been carried out in the British Army by a transport officer.[25]

Keen, brave and resourceful, he accompanied Fred Copeman, the battalion commander, 'wherever he went'. Copeman was quoted by Read and Fisher as saying that Foote was particularly useful in resourcing materials and facilities such as beds, food and headquarters. This took the weight of this type of activity from Copeman's shoulders and allowed him to get on with his duties commanding the battalion.[26] While in Spain, Foote mixed with all the leading British Communist Party members, not just Fred Copeman. This included Dave Springhall and Peter Kerrigan, who were both political commissars.[27] Copeman was quoted in Read and Fisher's book as having the highest regard for Foote's hard work and courage under fire. He was also known to Copeman as a 'fixer' who could make things happen. Good in a tight spot and able to think quickly on his feet, it is not surprising that Copeman thought Foote to be a good fit for his mission abroad.

Foote was variously described in different sources as a 'batman' or as a 'driver' in thumbnail descriptions of him in Spain. The International Brigade Archive of volunteers lists him as a batman. But to be so close to the leadership of the brigades must have meant that he was a man of solid reputation, trusted with valuable information at this crucial time. Late in the war he was given the job of driving an ambulance transporting wounded men back to the UK and using the return journey to Spain to courier messages and cash from the Communist Party leadership in London to the front line. With sixteen others, he re-entered Britain on 16 October 1938; but history intervened with this plan to return to Spain, however, and in 1938 the International Brigades were withdrawn when defeat for the republican government was seen as inevitable. This scattered the Brigade volunteers who had managed to evade the prisons of General Franco and quashed Foote's intention to return.

In Britain after the war, Foote played down any burning political zeal which had driven him to Spain. In his autobiography published in 1949 he said 'I joined the International Brigade and fought in Spain partly because of a love of adventure and partly because I felt the cause was right.'[28] By the time of the publication of his book he had come to a different view of the role of the USSR in Spain. He frequently, and in detail, made the claim that Stalin was keen to use the battles on the peninsula as a testing ground for his armed forces, their tactics and their weapons. He made the claim on numerous occasions that Spain was 'the European Salisbury Plain for trying out their own war machines'. An example of this was something Foote referred to as the 'Moscow Operation' during the battle of the Ebro, which he thought would be 'long remembered by those who were lucky enough to survive it'. In this operation the Russians supplied tanks to the republicans to be used in an innovative battle strategy. They were manned by German volunteers who had been trained in a Soviet tank school. Whatever the virtues of their strategy, it was pointed out to the Russians that artillery bombardment had caused irrigation ditches to leak and the battlefield was now a tank-hostile quagmire. The Chief of Staff of the International Brigade, Malcolm Dunbar,[29] pointed this out to anybody who would listen. But, as Foote drily put it: 'Moscow orders were orders'. Twelve out of the forty tanks returned. The rest were captured intact. 'I trust that the lesson was instructive to the Russian observers. It certainly was to the surviving tank crews, who drove their Russian commander back to the base area never to be seen again.'[30]

The most comprehensive description of Foote's time in the International Brigade is in Read and Fisher's *Operation Lucy*. Again, there is no reference and little to convince the reader that their account was a verbatim record. Assuming that what they wrote was the transcript of a conversation with Fred Copeman, a picture is painted of a man used to military discipline, a man already a non-commissioned officer and a man of intelligence. They portray a man of great courage. For instance, on one occasion Foote assisted Copeman and a wounded comrade to escape from a trench while under fire. Copeman needed such men around him and appointed him as his personal driver. This meant transporting people and equipment, sometimes at great personal risk.

It was Foote's ability to 'fix' things which appealed most to Copeman, argued Read and Fisher. He could lay his hands on food, drink and equipment almost at will. They quote an instance where he managed to acquire a car he had found 'abandoned' in Madrid. It carried a plaque saying that it was the donation of the students at Oxford University. This was the car he drove Copeman around in. Read and Fisher describe several instances of Foote's derring-do adventures with Copeman, including driving the 'Al Capone style' (Read and Fisher) car over irrigation ditches with Franco's Moorish soldiers in hot pursuit.

In 1938 Copeman was sent home after an operation to remove a gangrenous appendix. Foote would follow him home later in the year driving an ambulance.[31] They would meet up again in London.

When he signed up for the International Brigade in 1936, Foote's politics were vague. By the time he got to Moscow in 1944, however, he enthusiastically played up the political side of his decision to go and fight. In Moscow he knew that a strong political pedigree might keep him out of a labour camp. Foote was nothing if not adaptable.

Chapter Three

London

Recruitment to Soviet intelligence

Back in Britain in 1938, and with a record of desertion from the RAF, Foote was invited to a chat at 16 King Street, where he was interviewed by his old pal Fred Copeman:[32]

> He invited me to his flat in Lewisham for a meal with him and his wife. After supper, the next move was made. 'Springhall has been asked to recommend someone for an assignment. We have discussed various people and think that you might fit the bill. I know nothing about the assignment save that it will be abroad and will be very dangerous.' I think that was all that Fred Copeman did in fact know.[33]

In Agent Sonya's autobiography she said she had requested a comrade 'from Austria or Czechoslovakia' for a recommendation of a likely candidate for this mission. Sonya's biographer states that she was probably referring to Austrian communist Fred Uhlman. He in turn passed on to Dave Springhall the request for an ex-Brigadier nomination for the job. Springhall and Copeman settled on Foote as the ideal candidate. Foote's agreement in principle with this suggestion led to a further interview in Belsize Park, Hampstead. Here he met Brigitte Lewis (née Kuczynski, pronounced Ko-chin-ski).

In a later interview with MI5 Foote said that he also thought Dave Springhall[34] was behind the recommendation for the new role. Springhall was later expelled from the Communist Party for engaging in espionage for the USSR. He also received a seven year prison sentence.

Characteristically, Foote got on well with Brigitte and it is suggested in his MI5 files that his relationship with her bordered on flirtation. There is a note in his file which says that Foote seemed surprised to hear that Brigitte was married as he felt that he got on so well with her.

The assessment of his political reliability was stretched over a number of informal interviews by shrewd and experienced comrades. Copeman, Brigitte Lewis and finally Brigitte's sister, Ursula Kuczynski (codename Agent Sonya), all assessed Foote and found him politically and personally suitable. In Sonya's case this meant choosing Foote for espionage work when she knew that her life might depend on Foote's reliability. Foote later recalled:

> Despite the vagueness of the offer I jumped at it. Looking back on the whole affair in cold blood, it is a little difficult to understand why I should have accepted such an assignment with no notion whom I was working for or for what purpose.[35]

And yet ... even at this stage there were reasons to doubt whether Foote's devotion to the cause was entirely wholehearted. When the Nazi-Soviet pact was announced in 1939 it came as a shattering blow to Sonya and Len Beurton (codename John), the Independent Labour Party comrade who had come from Britain to join the group on Foote's recommendation. Their entire worldview was compromised by the apparent cynicism of this Soviet manoeuvre. But, according to Sándor Radó, the Red Army intelligence Resident Director in Switzerland, Foote was hardly bothered by it at all. Radó was not impressed by Foote's political education in the least and seemed to regard Foote as something of a political dunce:

> Shortly before she left Sonya introduced me ... to Alexander Foote (codename 'Jim') ... thanks to what Sonya had told me, [I] was able to form a pretty clear picture of the Englishman. The impression I received was a rather mixed one. Foote was undoubtedly an

intelligent and determined man ... His schooling was only moderate and he had never learned a trade ... What most surprised me was his total lack of political education ... the man had trouble finding his bearings in the complicated international situation and probably had only a vaguest notion of the working class movement.

In other ways he admired Foote for his enthusiasm and his prodigious capacity for work:

Resourceful and ingenious when it came to tackling problems of a technical or economical nature ... Jim was a talented pupil of Sonya's and became an outstanding radio operator. He had an extraordinary capacity for work and could transmit large numbers of telegrams in a night.[36]

But however much he admired his technical skill and work ethic, Radó regarded Foote's political outlook as primitive. This view was echoed by the MI5 officers who interviewed him in 1947, who described Foote as, politically, an 'innocent abroad'. He was not alone in this estimation. This was how Foote referred to himself in his autobiography and 'An Innocent Abroad' is the title of one of its chapters. It is worth repeating, though, that the biography was written on Foote's behalf by an MI5 man.

This estimation of Foote as being intellectually poorly developed as a communist could be explained as an example of the British suspicion of over-theorising. British communists frequently complained of the tendency of the British working class to anti-intellectualism and suspicion of overarching political theories. Perhaps this was what Radó detected: keenness to get on with the job instead of faffing around with theoretical posturing. The ignorance that Radó complained of was illustrated to him when he invited Foote for a drink on the anniversary of the October revolution. The date was of no significance to Foote whatsoever.

Brigitte Lewis, Sonya's sister, was Foote's first contact with espionage. She had married a communist Englishman, but her maiden name of

Kuczynski indicated a very mainland European heritage. She was from a family of German, communist, Jewish writers and academics who had fled their homes just before the accession to power of the Nazis. Her brother Jürgen was the head of the Kommunistische Partei Deutschland (KPD) in Britain after its annihilation in Germany. The KPD had been the largest communist party outside of the USSR prior to the Nazi takeover. The leaders who had not escaped from Germany were in concentration camps. Those who did escape frequently went to the USSR, which, ironically, was in some respects a more dangerous place for them. More members of the KPD politburo were killed in Stalin's purges than were killed under Hitler; some seven in the USSR compared to five in Germany.[37]

So without understanding what his job would be or who he would be working for, Foote accepted the offer made by Brigitte. After a second interview Mrs Lewis informed Foote that he was to go to Switzerland to meet her sister Sonya, who would let him know what the dangerous mission involved. In Geneva he met Sonya (née Ursula Kuczynski, but now Hamburger by marriage) using the complicated rituals by which Soviet agents met each other for the first time. They were to meet outside the main post office in Geneva. This was an easy place to find for a foreigner and nobody would notice someone loitering.

> I was to be wearing a white scarf and to be holding in my right hand a leather belt. As the clock struck noon I would be approached by a woman carrying a string shopping bag containing a green parcel, and holding an orange in her hand ... The woman would ask me in English where I had bought the belt; and I was to reply that I bought it in an ironmonger's shop in Paris. Then I was to ask her where I could buy an orange like hers, and she was to say that I could have hers for an English penny.[38]

Sonya told him that he was to take up residence in Munich and to get to know as many people who worked at the BMW plant as possible. She gave him 2,000 Swiss francs (approximately £4,500 in 2010 values) for his living expenses. This was a considerable amount of money in 1938. He was also at this time paid a salary of $150 a month. This was the approximate equivalent of £1,465 in 2010. Accordingly, Foote obtained a passport and travelled to Munich on 10 August, obtaining rooms originally in the Pension Kalterdo, and subsequently in Elisabethstrasse 2.

The Agnes Zimmerman affair[39]

While he was in Munich, Foote met a young woman at a dance. Her name was Agnes Zimmerman. She was described as a 'mannequin' in his later interrogations, but she worked for a Munich fashion house. Foote came to know her and her family, who were Catholic and anti-Nazi. Agnes and Foote would visit each other until the outbreak of war made this impossible, then they would write about once a month. In one British intelligence report she was described as being Foote's' fiancée.[40] Agnes herself became a minor anti-Nazi Soviet agent in Germany (codename Mikki) and became a contact point in Munich for a group centered on a 60-year-old Swiss woman called Anna Müller, a 'cut out' for Foote's team in Lausanne.[41] Müller was the liaison officer for Soviet agents in Switzerland and was engaged in procuring passports from a source in the Swiss passport service who had himself been in the Soviet secret service for many years: Agent Max.

Agnes Zimmerman had managed to stay in touch with Foote using a contact in the German legation in Berne, Madame Brand-Roth, who was a friend of Agnes' mother. One letter from Agnes brought alarming news, not about her relationship with Foote, but something far darker.

Agnes had made herself available as a contact for two Soviet agents dropped into Germany by parachute. In 1943, one of these – a young woman codenamed Inge – had become separated from her comrade, who was quickly captured by the German authorities. She had also lost a suitcase which contained her clothes and her radio transmitter. Inge went to her first contact in Germany: Anna Müller's brother Hans in

Freiburg. Hans got in touch with his sister Anna in Switzerland and told her what had happened. Foote duly passed this information on to Moscow, in the hope that another suitcase could be sent out. Meanwhile, Inge went to Munich to meet Agnes. A new radio for Inge was provided and was sent to Hans, and Inge was instructed to return there to pick it up. After a couple of months' wait she had not returned to Agnes, who became increasingly worried about her fate. She wrote to Foote to outline the problem. All attempts by Foote to contact Anna Müller about the problem failed. Getting desperate, he travelled to Müller's home in Basel to check on her. She was not there and there was no way of him discovering where she was. More problematic developments in the case presented themselves. Foote received a letter from Agnes Zimmerman. This was not like her usual handwritten *billet doux*. It was typed and did not sign off with her usual hand. His address was written, in full, on the envelope. The letter informed Foote that Inge had gone to northern Germany and had not returned to pick up property from Agnes in Munich. Foote was extremely suspicious of the letter. More bad news was to follow. Foote received this telegram from Centre:

14.8.1943
No news of Inge. It is important to find out what Mikki [Agnes Zimmerman] knows of her. You must reassure Anna, but if you go to see her be very careful: we have been informed that her brother, Hans, has been arrested by the Gestapo. Director.

The Gestapo had arrested both Anna Müller and Agnes. Both women were severely interrogated and both did not reveal what they knew about the network. Anna's life was saved because of diplomatic pressure brought by the Swiss authorities, but she was confined in atrocious circumstances in a concentration camp and required months of rehabilitation before she could go home. Her brother Hans and his wife were executed.

Inge never resurfaced and was presumed dead. The prison experiences of Agnes left her with severe mental health problems from which she never recovered. Her relationship with Foote never recovered either.

In 1947 Foote met his sister Margaret, a meeting which was bugged by MI5, in which he showed considerable concern for Agnes. Margaret asked if her name indicated that she was Jewish, and Foote replied that she was classically Aryan. Margaret had kept herself informed about Agnes because she knew Agnes' sister, who now lived in Chislehurst. Agnes' mother had contacted Margaret; she found the letters hard reading. She said to Foote:

> She [Agnes] had arrived back, heartbroken, in a terrible condition. A terrible time she had. And all she wanted to know was if you cared for her and wanted her etc ... I had some terrible letters you know; a terrible letter from her, it was really, you know, heartbreaking.

Although Foote asked Margaret about Agnes' sister in Chislehurst and how far it was from her home, there is no indication that he ever went to see her.

When his book was published, Agnes' sister Marianne wrote to Foote. The letter was friendly enough on the surface, but it had been intercepted by MI5 and summarised for Foote's records: 'Writer says that Allan probably doesn't know but Agnes was arrested by the Gestapo on 4 November, 1944 because of her contact with Allan.' Marianne begged him to get in touch with her sister, who was now living with her mother in Munich. She had not recovered mentally from her experiences at the hands of the Gestapo.

In 1951 Foote's MI5 file recorded that Agnes had applied to enter the country to see her sister Mrs Foyer (married to a man previously known as Feuerberg). MI5 said that they did not consider her or her family to pose a security risk. It is not recorded whether she met Foote during her proposed stay, or even if she actually arrived. An entry in Foote's file casts doubt on the idea of her admission to Britain: 'Although it is impossible to make an absolute rule my view is that persons known to have a history of Soviet espionage should not normally be granted visas to visit this country.'[42]

Foote told a version of the story of the events surrounding the fates of Hans and Anna Müller and Agent Inge in chapter twelve of his book, but neglected to make any mention of Agnes in his account.

Chapter Four

Germany

Agent Sonya: Superspy

Although he was unaware of it, in Sonya, Foote had met one of the USSR's most formidable secret agents. In 1947 she was described in an internal secret service report by Roger Hollis of MI5 as 'a Soviet intelligence agent of considerable standing'.[43] She had already risked her life undertaking dangerous missions in China, Shanghai and Mukden, under the noses of the fiercely anti-communist Chinese nationalists and Japanese invasion forces. She had been recruited into the Soviet military intelligence by master-spy Richard Sorge in Shanghai. He, in turn, was possibly the most important Soviet spy in the Far East. Sorge managed to obtain and communicate Japanese war plans and reveal these to the USSR at a crucial point in the war.[44]

The Franz Obermanns affair

Foote was not the first person to be recruited into Sonya's spy ring in Switzerland. She had met another agent in Moscow prior to her transfer to Switzerland. In her book she called him 'Hermann', but his real name was Franz Obermanns. Foote called him 'Alex' in his memoir. The son of a waiter and himself a factory worker and trade unionist, he had been a member of the KPD before its abolition in Germany and had remained active until the Gestapo arrested him. He spent two-and-a-half years in a prison camp in Emsland. When he was released, he went back to working for the KPD until, under threat of re-arrest by the Gestapo, he escaped from Germany and subsequently went to Spain to fight in the

International Brigade. He served with the Chapaev division of the 13th International Brigade.[45]

In 1937 Obermanns went for training in Moscow. It was here that he was introduced to Sonya. Obermanns became a highly trained radio operator and spy. But he carried a number of disadvantages which later came to render his services useless. Foote said that he was 'far more of a liability than an asset'. In what Sonya described as a 'chemical experiment' in his Moscow training school, Obermanns was wounded by an explosion which caused a gash on his face. The wound successfully healed on its own but it left a very noticeable scar. 'A vivid red scar is not exactly an advantage to anybody involved in secret work', as Sonya unsentimentally put it. A second problem for Obermanns was his Finnish passport. This had been produced by contacts in Canada in the name of Eriki Noki and was perfect in every way but one: Obermanns could not speak Finnish, nor English for that matter. He knew nothing about Finland either. Despite this he managed to evade the Swiss immigration service and successfully entered the country.

Matters came to a head when the Swiss secret services visited Sonya's house and Obermanns was on the premises – scar and all. They made little fuss about this at the time as the neighbours were used to seeing gentlemen callers visiting her home. 'I acted the young woman caught in an embarrassing situation with a young man while pressing her husband for a divorce.' Later, after a routine check of foreigners papers, the police raided Obermanns' flat and found bits of radio transmitter scattered about the place. He was arrested on 11 December 1939. For the first three months he gave nothing of his identity away, not even confirming his name. Because of his accent the Swiss made a check with the German authorities. The Germans knew exactly who he was and requested an extradition. This was refused by the Swiss, and Obermanns was later interned in agreeable circumstances until the end of the war.

The impact of his arrest on Sonya was profound. Her transmitter was boxed up and buried in the garden. Foote summed up the problems that this brought:

This increased the security of operations immeasurably but added equally greatly to the difficulty of working. For anyone who wishes to indulge in espionage I do not recommend digging in a flowerbed for a biscuit tin containing the essential bits of a transmitter with the scheduled time for a transmission fast approaching. It may be romantic and in the best tradition, but it is also exceedingly difficult and rather humiliating.

Foote thought that the reason the police did not link their findings at Obermanns' flat with Sonya, the mysterious foreign-sounding woman in her isolated cottage, was that the police officer in charge of his case had been 'blown up by an infernal machine which ... he was attempting to immobilise ... We never knew whose bomb it was.'[46] Sonya herself described it as a 'fatal accident'. But she was struck by the fact that, from the officer's notes, nobody came to check out Franz Obermanns' last known associate, Agent Sonya. In a statement which could have served as a foreword to her later experiences in Oxfordshire she wrote: 'Where security officials are concerned, I have experienced so much incompetence alongside their thoroughness in every country I have worked in, that I have long since given up trying to puzzle them out.'[47]

The circumstances of Obermanns internment were mild, certainly compared to what he would have faced in Germany. He was even allowed out of detention and during the trips out he met both Beurton and Foote. According to Foote, 'He spent a pleasant if tedious war'.

The arrival of Len Beurton

Foote made three visits to see Sonya between 1938 and 1939. It was during these interviews that Sonya revealed the real reason that he had come to Europe – to engage in espionage and possibly sabotage in Germany on behalf of the Red Army. Later on, when in Moscow, Foote was to discover that originally, part of the Swiss network's efforts were to be directed against Britain, but that the growing danger of Nazi Germany caused it to switch its attention and efforts.

Sonya informed Foote that the intelligence network would need at least one more operative to gather information useful to Russia. Out of the blue, this second man appeared at Foote's door in Munich. He was the old International Brigade comrade and Independent Labour Party member Leon 'Len' Beurton. Foote had recommended him to King Street as a possible replacement for him as a transport officer, carrying material to Spain. He was therefore indirectly responsible for his recruitment to Sonya's team. In her book, Sonya states that Beurton was also a member of the Communist Party at this time, in addition to Foote. Nobody else supports this assertion and Foote actively denied that this was the case. Foote referred to Beurton in his book by the name of Philips, while Read and Fisher claim that his real name was Brewer. Nobody else used this name for him. MI5 used the name Beurton in their files, and this is the name that will be used here.

Beurton followed Foote to Germany in May 1939, posted in Frankfurt rather than Munich. In his initial interrogation after the war in 1947, Foote suggested to MI5 that Beurton was outraged to find that he would be working for the Russians after his negative experiences with them in Spain.[48] But later in the same weekend's interviews, Foote said that Beurton had gone to Germany thinking he was to be involved in some sort of international swindle. He was disappointed to discover that the mission was political in nature, and not because of the Russian connection.[49] In Switzerland vague projects and plots were discussed, including a half-baked plan ('which I had no intention of doing') to assassinate Hitler in the Osteria Bavaria, a Munich restaurant he favoured. There was another foolhardy plan suggested by Beurton to set fire to a Zeppelin. Of these, the Zeppelin plan came closest to implementation. According to Agent Sonya, while Beurton was in Frankfurt preparing the planting of an incendiary device on the airship, the hotel he was staying in was rapidly emptying of all its foreign guests as the international situation deteriorated. Foote was with Sonya in Geneva when the message came through from Moscow to abandon the plan. This was because by late August 1939, Moscow had decided to halt any anti-German espionage or other activities because of the recently signed Molotov-Ribbentrop non-aggression agreement. In his book Foote described the pact as 'a thunderbolt out of a clear sky' to his little network, although Sándor Radó was later to offer Foote's blasé attitude to this event as proof of his political naiveté. The volte face in Soviet foreign policy came as a devastating blow to both Sonya and Beurton too, whose lives had up to this point been premised upon the USSR being the last, best bulwark against the Nazi menace.

Beurton was evacuated from Germany and joined Sonya and Foote in Switzerland on 3 September 1939. This sounds an easier process than it actually was. Foote had to try to contact him by phone at his holiday destination where he was sunbathing next to a lake at Titisee. International telephone calls were not easy to make in 1939, and certainly not in the atmosphere of summer 1939. In this case Foote was lucky. All it took for him to track Beurton down was 'the waste of several valuable hours, an uncounted number of francs and the last remnants of what had once been a placid temperament'. At this time Sonya was living in Caux near Montreux in a cottage named La Taupinière, which – ironically for spies – translates as The Molehill. The two men were living close by in the Pension Elisabeth. As well as the ideological confusion caused by the Nazi-Soviet pact, this left Soviet agents in Switzerland with very little to do except to wait for further instructions. They entered a period of limbo.[50]

They spent the weeks instead learning many of the basic techniques of espionage, including the operation of wireless transmitters. Sonya was a trained radio operator who could manufacture a radio transmitter from parts obtained from various retail outlets. This was basic training for Soviet spies. Kitchen table manufacture of sets would be unlikely to alert the authorities to her activities. She was also skilled in coding and transmission technique.

Matters were not eased for the team by the declaration of war by Britain and France on Germany, one month after the Nazi-Soviet pact.

Foote was instructed by Moscow to cultivate contacts with the Romanian population in Switzerland with a view to moving Sonya's network to Bucharest should it become necessary. Many histories of the period hold that the entry of Italy into the war put an end to these plans.[51] Foote directed the blame for this elsewhere. He stated that it was Moscow Centre's inability to find the necessary dollars to grease the clandestine wheels for the arrangement which was the problem. Unconventionally sourced passports were expensive.

There were pressing personal problems for Sonya to attend to at this time. She was a German, a communist and a Jew, and she knew that she and her children would be ripe for arrest at the earliest opportunity should Germany invade Switzerland. The fear of invasion by Germany was widespread in Switzerland; they had invaded Denmark in April 1940, Holland and Belgium in May 1940, and by June 1940 France had also fallen. Sandwiched between Nazi Germany and fascist Italy, the Swiss looked a very likely target of a German attack. To undermine the temptation to invade Switzerland for its gold, the government moved its reserves to Fort Knox, and had communicated this fact to the world at large. If Switzerland were to be invaded, Sonya and her two children would be returned to Germany and a concentration camp. As if this was not bad enough, her residence permit in Switzerland was due to expire. She had a Honduran passport which she had obtained through unofficial and expensive means, but this was unlikely to be of much use. She had therefore taken steps to obtain a British passport in order to come to Britain with her children as refugees. In the circumstances of the time it would be hard to persuade the British authorities to issue a passport to someone with known communist connections in her own family. One way around this problem was to obtain a passport by means of an unconsummated marriage, a 'mariage blanc'. A huge number of these marriages of convenience were taking place in Switzerland as others tried this route of escape. The problem for Sonya was that she was already married to a fellow Soviet agent called Rudolf 'Rudi' Hamburger. He was at that moment in China working for the USSR, having departed for China from Marseilles a year earlier on 24 April 1939.

The potentially fatal nature of Sonya's situation led to a desperate plan. Different accounts are put forward about the details of this plan. According to Sonya's autobiography, she proposed marriage to Foote. He was a likelier partner for her than Beurton as he was closer to her age. Initially Foote agreed (she said) but later on changed his mind. He made up some (unverifiable) story about him promising to marry a girl he had got pregnant prior to, and possibly the reason for, his time in Spain. Len Beurton stepped into the breach and accepted Sonya's proposal of marriage. This seems to be the version of events which most historians have accepted. In Foote's account there is no mention of his initial promise of marriage, nor of the wronged maiden, either in his book or in any of his MI5 interrogations in the years 1947–1950. Whatever the truth surrounding this *ménage à trois*, Sonya and Len created an apparently happy marriage out of these dismal circumstances which lasted for the rest of their lives in the GDR.

To facilitate her marriage to Beurton, Sonya divorced Hamburger on the grounds of his supposed adultery with her sister Brigitte on 26 October 1939. Foote stood as witness to this imaginary and perjurious affair and the divorce went ahead. By this time Rudi was about to be captured by Chinese authorities, incarcerated under the harshest of regimes and probably tortured in a Chinese prison.

Sonya and Beurton, on the other hand, were married on 23 February 1940. A British passport application was made the following day. Plans were also made for the escape. Once the passport was obtained, the plan was for Sonya and the children to travel across Vichy France, pass legally into fascist Spain, and travel to Portugal to get a boat for England.

There were two problems with this plan. The first was that Len Beurton would under no circumstances be allowed to travel through Spain. As an ex-International Brigadier he would have little chance of obtaining a visa. For the moment, he would have to stay in Switzerland.

The second problem was more serious. Sonya had a nanny who had looked after her two children while she was building up her espionage network. Now in her fifties, she had been a loyal family retainer since Sonya was tiny. The problem for the nanny, Olga 'Ollo' Muth, was that there was no room in Sonya's escape plan for her. She was not likely to be arrested or punished in Germany and thus could not claim to be a refugee in Britain. Also, the thought of her separation from Sonya's little girl was too much for her to bear. Though not heavily involved in Sonya's activities, she had a pretty shrewd idea of what was going on. On one occasion she accepted the job of entering Germany and delivering a sum of cash to the wife of Ernst Thaëlmann, the incarcerated leader of the KPD.

Familiar with Sonya's secret activities, she decided to scotch her escape plan by informing the British embassy that they were about to give a passport to a senior officer in the Soviet secret service. Unfortunately for her the embassy, swamped now with desperate people trying to get away from Switzerland and the anticipated invasion, could not make head nor tail of her garbled story, which was conveyed in a mixture of German and pidgin English over a telephone line (Sonya says it was a face-to-face interview).[52]

Ollo was dedicated to, as she saw it, the wronged husband Rudi Hamburger. For all Sonya and Len's talk of a marriage of convenience to allow for an application for a British passport, it soon became clear that the marriage was all too convenient. It was clearly a love match that ran with all the enthusiasm of any newlywed couple. As long as Ollo was there, disapproving of the direction in which things were moving, she was a danger to them all. Foote expressed a lot of regret at this turn of events:

> She was a faithful old thing and I was fond of her. Had sex not reared its ugly head she would have been with us to the end ... It was bad enough to have the head of the network and your fellow operative acting like a honeymoon couple, without the thought

that at any moment the faithful retainer might try yet another denunciation – and perhaps with more success.[53]

In his otherwise excellent biography of Sonya, Ben Macintyre makes an extraordinary claim. At the end of chapter fourteen he quotes Len Beurton as saying: 'Len turned to Ursula [Sonya]. "She has already spoken to too many people. We have to do something before she turns you and the others over to the police and kidnap Nina" he said. "You will have to kill her."' At the beginning of chapter fifteen Macintyre warms to his theme:

> Ursula lay awake, wondering whether to murder her nanny. Len was firm. 'During the Spanish Civil War he had looked death in the face many times.' Unless she was stopped, she could get them all killed ... Espionage is a lethal profession as Ursula was well aware. 'The past had required me to deal with death more than once.' But the idea of 'liquidating' Olga Muth, whatever her treachery, was more than she could bear. 'We were not terrorists or criminals, neither unfeeling or cruel' ... They could not kill her, and she would not give Moscow the opportunity to order her to do so.[54]

Nobody else that I can find has a record of these deliberations. Macintyre gives little clue as to where this assassination plot was described. Certainly nothing of this nature is in the autobiographies of either Sonya or Foote, nor is there any reference listed to another source.

Olga Muth's indiscretion raised in Moscow Centre's view the unnerving possibility that at least two people outside of Sonya's spy ring knew of its existence: the nanny and the British consular official in Geneva. To this was added a third. Ollo had chatted about her suspicions to her hairdresser, who – luckily for Sonya – was an ardent anti-Nazi and kept his mouth shut.

The passport application went ahead. In Britain, the secret services became aware that Sonya had applied for a passport and sent a message to the consul in Geneva to block the application, but the document had already been issued, on 24 April 1940.[55]

Taking account of this jeopardous security situation, Sonya removed her transmitter to a flat in Geneva which had been sourced for her by communist leader Léon Nicole,[56] later to become the leader of the neo-communist Swiss Parti du Travail. She made periodic visits there to transmit her reports twice a month. With her group now potentially compromised, Moscow Centre told Sonya and Beurton to leave Switzerland as soon as possible. She applied for a visa to enter Spain, but before she left she was asked by Moscow to contact a man called Sándor Radó.[57] Prior to leaving for England in December 1940, she gave Foote his own cypher which enabled him to communicate directly with Moscow. He was then instructed to move to Lausanne with a view to eventually starting his own independent organisation. According to Tony Percy, Sonya instructed Foote to communicate to Moscow the venue, dates and times that Soviet agents could meet her in England should they wish to get in touch: The Wake Arms, Epping. Rendezvous times were the first and fifteenth of the month at 15.00. This arrangement was discovered in a notebook of Foote's and was noted by MI5 on 27 June 1950.[58] The notebook was in the belongings left by Foote in the Hotel Central in Lausanne in 1944, when he broke his bail conditions and flitted to France. It therefore acted as something of a time capsule, predating his escape from Switzerland and his sojourn in Moscow. The presence of this in Foote's archive somewhat undermines his claim in early MI5 interviews that she had put her old ways behind her when she left Switzerland for Oxfordshire and a life of pastoral innocence. Of course he might have transmitted this information to Moscow at Sonya's request, just in case she needed a point of contact in an emergency. But uncharitable observers of these events have drawn the conclusion that Foote knew Sonya was returning to Britain *on a mission*. This would suggest that Foote knew, when he told MI5 that she had hung up her headphones and retired, that he was knowingly misleading his interrogators.

Another entry in Foote's MI5 file dated 11 April 1948 reveals that as late as April of that year Hélène Radó was writing to Sonya using the name Maria Arnold, and was asking her about the whereabouts of 'Jim'. This letter, intercepted by MI5 might have been more to do with the frantic Mrs Radó trying to find out where her husband was and if 'Jim' had shared a similar fate in the USSR, but that they were still in touch raises an eyebrow to say the least.[59]

Sonya would later go on to be a key member of the spy network in Oxfordshire which transmitted atomic secrets supplied by Klaus Fuchs and Melita Norwood.

Chapter Five

Switzerland

'As a base of intelligence operations against Germany, the Soviet network in Switzerland rendered better service to Soviet strategy than that in any other single country, and the contributions to the Soviet victory was of paramount importance; if, as Moscow claimed, it was Stalin's genius that won the war, he was at least ably aided by the Swiss network...'

David Dallin, 1955[60]

Sándor Radó (Codename Dora): Resident Director, Geneva

Sándor Radó was a Hungarian communist of some standing. He had been one of the first communists in Hungary and had been a member of the short-lived Hungarian Soviet government in 1919. He had taken on some very risky assignments for the Comintern and the USSR and had met Lenin. But he was also a gifted academic geographer, and this became his cover for the time he was a spy both in France and later in Switzerland, where his wife Hélène joined him. She was also a veteran communist who had found her way into espionage work via the German Young Communist League and later the KPD. She was also part of the Soviet espionage team. She struck Foote as being 'in some ways the more dominant of the two in that partnership'. When Radó 'lost his nerve' later in the war it was Hélène who held him together and prevented him from breaking down under the pressure. They were a devoted couple and, from her home in Paris, she stood by her husband during his imprisonment in the USSR. But this came later.

Radó arrived in Switzerland in 1937 and took over the post of Resident Director for the Swiss network from someone Foote knew as the 'woman Major'. Foote was to meet this woman in Moscow years later. In Geneva, Radó ran a company called Geopress which supplied European newspapers, including ones in Germany and Italy, with maps intended for publication. He claimed to have been the first person ever to coin the name 'Soviet Union' for the USSR. His maps were in constant demand as Europe drifted towards war and his reputation in the Geneva community was very high. David Dallin underscored this point in his book *Soviet Espionage*:

> Later, when he had to flee voices were raised in indignation: 'How could the police suspect this pure scientist?' 'Various persons' the Gazette de Lausanne reported [Feb 2, 1949] 'energetically protested against this offense to a well known geographer whose presence had been an honor to Switzerland.'[61]

But Geopress was a cover for his activities as an intelligence officer for Soviet military intelligence. Radó was the lynchpin of a network of informers in Italy, Spain, Switzerland but mostly Germany. Many of his sources were of the highest standing in the political, military and cultural elite. Later, Radó's sources would include Rudolf Rössler – who would go by the codename Lucy.[62]

Rössler lived in Lucerne, hence his 'Lucy' codename. In Germany, Lucy's sources included men of the highest rank in the armed services of the Reich who were opposed to, and horrified by, the Nazis since and before their rise to power. In many accounts of the work of Radó's network it is contended that decisions made by the German General Staff, the Oberkommando der Wehrmacht (OKW), would be communicated to Lucy on the same day that they were made and were in Moscow's hands within twelve hours. One of the reassuring qualities of Radó's autobiography, *Codename Dora*, is that he discounts these embellished claims. The unvarnished facts about Lucy as a source were remarkable enough. Some

42 per cent of the intelligence transmitted to the USSR from Switzerland came from Lucy alone.[63] The information would be passed to Rössler then on to Radó's network through a series of 'cut outs', notably agents Sissy and Taylor. These were people who knew neither the names nor the addresses of the people who gave them information. They would be equally ignorant about the people who they handed the information on to.

The network that Radó administered was one of a number of organisations around Europe which became known to German intelligence as *die Rote Kapelle* – the Red Orchestra. They were all independent of each other and deliberately knew little of each other's existence. Groups were transmitting information to the Centre from Belgium, France, Germany, the Netherlands and Switzerland. The communication team of the Swiss arm of the Orchestra was called the *Rote Drei* (Red Three). The Swiss operation is regarded by many as the most successful group of them all. Radó was the key officer in Switzerland of the *Rote Drei*. The 'three' did not refer to people, but rather to transmitters.

Before the war Radó's normal practice had been to collect information, encode it, photograph the encoded documents on to microdots and to send the documents by courier to the Soviet embassy in Paris. From here it would be transmitted to Moscow. The fall of Paris to the Germans made this line of communication impossible. The border between Switzerland and France was hermetically sealed. This meant that Radó had information from various sources piling up, but no means of communicating it. By now Sonya, on the other hand, had two trained radio operators with no information to communicate.

Until Moscow gave her instructions to meet Radó, she had no idea that a parallel Soviet network was in operation in Switzerland. Moscow Centre sent her directly to Radó's home. This in itself was unusual and compromised Radó's own security. In *Codename Dora*, he described how this made him feel uncomfortable. In all their time working together, Foote never visited Radó's home and Radó visited him only once. This was considered a basic security precaution.

In March 1940 the Centre sent Radó a message via Sonya that a courier from Belgium was to visit him with information about starting a shortwave radio transmitter station. He was also supposed to have money to support his network. Funds generated by Geopress were drying up as the war had cut off the cash from foreign subscriptions. The courier had been given Radó's address and was heading his way. This too made Radó bristle. In normal circumstances the address of everyone in a network is kept especially confidential. And for nobody was this more true than the Resident Director. The agent sent by the Centre went by the codename Kent (real name Viktor Sokulov),[64] the director of another of the branches of the Red Orchestra in Brussels. Kent showed up at Radó's flat, unannounced, and immediately struck him as an arrogant know-it-all type. He gave Radó basic instruction on coding, enough to transmit information on his old, battered and unreliable transmitter. When it came to financial matters, Radó was in for a shock. Kent told Radó that he had no money, even for his stay in Geneva. He even asked Radó how much money he could give him to get home. Shocked by this proposed reversal of cash flow, Radó was informed by Kent that his journey was to test the feasibility of bringing cash across two occupied borders. It turned out that the authorities would have rumbled him if he was carrying a large sum, meaning he did not have any money to get back to Belgium.

In the winter of 1942 Kent was captured by the Germans. He heroically held out against his interrogators despite some severe techniques applied to him. It was only when his partner was brought into the room and threatened with torture that he broke down. Sobbing like a baby, he was turned by the Germans and revealed everything he knew about Radó and Foote's activities. He was later involved in the 'phoney courier' attempt to entrap Foote (more of which later). Kent was not the only radio spy to be successfully turned by the Germans, in fact in occupied countries it was almost the rule that radio operators would be brought to work for their former enemies. Bribes, torture and threats to families were too much for many and they would give the Russians bad information, or obtain from the Centre the names and addresses of resistance, and particularly communist resistance networks which they would then hand over to the Nazis. David Dallin is particularly interesting on this phenomenon.[65] As he puts it, turned operators 'also denounced and delivered up a large number of their friends; their collaboration was so enthusiastic that it surprised and disgusted even the German officials.'

Sonya's visit to Radó in June 1940 was to re-establish his contact with the Centre by setting up new shortwave radio connections from Swiss soil. Needless to say, with Switzerland jealously guarding its own much vaunted neutrality, this effort would be highly illegal. Len Beurton and Alexander Foote were to take up the role of radio telegraphists.

One of the first tasks of the group was to expand the base of their operation by recruiting more radio operators and building more radios. On 1 August 1940, Foote took rooms in Geneva and began training Edmond Hamel in wireless operation. Hamel (codename Edouard) was ideally suited for this role, although he did not prove to be as capable a student as his wife Olga (codename Maude). Mr and Mrs Hamel owned a radio sales and repair shop in Rue Carouge in Geneva, so the ownership of radio parts and aerials was only to be expected. Although neither Edmond nor his wife Olga were members, both had connections with the Swiss Communist Party, which was made illegal in November 1940. Edmond's brother in law was a well-known member and the Hamels were both well disposed towards the party. They became prolific radio operators, the second arm of the *Rote Drei*.

Despite the embargo from Moscow on German intelligence-gathering during the period of the Nazi-Soviet pact, intelligence had continued to arrive and was backing up. The network now consisted of Radó, responsible for collating, assessing and coding the intelligence, and two teams of radio operators who were trained in transmitting, receiving communications and constructing new radios from obtainable and hard-to-trace sources. Sonya and Beurton were in the Geneva area. Foote now moved to Lausanne, where he would remain for the rest of his war. Sonya officially handed over her network to Radó and prepared to leave.

Speaking of their disillusionment with the Nazi-Soviet pact and abandonment of the network that she had painstakingly created, Foote said:

> In a way she was lucky to have received her disillusionment early in the war. She had worked for many years for what she thought was a righteous cause, and she was spared the final discovery that the cause was not an idealistic crusade but merely power politics in its crudest form.

Little did Foote know that Sonya was yet to achieve her highest significance from a new base in Oxfordshire.

On Christmas Eve 1940, Sonya and the children left Switzerland for the UK, travelling through France, Spain and Portugal. Despite delay after delay she arrived in Liverpool on 4 February 1941, aboard the cargo ship *Avoceta*. Beurton, now a lovelorn newlywed, lost interest in the work of the group and began falling out with people. According to Foote he had only one desire and that was to return to England and rejoin Sonya. But Foote made a statement in his book which revealed the true nature of their relationship: 'but this [return] I could not allow until the organisation could carry on without him. So he remained with Hamel until March.' How he could have stopped Beurton, or what sanctions he could have applied, Foote does not make clear.

Beurton had a more difficult journey home than his wife and it was only after lobbying from Eleanor 'The Minister For Refugees' Rathbone that he came to Britain on 30 July 1942 with a passport which carried the name John William Miller. In his autobiography Foote put it like this:

> [Len] then pulled out of the organisation, and though he remained in Switzerland until 1942 he had no more official contact with us after March 1941. Moscow allowed him to try to make arrangements to leave at the end of 1941 and even assisted him in obtaining a British passport by getting a leading British politician

to intervene on his behalf. The politician concerned acted, I am sure, quite innocently in this as worked through a number of cut-outs, and the person in question would probably have been horrified at the thought of assisting a Russian spy.[66]

His passport had been issued courtesy of a secret service man in the British consulate in Geneva called Victor Farrell, in return for 'intelligence material'. What this consisted of was an introduction to a Chinese journalist called Wang, who was one of Radó's contacts. Wang was a friend of a German general who was now the governor of conquered Belgium. Although Beurton had been a Soviet agent, the fact that Britain and the USSR were now allies meant that an intelligence-for-passport exchange was feasible.[67]

This meant that by 1941 Radó had three radio operators and two transmitters: one for the Hamels and one for Foote. In 1942 a third operator and transmitter were established when Radó recruited a young woman called Margaret Bolli[68] (codename Rosy) to the network, and she operated a transmitter constructed by Edmond Hamel from her home in Geneva. Bolli was a ballerina and a leftist anti-Nazi. It was Foote's repeated assertion that Radó was having an affair with the younger woman.

From being an agent in a state of limbo, Foote became a hyperactive telegraphist. 'From mid-March 1941 until my arrest in November 1943 I was in constant radio communication with Russia except for a period of about six weeks in Oct/Nov 1941 when Moscow was in danger.'[69]

As for the personal relations within Radó's network, they were not always good. Foote did not have a lot of time for Radó. In the bugged meeting with his sister Margaret after the war, Foote said of him that he was a 'rotter' and that he swindled the Russians out of 'about one hundred thousand dollars'. Whether this was how the Russians explained Radó's incarceration, or whether Foote had independently observed his fiddling is not clear.

Structure of the *Rote Drei*

'We all have our prejudices and radio men are mine. They're a thoroughly tiresome lot in my experience, bad fieldmen and overstrung, and disgracefully unreliable when it comes down to doing the job.'

    George Smiley in John Le Carré's *Tinker, Tailor, Soldier, Spy*

Each of the radio operators had their own radio signature; their own call sign. Each had their own key for encrypting information, which had to match their call sign. They were all given a timetable by which to communicate with the Centre in Moscow and the changes in wavelength that they were to observe during transmissions, to shake off nosy detectors. Any discrepancies in this discipline would arouse the suspicions of the Centre who were always alive to the possibility that a radio had been captured and misleading information was being transmitted. This practice, known in German as *funkspiel*, could result in Soviet military resources being misdirected and to battlefield disasters. The rest of the Red Orchestra had been taken over in precisely this way.

In addition to these security measures the radio receiver operators in Moscow had one more clue as to the identity of the person sending a signal. Each transmission was tapped out in Morse code and the hand that operated the Morse key inevitably developed its own style, much in the same way as a person develops a handwriting style. Foote had a particularly recognisable style; rapid, accurate and unchanging. The speed of his Morse code was one of the things which made him such a good operator.

There were many sources of the information which flowed through Alexander Foote's Morse key and there were other keys from the same network communicating information to Moscow; the traffic was too great for one person to handle. The chart on the following page represents a simplified diagram of the structure of the Soviet network in Switzerland.

There were three main sources of information. One was the PAKBO group. This was organised through Otto Pünter, a Swiss journalist and luminary in the Swiss Socialist Party.[70] He had sources adjacent to British intelligence in Switzerland. Most of his material went through the Hamels. Pünter had been a journalist working in Spain during the civil war and it was here that he made many of the connections that would become useful in the struggle against Nazism later.

Simplified diagram of the structure of the *Rote Drei* espionage ring.

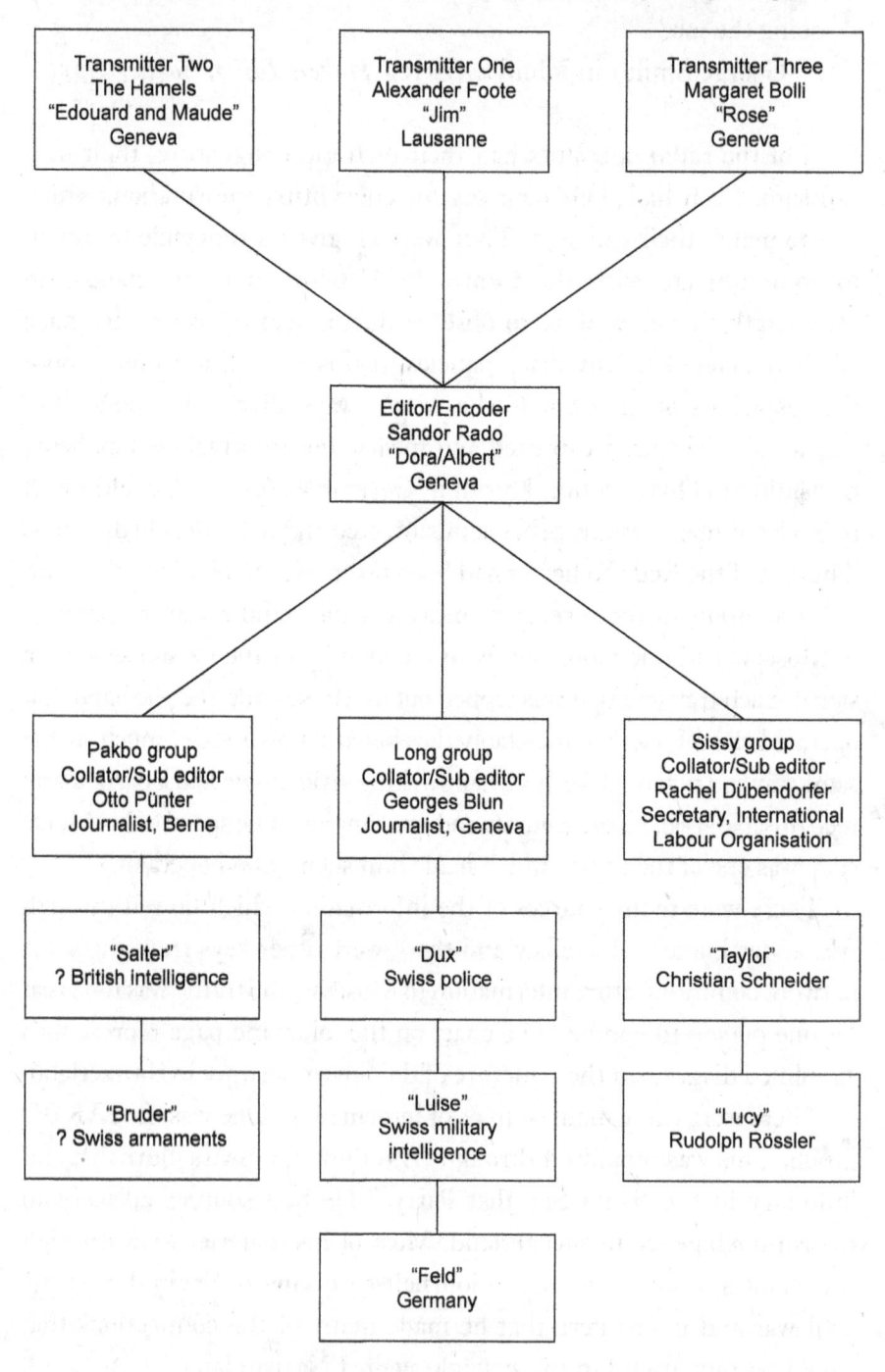

```
┌─────────────────────┐   ┌─────────────────────┐   ┌─────────────────────┐
│   Transmitter Two   │   │   Transmitter One   │   │  Transmitter Three  │
│     The Hamels      │   │   Alexander Foote   │   │   Margaret Bolli    │
│ "Edouard and Maude" │   │        "Jim"        │   │       "Rose"        │
│       Geneva        │   │      Lausanne       │   │       Geneva        │
└──────────┬──────────┘   └──────────┬──────────┘   └──────────┬──────────┘
           │                         │                         │
           └─────────────────────────┼─────────────────────────┘
                                     │
                        ┌─────────────────────────┐
                        │    Editor/Encoder       │
                        │      Sandor Rado        │
                        │    "Dora/Albert"        │
                        │        Geneva           │
                        └────────────┬────────────┘
           ┌─────────────────────────┼─────────────────────────┐
           │                         │                         │
┌──────────┴──────────┐   ┌──────────┴──────────┐   ┌──────────┴──────────┐
│    Pakbo group      │   │     Long group      │   │    Sissy group      │
│  Collator/Sub editor│   │ Collator/Sub editor │   │ Collator/Sub editor │
│     Otto Pünter     │   │    Georges Blun     │   │  Rachel Dübendorfer │
│  Journalist, Berne  │   │ Journalist, Geneva  │   │ Secretary, International│
│                     │   │                     │   │  Labour Organisation│
└──────────┬──────────┘   └──────────┬──────────┘   └──────────┬──────────┘
┌──────────┴──────────┐   ┌──────────┴──────────┐   ┌──────────┴──────────┐
│      "Salter"       │   │       "Dux"         │   │      "Taylor"       │
│ ? British intelligence│ │    Swiss police     │   │ Christian Schneider │
└──────────┬──────────┘   └──────────┬──────────┘   └──────────┬──────────┘
┌──────────┴──────────┐   ┌──────────┴──────────┐   ┌──────────┴──────────┐
│      "Bruder"       │   │      "Luise"        │   │       "Lucy"        │
│ ? Swiss armaments   │   │   Swiss military    │   │  Rudolph Rössler    │
│                     │   │    intelligence     │   │                     │
└─────────────────────┘   └──────────┬──────────┘   └─────────────────────┘
                          ┌──────────┴──────────┐
                          │      "Feld"         │
                          │      Germany        │
                          └─────────────────────┘
```

The Pakbo and Long groups had been collecting intelligence for a considerable time before they came into contact with Radó's network. Their information went by coded messages to London. After the start of the war Pakbo had to send his materials via Porto in Portugal to be forwarded on to London from there. Much of the information during this time went by the only airline still operating between Switzerland and Portugal: Lufthansa. In his 1967 book *Guerre secrète en pays neutre* (*Secret War in a Neutral Country*) Pünter stated that he was always surprised German counter intelligence did not pick up on this transfer, which amounted to a considerable volume of material. During the winter and spring of 1942 the most reliable information and in the largest volume came from the Long and Pakbo groups. In his autobiography Radó singled out the information gathered by a Swiss intelligence officer who went by the codename Louise in the Long group. His sources in Berlin had contacts in the German high command. As an example of the usefulness of the information that Louise was passing to the transmitters of the network, Radó quotes a telegram sent to Centre on 6 April 1942. It relates to plans being made by German forces for a summer offensive against Russia:

6 April 1942. To the director.
From Louise.
1. Paratroops, SS units and armoured units are arriving in Nikolayev daily.
2. Köningsberg, Warsaw and Insterburg are full of troops waiting for the attack. These areas are being made increasingly secure against air attack.
3. Large numbers of troop-transport planes have been concentrated in Zaporozhye. The chief assembly area for tanks is Stalino in the Donets casein. It has been established that Smolensk has a large number of trains and a big camp for engineering units.

Dora[71]

What the chart on p.44 fails to convey is that there was a degree of intermingling of intelligence traffic between the Swiss police, the Swiss armed services, Swiss intelligence and the Swiss Soviet network. There was also traffic between many of Radó's sources and Allied intelligence, particularly British intelligence. This was especially true of the Sissy group.

The Sissy group was run by a communist secretary in the International Labour Organisation called Rachel Dübendorfer (Agent Sissy). She did not know who the source was for her information as it came through a third party. His name was Christian Schneider (codename Taylor). A translator at the International Labour Organisation, Taylor started to deliver information just after the German invasion of the USSR. For a while he was the object of Radó's mistrust as he had no obvious connection to a source of high-grade military intelligence. It later emerged that the source who was giving Taylor his information was to become the Radó network's most vital source of information. Taylor was the link to Lucy, Rudolf Rössler. Who Lucy got his information from has been lost to history. See Chapter Eleven for some of the outlandish claims intended to fill this loss.

Codename Lucy

> Who was Lucy? He was the most important actor in this peculiar drama, but he never came into the limelight … [he] held in his hands the threads which led back to the three main commands in Germany and also could, and did, provide information from other German government offices … I can only give the facts as known to me and the deductions I can draw. The rest of the story is Lucy's, and Lucy isn't talking.[72]
>
> Alexander Foote *Handbook for Spies* 1949

Rudolf Rössler was an ardent anti-Nazi German who had escaped from Germany and settled in Lucerne. He ran a publishing house from the city, issuing books written by authors critical of the German regime. In his youth he had been among a group of friends and comrades in the First World War who had formed firm loyalties one to another through hardship and deprivation at the front. Many of these old friends went on to high office in the German armed forces. It is thought, though nobody is certain, that these contacts supplied Rössler with information which he duly passed on to Swiss intelligence. According to Radó, Rössler had been supplying military intelligence to the Swiss since before the war, via a secret (and frequently described as semi-private) branch of Swiss intelligence called the Buro Ha, named after its founder Major Hans Hausamann.[73] At first he worked exclusively for the Swiss, but the Swiss military had more information about all the theatres of war than they knew what to do with. The Swiss were in an ambivalent position at the outbreak of the war, especially when it looked as though the Germans were winning. On the one hand they feared the Germans intensely, but on the other hand, in the un-referenced words of General Guisan, the head of the Swiss army general staff, quoted by Accoce and Quet: 'the only thing that could stop the conquest of all of Europe by the Nazi regime was a military defeat in the field ... and there would be no prospect at all if the Russians collapsed. Could the Swiss do anything to help them in holding out?'[74]

At first the information that Lucy obtained concerned the fighting in the West before the Nazi invasion of the USSR. The information came from agents with codenames Werther, Teddy and Olga. Little attention was paid to Rössler's information by the intelligence services of the Western Allies, Britain and France. They were suspicious of the source, and they feared that the Germans may have been giving them some genuine material in the hope that they might, by misinforming the British, be able to out manoeuvre their forces later on. So despite the high quality of the information emanating from Rössler and the risks his contacts took in obtaining it, little use was made of his information.

In numerous histories of these events it is frequently stated that the team supplying Lucy furnished the USSR with the date and location of the German invasion. But according to Radó's autobiography the Lucy information did not come on tap until the Battle of Stalingrad. Radó's group were still able to predict the date and time of the invasion of the USSR, but these sources were furnished by the Pakbo and Long groups. After Germany attacked Russia, Lucy's contacts increased their traffic about developments on the Eastern Front. So much information came through about the Eastern Front that Rössler sought some form of contact with the Soviet government so he could pass it on. He managed to do this through a communist contact of his: Christian Schneider.[75]

Taylor became the 'cut out' between Lucy (Rössler) and the key link to Radó's network. He did not have direct contact with Radó; his contact with Radó's network was through Rachel Dübendorfer. She offered the Taylor information to Radó, who was curious about the quality of the material in just the way that the British had been. Rachel Dübendorfer was sworn to resist any attempts to discover Lucy's identity. This was a duty she observed in spite of the strongest instructions from Moscow to identify her sources for the purposes of independent verification. Rössler himself took the secret of his sources to the grave. This has led to endless speculation as to who they might have been ever since.

The information that came from Lucy was so timely and so precise that the Russians considered it to be too good to be true. For a time Radó was instructed to ignore Lucy's output. It was only persistence by him, against Moscow's instructions, which led the Centre to see the value of Lucy's information. So important did the Lucy material become that it was funnelled immediately to Foote, the network's most skilful and quickest telegraphist. This was not the only instance in which Moscow's suspicion of top grade material led them to doubt the authenticity of their source. In his biography of Guy Burgess, Andrew Lownie describes the same suspicion applying to the Cambridge Five spies in Britain:

> The extraordinary amount of intelligence supplied by the Cambridge Five rather than pleasing the Centre, however, only fed into their paranoia. A young intelligence officer, Elena

Modrzhinskaya, was asked to evaluate the information provided and determine its reliability. How possibly, given their communist past, could the Cambridge Spy Ring have been allowed to work for British Intelligence? The Centre couldn't believe the Five's access and how much secret material was being supplied, nor could they believe that British intelligence were not targeting the Soviet Union. 'Not a single valuable British agent in the USSR or in the Soviet embassy in Britain has been exposed with the help of this group, in spite of the fact that if they had been sincere in their cooperation they could easily have done', one report noted ... So suspicious was Moscow Centre about their star agents that the London residency was ordered to create a separate independent agent network.[76]

Everything changed for the Swiss group when Hitler launched Operation Barbarossa. When the Germans invaded Russia, the Centre issued this broadcast: 'Calling all networks ... The fascist beasts have invaded the workers' fatherland. The moment has come to do all in our power to help the USSR in its struggle against Germany. Signed The Director.'

Later on in the war, and using Foote's call sign NDA, the Centre sent Foote this message:

> NDA ... the Centre has decided that from now on dispatches will be divided into three categories. 'MSG' will designate routine communications, 'RDO' urgent messages and 'VYRDO' will preface messages of the greatest importance. From today on all information communicated by Lucy will be classified as VYRDO and be sent on immediately. The Centre will be available to receive communications twenty four hours a day. NDA alone will transmit Lucy's communications.[77]

The boy from Rockley Street in Liverpool was now responsible for handling the most valuable espionage material and sending it on to the

Soviet Union in its greatest hour of need. He gave them what was, in effect, a seat at the most secret meetings of the German army general staff, the OKW. His material covered army affairs, but this was combined with equally accurate material from the air force and navy. It was not just the accuracy of the material that impressed Foote and his Soviet comrades. It was its speed. Foote said in his book that he imagined their German agents went from meetings directly to radio transmitters and from there to Lucy.

> The technique of Rössler's collaboration with Radó's apparat was as follows: Rössler would write his messages in clear [plain English] and turn them over to Radó in Geneva through a liaison. Radó coded them and directed one of three radio operators to transmit them to Moscow; sometimes Foote did the coding. Moscow's messages for 'Lucy' had the same handling in reverse.[78]

In time, Russian generals would plan their campaigns around information obtained from Radó via Foote, the Hamels and Rosy. They knew where, in what strength, and what the state of morale was among the forces heading for the attack on Moscow and Stalingrad. Had they not been able to defend Moscow and Stalingrad, and had the Russians been defeated at the battle of Kursk, the war might have had a very different outcome for the Western Allies. Radó's transmitters operated by the Hamels and Rosy handled important but lower-grade information from the Pakbo and Long groups. This arrangement lasted until the sheer volume of Lucy material necessitated that they too handle VYRDO broadcasts.

In 1985 Nigel West quoted *Der Spiegel* on the quality of the material passing through Rössler's hands: 'The former chief of the German general Staff, Franz Halder, went on record to say in *Der Spiegel* on 16 January, 1967: 'Almost every offensive operation of ours was betrayed to the enemy before it appeared on my desk.'[79]

Chapter Six

Lausanne

Radio Station Foote, Apartment 45, Chemin de Longeraie 2, Lausanne

Life could not have been easy for Alexander Foote at the outset of the war. He was still a newcomer to Switzerland when he was transferred to Lausanne, a town where presumably he knew nobody at all. Looked at from a professional point of view, knowing no one would have been an advantage. Anonymity was the key to his business. In spy films the hero would play (and win, obviously) at roulette surrounded by beautiful women. The night might or might not conclude with a brawl in the bar and enough dead people to become an international incident. For Foote, behaviour such as this would amount to little more than professional negligence. The reality would be that a spy who behaved like this would not last long and would be useless up to the point that he was captured.

He would be followed and closely observed, particularly for details of who, where and when he was meeting people. His contacts would then be followed until any hint of espionage within this network was worn out. Then the whole lot would be captured in one early morning swoop. This was how German intelligence had captured all of the other other branches of the Red Orchestra and they were all considerably less conspicuous than James Bond.

Installed in his flat in a middle-class area of Lausanne, he was ready for action: 'I had overcome the two main hurdles a spy has to surmount. I had a fixed legal base, and my means of communication were secured. These two obstacles trip up ninety per cent of the spies who end their lives on the scaffold or in the cells.'

The aim of the professional spy was to be as inconspicuous as possible; to blend into the humdrum of everyday life, to not be noticed. For the sociable type of man that Foote was, this must have come at some personal cost. Perhaps he was lonely, but if he was it never came out either in his autobiography or in any of his interrogations. And he only needed to read the newspapers about the daily life of Russian soldiers during the period of Operation Barbarossa for him to realise how objectively lucky he was.

And yet Foote did stand out. Tall, burly and an Englishman of military age, his presence in Switzerland would require explanation to anybody he might meet. Why was he here? Why was he not in the British Army? Luckily for Foote, Switzerland at this time was awash with British people:

> Lausanne was full of such, ranging from the genuine, stranded resident or refugee down to the frank embusqué [person seeking to avoid military service] who had no intention of returning to England and military service and every intention of passing a comfortable and neutral war. I attempted to steer a graceful course between both extremes, my air of respectability being counteracted by my being obviously of military age.

There were retired army types, superannuated members of the diplomatic service and journalists trapped in the Switzerland that Radó described as 'The world's largest prison'. There were others there too. These were what Foote called the 'riff raff of the Riviera'; people living off their disreputable wits. These were an unpleasant crowd to mix with, but they provided a milieu in which Foote could camouflage himself. They would also be people who Foote could not, would not, trust with any clues as to his activities.

Foote was a late riser and his friends knew better than to call in the mornings. Perhaps they saw this as evidence of a louche and hedonistic lifestyle. In reality, following the German invasion of the USSR Foote was to all intents and purposes someone who worked permanent night shifts. His evenings would be spent coding the information he had been given by the agents in his own network. This might have been supplemented by material brought to him from Radó's network in Geneva. This would be mostly already encoded but often was not. The information was brought to him by 'couriers'. These would be Rosy, Olga Hamel, or occasionally Radó's wife Hélène.

In his book and to MI5, Foote described in detail how the encoding was done. He said in his book that although the system looked complex it was in fact easy when one got to know it. It does not look easy. It involved using numbers for letters and then recoding the message using details from a book known only to the Centre and the spy. Without knowing the agreed code book the code was almost impossible to crack, and for all the resources they threw at the problem, the Germans failed to crack it. Only mistakes among the *Rote Drei* let them in.

With the information encoded, Foote would be ready to transmit. He had set times for his emissions when he knew that someone in Moscow would be waiting for his call. In an emergency he could call outside of his schedule, but he knew that this would automatically raise the threshold of suspicion at the receiving end. Trivial information which was transmitted outside of the set schedule might suggest that the network had been breached.

Foote would start on one agreed wavelength to 'wake up' his counterpart in Moscow. He would send out his own individual call sign. Moscow would reply with its own call sign on a different wavelength. Then both transmitter and receiver would migrate over to a working wavelength to complete the night's broadcasts. Call signs, broadcast times and wavelengths would all be periodically changed to throw any potential eavesdroppers off the scent. The speed of transmission was also of crucial importance. As mentioned, one of Foote's most notable skills was the speed of his delivery of Morse messages and their unfailing accuracy. The longer the broadcaster was on the air the easier it was for the radio-finders to locate their stations.

Another advantage to night-time broadcasts was the effect that these would have on his neighbours. Foote lived in a built up area and before the television era people listened to radio for entertainment and information. A powerful transmitter in the neighbourhood could easily cause people's radios to splutter and squeak with interference. Foote's transmitter was indeed powerful. One of his comrades said that it could easily have been picked up in the USA or even South America. French-speaking Swiss had a word for the noises on their radios caused by interference. Their wireless, they would say, was infected by 'parasites'. Foote's kit was so powerful it could have given everyone in his quarter of Lausanne a bad case of the parasites. Interference on this scale might cause questions to be asked and investigations to be demanded. Restricting broadcasts to the hours between 01.00 and 06.00 would raise the likelihood that the neighbours would all be in bed and unlikely to be needing their wireless sets.

Nevertheless, communications were always, as Foote himself put it, the 'Achilles heel of any spy ring', and simple mistakes among the members of the network would allow them all to be scooped up by the authorities.

Short bursts of transmission were a good principle to aim for, certainly. But during the battles of Stalingrad and Kursk in 1942 and 1943, the Lucy material was coming in such volumes that the principles of caution were pushed to one side. In this period Foote was at his transmitter all night and his workload was prodigious. He would sometimes sleep in his clothes. When he was not at his Morse key he was attempting to arrange the network's finances. Thankfully, receiving messages from the centre was less of a problem than transmitting. Messages could be picked up on a regular wireless set, providing it was powerful enough. No doubt the Hamels were a valuable source of information of which domestic radio set would be best suited to his needs.

In an interview with historian David Dallin, Foote related a story about one night in August 1941. A very long VYRDO message came through to his radio receiver: 'Urgent, Open Immediately.' The message was in poor English and as Dallin said, the contents were 'anything but urgent', but were rather commonplace observations on the need for strict security.

During the tiresome night transmission [Foote says] I twice asked Moscow to postpone the rest of the message to another night but the Centre refused and I had to receive it complete ... We never understood the real meaning until, four years later, it was revealed to me when I was in Moscow. It turned out that the message was written personally by Stalin after a meeting of the General Staff ... Since Stalin himself had dictated the verbose message nobody dared to translate it freely, hence the pidgin English ... and it had to be completed without interruption.[80]

When Foote was up and about his days would have been filled meeting couriers, and cut outs bringing him material and other network-related information. These would be met away from his address if possible, in case they were followed. They would meet using different venues for each occasion. Often, for important rendezvous, members of the network would meet in towns some distance from their usual haunts. Meetings in the homes of agents were kept to an absolute minimum. But they did happen. It is the result of one of these visits that we get an image of the inside of Foote's flat, courtesy of Sándor Radó.

He had taken a furnished flat on the fourth and top floor of a large apartment house. As a place for conspiratorial work it had a lot to be said for it. At the end of a long landing a double door fitted with heavy bolts offered protection against eavesdroppers as well as offering an obstacle to any unwanted visitors who might seek to invade Jim's privacy: by the time the police got both doors open Jim would have plenty of time to destroy the transmitter and destroy any secret papers ... The flat consisted of living room, one bedroom with recess, kitchen, bathroom and offices. A marvellous flat for a single person but expensive: it cost 200 francs a month, and the landlord demanded payment six months in advance ... The furniture was old and shabby. Jim's exceptionally powerful receiver stood on a table in the corner of the living room and the aerial ran diagonally across the room. There was no need for concealment because listening to the radio was perfectly legal. The rest of his apparatus – the secret part – fitted into a secret compartment at the top of the wardrobe. Jim had very skilfully built the transmitter into the body of a typewriter, and the secret compartment was so cunningly constructed that you would have had to smash the wardrobe to pieces to find it.[81]

One problem which did not bother Foote in his day-to-day practice of spying was trouble from the police. When he did run into trouble with the police during a raid on his flat in November 1943, it was game over for his branch of the network. But he did not live a life on the run. Such a life, he realised, would make for very bad spying. A spy constantly looking over his shoulder can not concentrate on his job:

> In real life, once the police are really after you, there is little you can do to avoid them. The average spy hopes to avoid police notice rather than evade it once awakened. His real difficulties are concerned with the practice of his trade. The setting up of his transmitter, the obtaining of funds, the arrangement of his rendezvous. The irritating administrative details occupy a disproportionate portion of his waking life and cut unwarrantably into his hours of sleep.[82]

Accordingly, Foote spent his time going about 'adopting the air of an idiot and a foreign child', as he himself put it. He even laughed along when his friends inadvertently joked about his secret life. When his true role was finally revealed, the *Gazette de Lausanne* printed a series about Foote's life featuring the memories of the people who knew him. One said:

> We kidded him about being a British spy. 'Listen, where are your secrets, your messages in invisible ink and your attributes of the perfect spy?' we used to ask him. He enjoyed these jokes immensely

and took part in the game with dry humour. Someone asked him once: 'In fact what are you doing for a living?' Unperturbed he answered 'Dont you know? I am a spy.' He gave the same answer to a young lady who told him: 'Allan, you really look like a spy.' 'Oh my dear,' he answered. 'It is awful, nothing can be hidden from you.'

In fun his friends had his handwriting analysed. Unfortunately they did not keep the report, but they poked fun at him, calling him a rotten hypocrite. He was plainly overjoyed: 'Oh this is wonderful! Great! What did the graphologist say? That the writer pretends to be someone else than he really is?'[83]

In the above article an insight is gained into Foote's social life. Despite his home being his radio station he was not afraid to bring friends there. To his friends he always seemed to be well provisioned. He would make them 'exquisite rice puddings', even though rice was hard to obtain. They were also quoted in the newspaper as saying that he ate butter in 'unnerving amounts'. Looking back on his time with them, suddenly certain aspects of his behaviour made sense to his friends. One time his telephone rang and instead of speaking normally he just responded with clipped 'Yes', 'No', 'Yes' replies. On another occasion he said that he would have to ask his friends to leave because somebody was coming to see him. At first they refused to go, saying that they 'wanted to hang on to see his mysterious contacts'. He pressed them, insisting that they would have to shove off. They said that if he insisted on throwing them out they would hang around in his corridor to see who was coming. At this point 'he became so annoyed and so furious that we didn't pursue the joke and we left'. On one occasion he asked his friends to see whether they could look back into his flat using the peephole in the door.

The *Gazette de Lausanne* article also commented on his relations with his landlady and his *femme de ménage*. With both he was kind, considerate and well paying. The concierge of the building liked him:

> He wasn't very chummy, but he always had a kind word. And he was well informed too, you know? I always knew where the war was up to. 'Eh Monsieur Foote, what do you think about the news this morning?' With two words he would bring me up to speed. His arrest caused me a lot of regret and I miss him. I'm not nearly as well informed now.

The friendly relationship he had with his concierge paid handsomely when German intelligence in the shape of Lorenz and Laura (see below) came calling. She was asked by the *Gazette* journalist to confirm Foote's claim that they had come to his building looking for information:

> Mais oui! I well remember a couple coming to me with some story about a sister who was supposed to be getting married. I told them that I didn't get mixed up in the lives of my tenants ... They gave me their telephone number and asked me to ring them when he came in but I didn't keep the number. Too bad! They also visited Hélène, the cleaner, and tried to get her to speak. But they didn't offer either of us any money.

His friends knew that his sympathies were to the left, politically speaking, because he acceded to any pay demands his cleaner made. He also paid her while he was not around; 'You still have to eat even if I am not here!' To his friends he expressed admiration for the Russians: 'the people of the future', and did not seem unduly perturbed by the reports of bombs dropping on London; 'Perhaps they will destroy some of the slums. At least the people will come out of it with better homes!'

Echoing the estimation of him made by Sándor Radó, his friends noticed how high-falutin discussions about art and literature bored him. They described him as being 'matter of fact'. Certainly he liked to go to the cinema, but always for the matinee. Now they knew that he did his transmission in the night *'ce qui explique bien des choses'*, this explains a lot.

One item in the daily life of Allan Foote that gets no mention is any type of gun. At no point in his autobiography or in his many interrogations is there any reference to firearms. In fact, none of the rest of the autobiographies of his fellow conspirators mention guns either. Europe was awash with firearms during the war, so it is conceivable that they were available. There is not even any discussion as to why the actors in this drama did not wish to carry a gun. They simply do not feature in the story.

Foote's network in Lausanne

Foote's removal to Lausanne was to set up a subnetwork, independent of Radó's, which could gather information on its own account. Foote recruited three main sources, which proved to have varying levels of usefulness. The first source was codenamed May, who acted as a cut out for Jules Humbert-Droz. An ex-priest, he had been a leader of the Swiss Communist Party before it was declared illegal in 1940. Previously, he had been the secretary of the Comintern before Georgi Dimitrov.[84] Dimitrov was a celebrated defendant in the court case where he and two others were accused of conspiracy to set fire to the Reichstag. Foote's second agent was codenamed Anna (see the Agnes Zimmerman affair, p.21). She was an important cut out in that she was in touch with Agent Max, a Swiss official who manufactured illegal passports. His third source was a married couple. In Foote's words they were 'never really a source of mine but were an unpleasant incubus thrust on me by the Centre'. Their codenames were Lorenz and Laura. More about those two later.

His other reason for going to Lausanne was to establish a transmission centre at a safe distance from the other ones in Geneva. In his book, Foote divided his time up into two distinct phases. The first was the spring of 1941 up to the German invasion of the USSR. In this first period he made two transmissions to Moscow per week at 01.00, and then would wait for Moscow's response. They were 'easy, carefree days'.

Foote's role in the network included the following tasks: 1. encoding information. 2. transmitting information over his shortwave transmitter. 3. training new recruits to the network in radio operation and in the rules of undercover work. 4. the organisation of finance.

On 12 March 1940 Foote started broadcasting to Moscow from Lausanne. Prior to this date he had some technical difficulty with his transmissions. His 'address' receiving signals from Moscow was the call sign NDA. He was to respond with the call sign FRX to show that he was receiving their signal. For the first period in Lausanne he could hear Moscow tapping out NDA, NDA, NDA, calling him to respond. His own call sign was going out into the ether FRX, FRX, FRX and receiving no response. Then one night he heard 'NDA NDA OK QRK 5'. This was the signal he had been waiting for and confirmed that he was being picked up loud and clear.

His career as a radio operator got off to an inauspicious start. In June 1941 Germany invaded the USSR and made rapid progress in the country. He became the main thoroughfare for information to Russia, and the information he sent was of the highest quality. His transmitter had predicted the date and the location of Germany's attack on the USSR, even though this warning was not heeded in Moscow Centre. Stalin apparently could not accept that Hitler would be foolish enough to start a war on two fronts, East and West. It was not just the Radó team whose warnings were ignored. The Great Helmsman was ignoring equally alarming messages coming from master spy Richard Sorge in Japan. The progress of the Germans was so rapid that they quickly came to threaten Moscow itself. This resulted in a bewildering series of events for Foote and his colleagues. Moscow Centre just disappeared from the airwaves half-way through a transmission. Without any warning or explanation they simply stopped broadcasting. The Swiss team tried and tried to elicit a response but the line was dead. Behind the scenes in Moscow there had been an impulsive, panicked evacuation ahead of a possible German takeover; many of their governmental functions were moved to the interior of the USSR, away from German attack.

Intelligence was one of the departments evacuated to Kuibyshev. When they re-established themselves, far to the east of Moscow, the Centre finished the sentence they had been tapping out, with no explanation for their absence.

Foote was by now nestled in an expensive flat in the Chemin de Longeraie in Lausanne. This was not as easy to achieve as it might sound. It was against the law for foreigners to take flats when the war started. There had been a collapse in the tourist industry and the Swiss insisted that foreigners occupy hotel rooms rather than permanent addresses, in order to preserve their hospitality sector. This was not an option for Foote. He needed to have somewhere he could broadcast from in the middle of the night without nosy guests in the next room alerting reception. More than that, he needed somewhere he could erect an aerial. No aerial meant no transmission or reception. Playing the part of the eccentric Englishman of generous means, he deliberately took an apartment on one of the upper floors of a well-to-do block of flats. His flat had the added advantage of a short corridor outside his front door which would allow him to hear footsteps leading to his home. At this address he played the role of an *homme du monde*, living the life of a man trapped by the war in a foreign country, working his way through private means from whist drive to whist drive. Otto Pünter said of him *'il menait la vie d'un Anglais un peu snob'* (He led the life of a somewhat snobby Englishman). Friends knew not to look for him in the mornings due to his habit of rising late. In reality he was a man often close to financial disaster and his late rising was due to him broadcasting through the early hours and on some occasions, such as during the battles of Stalingrad and Kursk, not going to bed until six or seven in the morning.

From June 1941 to October 1943 more than 6,000 messages to and from Moscow went through Foote's radio (although this figure is disputed in later CIA studies).[85] He was decorated four times during the war and rose to the rank of major in the Red Army. Here is an example of the material that, with Stakhanovite dedication, Foote was broadcasting for sometimes twenty hours a day. It comes from Radó's autobiography. It is not certain, only likely, that Foote transmitted it:

13 June 1943. To the director. Urgent.
From Werther.
Drawn up on the Soviet-German front including the far north at the beginning of May, after reorganisation and reinforcement, were a total of 166 divisions of the German army. They include 18 armoured divisions, 18 mobile and light divisions, 7 mountain infantry divisions, 108 infantry divisions, 4 Waffen SS divisions and 3 air-force divisions.

In addition there are 3 armoured divisions and 6 infantry divisions at the disposal of the army high command and 1 SS division at the disposal of the Wehrmacht high command.

There are a further 122 policing and replacement divisions in the occupied hinterland.

An endless stream of information passed through Foote's radio. Supply statistics, morale, hospital shortages, food supply and casualty figures all accurate and all timely. This information enabled the Soviet high command to simply disappear from areas where the Germans were planning to surround their armies. It enabled the Russians to attack with confidence the sections of the front where the Germans were especially weak.

But in the middle of this effort, Foote had to deal with day-to-day troubles involving his citizenship and his residency. On one occasion he was visited in his flat by a detective who wanted to know why he was in an apartment and not in a hotel. The interview was polite and non-hostile and was livened up by Foote's provision of some first class scotch:

> He explained in the politest way that there was an ordinance which forbade foreigners to rent apartments and, perhaps, I would be good enough to explain myself. I explained that I had not been aware of the order when I took the apartment ... I was perfectly prepared to give up the flat, inconvenient as this might be, and

retire to a hotel, but felt I had to point out that it was an expensive flat in an expensive block of flats and that I was spending far more occupying it than I would living quietly en pension in a hotel ... any change in my present mode of life would decrease the flow of sterling from my pocket into the Swiss coffers.[86]

This explanation seemed to satisfy the officer.

Foote constructed his own transmitter from parts supplied by Edmond Hamel. As mentioned earlier, Radó recalled how Foote disguised the radio by fitting it into a portable typewriter case. This in turn was hidden in a special compartment built to Foote's own specifications in some fitted wardrobes. The entry to the cavity was invisible to the naked eye. It was filled with material that would not reveal it was hollow if it were tapped. But the main problem facing Foote in his new home was the construction of the aerial. To have a wire sticking out from his flat would arouse suspicion and awkward questions might be asked, but without an aerial his equipment was useless. He tackled the problem head on. Explaining that he was a lonely Englishman eager to follow the news on the BBC on the mediumwave band, he employed a technician from a local radio merchant to fit an aerial professionally. This not only gave his apparatus some respectable provenance but with some minor tweaking he could arrange it to suit his own specialist needs. When the technician came to fit the equipment, access to Foote's supply of scotch left the man well disposed to his customer. And unlikely to inform the police.

Political pressure on the Swiss

The best account of the pressures that the Swiss government were under during the war is contained in the book *La guerre a été gagnée en Suisse* (The War Was Won in Switzerland). Published in 1966 and written by journalist, historian and novelist Pierre Accoce[87] and Pierre Quet, the English translation was published in 1967 under the less glamorous title *The Lucy Ring*. The book was savaged by Sándor Radó as being more of a novel than a history. It was also poorly received, on different grounds, by Malcolm Muggeridge, who published a full page critique of it in *The Observer* on 8 January 1967 (see Chapter Twelve). Despite these critiques over details, the book gives a vivid description of the complexities which faced the Swiss in their dealings with the warring nations surrounding them.

The Swiss government was quite naturally protective of its reputation for scrupulous neutrality at the outbreak of the war. They were terrified at the prospect of invasion from their aggressive neighbour. But even beyond the threat of invasion, Switzerland was dependent on imports of key materials from Germany and Italy. Life would be very difficult in the federation without these imports. Germany had already invaded most of the smaller nations of Europe: Denmark, the Netherlands and Belgium. They invaded the Netherlands precisely because they had 'abused the privileges of neutrality', according to the invaders.

The Swiss had a large German-speaking population in their own country and were afraid that Germany might seek to swallow them into a Greater Germany as they had with the Sudetan Germans in Czechoslovakia.

Swiss military intelligence were keeping a nervous eye on their northern neighbours throughout this period. They were approached by the German émigré Rudolf Rössler who, through his contacts thought to be in Germany, had high volumes of accurate and up-to-date intelligence about intimate details of German war preparations. He correctly gave the Swiss the date and time of the German invasion of Poland. They saw the value of his information and took him on as an 'assessor' of intelligence. His base was in the Buro Ha, situated in the Villa Stutz, close to Lucerne. In this capacity he began to bring the Swiss intelligence agency information that he was obtaining from sources thought to be from inside the German general staff, the OKW. His informants in Germany had the codenames Werther (army), Olga (air force) and Teddy (navy). These are not to be understood as the names of individuals, but rather the names of the collected groups of his sources. Rössler made only one condition for his collaboration with Buro Ha: he was never to be asked about his German contacts.

Before the war broke out, the Swiss military – under the leadership of General Guisan and Brigadier Roger Masson in military intelligence – became aware not just about potential threats to Switzerland, but also about the plans Hitler had for invading the rest of Europe. Clearly, handing over this information to the Western Allies would be a gross violation of the principles of neutrality. Instead, information from Rössler's sources was allowed to reach them through a go-between in the Czech diplomatic service who went by the codename Uncle Tom. The pity was that in the West at least, the information they were receiving was ignored.

After the fall of France in 1940, Accoce and Quet put these words into the mouth of Hausamann (source unspecified):

> Switzerland is in danger and the Nazis are drunk with victory but all is not yet lost. A resistance movement has begun in Norway and before long a similar movement will begin in France ... Great Britain will not give in. We must therefore continue our work. It is Rössler's duty to do so. The Confederation opened its frontiers to him when misfortune struck his country. He in turn should help them in the trials that lie ahead.[88]

With the Germans in occupation of France and Britain confined to base following Dunkirk, Hitler turned his attention to the East. He planned a swift knock-out of the USSR; his plans for the invasion of Russia were laid out in Operation Barbarossa, of which, according to Accoce and Quet in 1967, only nine copies were printed. One week later, they said, Rössler had a copy.

The question for Rössler was now: how much and when should he deliver intelligence to the Russians? He could be pretty certain that the Swiss would not like it. They might have been well disposed to the Western Allies, but the USSR was something quite different. He sounded out a communist friend of his, Christian Schneider (codename Taylor), who contacted another communist friend who ultimately contacted Sándor Radó. Rössler (Lucy) would pass information on to Schneider (Taylor), who would in turn pass it on to Dübendorfer (Sissy), who would take it to Radó. He would then have it couriered to Foote (Jim) for transmission. In *Codename Dora*, Radó contended that the Lucy team did not start to deliver their vital information until just before the battle of Stalingrad.

During the course of the war the Germans became convinced that they were leaking intelligence from the highest reaches of the Reich. There have been numerous published claims that their soldiers found German battle plans on the bodies of dead Soviet officers. The Germans leaned on the Swiss in all manner of ways for concessions about a variety of matters and the Swiss, through their military leadership, did whatever they could to comply from fear of the consequences. The Swiss gave the Germans everything they could except the thing that the Nazis wanted most: the source of the leaks.

Tracking down the sources of the intelligence breaches was one thing. But as the war dragged on the Germans also became aware that the information they were losing was not just travelling into Switzerland. It was also being transported out to the Reich's enemies, in particular the USSR. The Swiss walked a tightrope: they had to spy on their neighbour and collect evidence of their plans towards them. But they could not be seen to be breaching their neutrality by revealing to anybody else what their spies were telling them.

There was an ambivalence in the Swiss policy towards the events raging around them. On the one hand, they had to demonstrate their commitment to neutrality. On the other hand it was obvious to them that, were Germany to win the war, Switzerland would be poorly placed to resist any demand from their emboldened northern neighbour. So, while scrupulously neutral in their official attitude, their military intelligence took something of a relaxed attitude to Allied intelligence-gathering on their soil, while coming down hard on German intelligence-gathering. It could be described as benign neglect of the activities of the democracies.

Whatever the attitude of the military, the police took a somewhat different attitude – at least officially. Their job was to uphold the law, and unofficial transmitters were definitely on the wrong side of that line. They were constantly on the lookout for illegal transmitters and did their best to arrest operators. The Germans had a shrewd idea of where and when the illegal broadcasts were happening. Improvements in triangulation and radio finding techniques meant that the location of transmitters could be pinpointed with accuracy. With this advice handed over to the Swiss police, any hesitation at suppressing them could have serious political consequences.

Up to the end of 1943 the flow of information to the *Rote Drei* was incessant. It was brought to Foote and his colleagues via couriers who they would meet in public, and who would not know the real names or addresses of either Radó nor Foote. This information did not just consist of military matters. Information about morale in Germany, industrial output, the effects of bombing on cities and disaffection among the troops. Anti-fascist police officers would make notes of remarks made by deserting German soldiers who were attempting to enter Switzerland looking for asylum. Anti-Nazi nurses would listen to the conversations of German servicemen under treatment in Swiss clinics and pass on their information. Members of the Swiss Communist Party who went across the still-open border to work in Germany would bring back their own observations. In this way a picture could be built up of the situation in the Reich.

Foote and the financing of the *Rote Drei*

The main preoccupation of the network at that time was finance. An espionage organisation without finance is almost as useless as one without communications ... The majority of my communications with Moscow at this time were over this financial question, and in the end it turned out that I had to do all the organisation for the financing of the network.[89]

To the unprepared mind it might seem as though espionage in the Second World War was fuelled mainly by ideology and the belief in what was right. But on the slightest reflection it is obvious that espionage requires considerable funding. Foote, for instance, did not have a job. He had to maintain a facade of respectability. He had travel expenses. He had to meet in cafes and restaurants, he had equipment to buy. He didn't mention this much in his book, but presumably on occasion, he had bribes to pay. When Rudolf Rössler was considering sending information to the Russians he wanted to do so without expecting remuneration. But Christian Schneider (Taylor), advised him against taking this approach. The Russians, he said, would not trust his information if it came at minimal cost. They would think he was a German agent provocateur. Taylor had his own story. He gave up his job at the International Labour Organisation to devote himself to working for Radó's network. The Russians said that they would support him for life when the war was over. They did not keep their promise.

The Pakbo group required little in the way of financial support as they gathered their intelligence in the course of their jobs as journalists and diplomats.

At the peak of its activity Radó's network was costing $10,000 a month[90] and it was Foote's job to deliver it. This translates approximately to £71,000 at 2010 prices. But of course, when money enters the equation so does fiddling. Even worse for morale than fiddling – possibly – is the suspicion of fiddling. In an operation like that of Sandor Radó, bookkeeping would be almost impossible:

> According to standing orders, agents abroad were required to obtain the Centre's authorisation for every item of expense and account regularly for funds expended. This system might have worked well for a small agency in normal times but in the case of

the Swiss agency which had expanded ... all over the country and had a multitude of new sub agents and sources, real accounting was impossible. Radó had to take on himself more than was permitted ... he kept some records ... contrary to regulations ... In 1943 when the police searched the house of one of his radio operators they found a set of Radó's papers which revealed to the authorities the financial history of the network.[91]

In his 'homework' written out for British intelligence in 1947, Foote said that although the Hamels were paid the occasional 100 francs for out-of-pocket expenses, they had been allowed a salary of $100 a month from the time of their recruitment, which Radó had not passed on. This amounts approximately to £700 at 2010 prices. He only found this out when he arrived in Moscow. Whether this was true is another matter. The veracity of the charges Moscow laid against the spies in their service is open to serious doubt. Even though he had contempt for how the Centre handled the financial affairs of the Swiss network, he was prepared to take this information directed at Radó at face value. In her memoir *Sonya's Report*, Ursula Kuczynski makes a not too subtle inference that Foote himself was not above neglecting to pass on an agent's money.[92]

Normally, funds could be sent by courier from the nearest embassy of the USSR but with the defeat of France that option was now closed. Moscow had no diplomatic base in Switzerland. The options for receiving money in 1940 were very limited – and closing down fast. Foote was scathing about Moscow's efforts in this regard. For Foote, the abortive funding mission of Agent Kent to Radó typified Moscow's financial incompetence.

It would not be possible to transfer cash in the normal way through a bank from a neutral country as, for Foote to retrieve the money, he would have to reveal his identity. In the end he came up with a plan which was foolproof, if costly to Moscow. Cost in the context of the Second World War was difficult to assess. The Russians had an open line of credit with the USA. Foote's scheme worked like this: Switzerland had a thriving black market in currencies during the war known as the 'black bourse'. People with relatives abroad, or companies with branches in America, could transfer money in and out of the country. This could be done through the National Bank and at a fair rate of exchange. For 'no questions asked' transfers, however, the same could only be achieved at an exchange rate which amounted to highway robbery. Money would be deposited with a Swiss firm in America in dollars and withdrawn in Switzerland in francs. Using this method Foote estimated that he transferred some $100,000 (some £712,165 in 2010 terms) to the Swiss network:[93] 'This system was one which I worked satisfactorily all the time I was with the network, and as a result some hundreds of thousands of dollars were transferred to our use through the intermediary of innocent firms.'

Later on the US authorities tightened up the regulations on the transfer of cash out of the country by businesses and Foote had to quickly think up another scheme. This time, instead of using firms he used the assistance of individuals with relatives in the USA. They would transfer the cash and deliver it to Foote at 'ruinous' rates of exchange. He had to remember what stories he had told to whom about why the deals were being done under these taxing circumstances. Playing once again the eccentric Englishman, Foote made 'some discreet enquiries among my more monied Swiss friends and the shadier of my English acquaintances', and put his plan into operation. 'The latter were not an attractive crowd but they turned out ... to be useful to me – though quite unconscious that they were indirectly assisting the Red Army.'[94]

The organisation of finances in this way was one of Foote's main achievements during his time in Switzerland. He took the strain off the rest of the organisation who were able to get on with their work without worrying about where their next franc was coming from.

The financing of a Russian espionage network in wartime in the face of currency and exchange regulations was no joke, and

I take a great deal of credit to myself that despite my original, pardonable ignorance of international finance and the black bourse and the lack of ideas from Moscow, I was able to keep the whole organisation solvent until my arrest.[95]

Foote remained highly critical of Moscow's attitude to the financial support of their Swiss network. He accused them of being entirely unrealistic in their proposals (one time they suggested that he travel to Vichy France to meet a courier, as if an Englishman wandering around would not attract attention), and of having no proposals at all.

Eventually the funding streams for the network dried up as the authorities in Switzerland tightened up their regulations. Radó was borrowing cash from wherever he could, especially the Swiss Communist Party and, at one point, from Pakbo himself. Radó borrowed 80,000 francs (approximately £132,000 at 2010 prices) from him. Later, when Foote was in Moscow being interviewed by his handler Major 'Vera', she said that the Centre had no intention of ever paying this sum back to their erstwhile comrade. They did not feel constrained to keep promises made to 'bourgeois' types.[96] Later on in the war, and when Foote was in a Swiss jail, it would be over matters of finance that one of his network colleagues took risks with security, bringing a network far away to its knees. This, thought Foote, was because of financial mismanagement by the Centre. At the risk of running ahead with the story, the details were as follows.

The Rachel Dübendorfer affair

Just prior to his arrest in November 1943 Foote had been on the verge of arranging a large transfer of cash to the network from the USA. Obviously, it was not possible to complete the transfer from his prison cell. The arrest of Foote and the fact that Radó was on the run and in hiding meant that Rachel Dübendorfer (Sissy) was now in effect the senior partner in the Soviet military intelligence network in Switzerland. The limitation of funds meant that payments could not be maintained to the network's sources. This was a particular worry for Sissy, from whom such glittering intelligence material arrived. She became so anxious about the financial strangulation of her branch of the network that she broke cover and sent a comrade in Canada an un-ciphered note. She had worked with the woman in the ILO and knew her to be a communist. She requested that her friend take a clumsily expressed and easy to crack message to the Soviet embassy in Ottawa. The transparency of these messages was such that it became possible for American counter intelligence to understand whole swathes of Soviet intelligence activity in their country. In fact, when news broke about the defection in Canada of a minor legation official called Gouzenko, the alacrity of the round up of Soviet agents in Canada and North America was due to the fact that the Allies had already been sensitised to their presence and were waiting to pounce.

As if this was not enough to get Dübendorfer into trouble with Moscow, there was more to come. When she was arrested by the Swiss authorities, they were very keen to know who she was working for and who her sources were. Their evidence about a connection with Rudolf Rössler was loose, and in any case was not strong enough to support any accusation of pro-Soviet activity. Rössler was, after all, an 'assessor' for the Swiss secret services, too. When pressed into a corner on the subject of acting for a foreign country, she claimed that she had been supplying intelligence to the British. This carried much less criminal opprobrium in the Switzerland of 1943 than admitting she was working for the Russians. It may also have been true. The British were, after all, allies of the USSR, and giving them intelligence may not have seemed as shocking as it did elsewhere.

But her admission of working for the British soon landed on the desk of the Director in Moscow. Pierre Nicole, the son of the leader of the Swiss Communist Party, got access to documents belonging to Sissy's defence lawyer, and communicated her admission to Russia.

Before her trial Sissy skipped out of Switzerland and it was some considerable time before she and her partner Paul Boetcher, an ex-communist minister in the government of Saxony, went to Russia to face the music. Why they agreed to go is anybody's guess. According to Foote the Soviets were 'after her blood'. In the summer of 1947 she vanished, and friends and family could find no trace of her; she had been given a hefty prison sentence in Russia. Released from prison in 1956, she lived the rest of her life in the GDR. Her imprisonment is not mentioned in Radó's or Foote's books.

Lorenz and Laura

At the instigation of the Centre a Mr and Mrs Martin (codenames Lorenz and Laura) were put in touch with Foote in 1942, with instructions that they were to become part of his group. On reflection in 1949, Foote came to regard their recruitment as the beginning of the end for his organisation. They had been agents for the USSR since the mid-1920s and had themselves been brought up in Russia, where their children still lived. The minute they met Foote, he mistrusted them. For one thing they were too sharply dressed for Soviet agents, he in flashy suits and her in expensive furs. But it was their flagrant disregard for the rules of spy-craft which bothered him most. They insisted on meeting Foote at their somewhat lavish home; handing out addresses was possibly the gravest mistake an agent could make. It was not until very late in the day that Radó had any idea of where Foote lived and vice versa. To be invited to a contact's home address on first acquaintance broke all the rules. Their house was always kept swelteringly hot and their first action whenever he arrived was to insist that he make himself comfortable by handing Laura his overcoat. This was then taken out of his line of sight. Then there was their habit of repeatedly pressing Foote on the subject of where he lived. All of this bothered Foote, and he told the Centre that it bothered him. But Moscow maintained that the couple were as good as gold and instructed him to maintain contact. Foote remained suspicious and when he attended meetings in their home he hid his identity documents in a pouch/pocket he had sewn into his trousers. When he arrived on one occasion, he deliberately left some pieces of paper in a specific order in one of his normally empty pockets. On leaving their flat he found that the newly shuffled papers had all the marks of having been examined. In the end Foote defied the Centre and cut off all contact with them. The breaking point came when he took a stroll in the gardens of their house at Lorenz's insistence. At one point during their walk Foote caught Laura surreptitiously taking a photograph of him. Foote did not discover the true nature of this event until he arrived in Moscow. His picture was on some German intelligence documents the Russians had captured.

Foote's attempted abduction by the Abwehr

Arrest by the Swiss was not by any means the worst thing that could happen to Foote. He feared being invited to meet bogus 'contacts' who were German agents who would bundle him into a car and take him over the border to Germany. At the end of March 1943 he was sent by the Centre to meet a French courier to hand over some money in Lausanne. Foote and the courier observed all of the complicated rituals required for them to recognise each other. Centre had instructed Foote to hand over the cash and to walk away without saying anything, but the courier was positively chatty, against the clearly expressed rules of the engagement. This immediately aroused Foote's suspicions. Further meetings were arranged because Foote had not been able to stump up the right amount of cash in time for the first meeting. His anxieties were not reduced when the 'courier' gave Foote a book wrapped in a brightly coloured orange envelope and told him it contained messages for Centre tucked between its pages. This had not been on the list of tasks given to him by the Director and Foote began to suspect that the book was intended as a beacon for German agents to follow when Foote was going home. The courier tried to make arrangements to meet the following week at a place conveniently close to the Swiss-French border, an ideal venue for an abduction. Now deeply suspicious, Foote took a taxi and sped away from the encounter. He stopped at a public convenience and tore up the envelope and flushed it away, noting as he did it that it was of Swiss, not French, manufacture. He then boarded trains and buses on a very circuitous route home and when he was satisfied that he was not being followed he alerted Centre about his suspicions. They advised him to find the telegrams hidden in the book, encode them into his own code (which was still unknown to his pursuers) and after transmitting their contents to burn the book. Two weeks later the Centre confirmed that Foote had actually met with an Abwehr agent and that they did in fact intend to abduct him. The entire network to which the courier was supposed to belong had been penetrated and its leader, Agent Kent, was now cooperating with the Germans. Foote's abduction is said by many sources to have been at least in part overseen by Klaus Barbie, known to the French resistance as the Butcher of Lyon.

The fact that Lorenz insisted on meeting Foote face to face and not through a cut out, and the knowledge that the Abwehr wanted to kidnap him added up to justification for Foote to cut off all links with the couple. Moscow Centre confirmed later that Lorenz had intended to use one of their meetings as the opportunity to kidnap Foote and remove him to Germany.

Foote and the rounding up of the Radó network

By assiduous detective work within Germany, the Abwehr had come to the conclusion that the broadcasting of intelligence was not coming from inside the Reich, even if the information itself was. They had concluded that the broadcasts were coming from Switzerland. How the information arrived in Switzerland they did not know (and to this day nobody knows), and while it might have contributed something to their war effort to lop off the branches of the espionage tree, until the roots had been dug out the whole tree might well regrow. But the leaks were damaging their battlefield performance on a daily basis and therefore something serious had to be done.

The Germans had had very little success in decrypting the messages broadcast by Radó's agents so they made tracking down their transmitters a top priority. The Swiss confederation was already flooded with German agents at all levels of society. This process had been going on for some time. In fact, Switzerland in this period was alive with foreign agents from many countries.

> Colonel Jaquillard, head of Swiss counter espionage, was to count with stupefaction 350 German spies on the nights of 14th and 15th May 1940 alone. They were sitting quietly on the German side of the frontier, awaiting the best time to slip into Switzerland.[97]

The German security forces were already experienced in detecting and closing down espionage transmitters. They had managed to silence spy networks in Belgium (run by Leopold Trepper[98]), the Netherlands and France using radio detection techniques. Improvements in the means by which radio signals were detected meant that, by turning an aerial on a specially adapted radio receiver within a van, skilled technicians could tell which direction a signal was coming from by a process called triangulation. The problem they had was that they could only tell that it came from somewhere on a straight line on a map. But by taking another reading from a distant site and mapping another line, the technicians could work out where the lines in the map crossed each other. This would be the source of the signal. In occupied countries the German practice had been to identify the source of a signal and then to carefully note everyone that visited the address of the source. Then they would follow the visitors to ascertain who they were meeting. In this way they managed to roll up an entire organisation. This was not so straightforward in a neutral country like Switzerland.

It is a measure of how serious the Germans were taking the threat posed by the *Rote Drei* that they put someone of the rank of SS-Brigadegeneral Walter Schellenberg[99] in charge of a unit responsible for tracking Foote and his comrades down. According to Accoce and Quet,

Schellenberg was placed in charge of the hunt for the Swiss transmitters by Himmler himself following the assassination of Reinhard Heydrich[100] in Czechoslovakia. Schellenberg held top secret meetings with the head of Swiss counterintelligence, Roger Masson. In these meetings Schellenberg offered the Swiss concession after concession. Nothing was requested of Masson in return, but the fact that the Germans were so keen on meeting them must have raised serious questions in the minds of the Swiss. It is possible that Masson was well aware of the espionage happening on Swiss soil. Commencing in 1942, meetings between Masson and his German opposite number came at a time when the Wehrmacht appeared to be invincible and everyone in Switzerland was on edge and fearful of their Nazi neighbour.

The German radio detection service was based in Dresden. From here and other sites they pinpointed the likely source of the trouble: Geneva and Lausanne. From this point on the Nazis piled unbearable pressure on the Swiss to suppress the illegal stations. As noted earlier, the Swiss had (some say) taken a relaxed attitude to the broadcasts from their soil, secretly seeing a German defeat as their best hope. But the fear of invasion among the Swiss political and military classes and in the general public itself meant that the German demands could not be ignored forever. In September 1943 the Italians had surrendered, and the possibility that the Nazis would invade Switzerland to create a buffer zone between the Reich and a possible Allied invasion through Italy was all too realistic.

Throughout 1942 and 1943, during the battles of Stalingrad and Kursk, the workload placed on the transmitters, and particularly on Foote, was colossal. Sometimes he would be called upon to work right through the night transmitting information directly lifted from the minutes of the German general staff. According to Radó this information would find its way to Moscow between three and six days after it had been decided in Berlin. Incidentally, Radó discounted some of the more dramatic timings of how long material took to arrive in Moscow. Accoce and Quet declared in *The Lucy Ring* that they could be there within twelve hours – even six hours at one point. Radó described these accounts of his work as being 'hepped up'.

After the incident with the Abwehr courier Foote had been ordered to stop all contact with Radó as he was judged to have been possibly compromised. This meant that he entered a relatively quiet period. His main activities vis-á-vis the Centre were organising financial matters and exchanging information about the fate of Anna Müller, now captured in Germany. On the advice of Moscow, Foote took a holiday in Tessin in September 1943. When he returned his concierge told him that a couple sounding suspiciously like Lorenz and Laura had been to his apartment asking searching questions. The concierge had the presence of mind to decline the sob story they offered in return for information (see Chapter Ten). But regardless, this meant that the Abwehr now had his address, name – and as he found out later, his photograph.

It was felt safe enough for Foote to contact Radó again in the summer of 1943, but the news from him was not encouraging from a security point of view. Radó said that he had been spotted 'by accident' in a restaurant by a man who had been a Soviet agent but had gone over to the Germans before the war. This in itself would have been disturbing enough, but according to Foote (whose word here has to be taken with the utmost caution) he had committed one of the worst faux pas in the spy's catalogue: he was mixing business with pleasure. In his autobiography Foote contends that Radó was in the restaurant with Margaret Bolli (Rosy), in the course of their *petite affaire*. This meant that two branches of Radó's network were possibly compromised: Radó himself and Rosy. Of these the Abwehr decided that the most promising results would probably come from Rosy. Thus a handsome blond Abwehr agent 'accidentally' engaged Rosy in conversation one day and one thing inevitably led to another between them.

Rachel Dübendorfer (Sissy) was having her own problems. She had been approached by people who said they had important information for her from Foote (Jim). Sissy had never met Foote or even heard of him, so this contact sent a shock through the network. How had this bogus informant come to know about her? What else did they know? Foote and Radó decided to meet as little as possible, and only during the hours of darkness. The Swiss Communist Party was alerted in case they might have to come up with safe houses, should matters get sticky.

With their plans to kidnap and assassinate their way into the network showing little in the way of return on their investment, the Germans tried another tack. They tried to get the Swiss Bundespolizei (BUPO) to enforce Swiss law and to close down the transmitters for them. They had been sluggish in their efforts to do this because, theorised Foote, they thought that the transmitters were broadcasting for the British. But when the Germans turned up the heat the Swiss had to do something. It was not as if they did not have the skills or the technology for the job. According to Foote they had an efficient monitoring system.

By late 1943 the outlook for the Swiss network was bleak. The first transmitter the BUPO honed in on was the one operated by the Hamels. They were no strangers to the attentions of the police. Their flat above the shop had already been raided by the Swiss police looking for Communist Party literature. During their search of the Hamels' flat they did not find the transmitter used for espionage, but they found another partially constructed one. With a straight face Edmond Hamel explained that while the machine in BUPO's possession had the *appearance* of a partially constructed radio transmitter, and while it contained many of the parts required for a radio transmitter (though fortunately for them not, at this stage, a Morse key), it was in fact a piece of medical equipment intended to send out precisely measured vibrations for the treatment of an uncomfortable condition: neuralgia. Edmond even had a doctor's note confirming he had this problem. When he was asked why the set was hidden Hamel told the police that he was aware of how much his kit resembled a radio transmitter and he thought its presence might be misinterpreted. Despite this, Edmond was taken away and held for three days. A shortwave transmitter was a shortwave transmitter after all. In the end Edmond had to face a court martial, but it failed to establish any serious criminal conduct and he received a ten-day suspended sentence.

At this point the authorities did not suspect the Hamels of espionage activity, but their close links to Olga's brother meant that they came under suspicion of being members of the illegal Communist Party, which was what occasioned the raid. To beef up their security Radó had them move into a posh villa – a detached dwelling in a park, with a 360-degree view, perfect for them to observe anyone hanging around. But it was also an easy catch for the BUPO detectors. There were no adjoining buildings from which a signal might be coming. Inevitably they caught Edmond in the act of transmitting. On 8 October 1943 they arrested the Hamels and took away their transmitters and the materials due to be transmitted. When interviewed about these events by Swiss TV in the 1970s, Hamel was asked if he was bitter towards the police who raided his home, arrested him and had him jailed. A quiet and humble man, he replied 'No. They were doing their job.'[101]

This in itself was a serious blow to the network, but they also captured material that Radó, in Foote's words, 'had been idiotic enough to leave' with them, fearing that he was also being tailed by the police. The haul included items waiting for encoding, financial records of the network, Radó's code book and Foote's name and address. Or, as Foote put it: 'The Swiss could now open up a good deal of the material that had been transmitted to Moscow. They had all the previous messages archived. The next on the list was agent Rosy.'

No account of this lapse in security made it into Radó's autobiography. Perhaps he considered this to be one of Foote's 'wild assertions'.

Agent Rosy (Margaret Bolli) had been hoodwinked into a 'honey trap' by a German agent. He was the eligible Abwehr agent called Hans Peters (codename, inevitably, Romeo). Peters was a hairdresser based in Geneva. Trusted by Rosy, who believed him to be a German Communist Party member, he was a frequent visitor to her flat and over time surreptitiously obtained access to her call sign and her cipher key. This helped the Germans to decode many of her messages too. She reported to Radó that she thought her flat was being observed by the Swiss police; she was instructed to stop broadcasting and to destroy any materials she had, in case she was raided. She was also told to find another flat and to move her transmitter to this other address. Disobeying her instructions she accepted an invitation from Peters to move into his flat. On the same day as the Hamels' arrest the police raided his flat and captured Rosy and Peters in bed, according to Foote (who seemed to take an uncomradely interest in Rosy's amatory affairs). Because she was staying in a built-up area, the only way the BUPO could pinpoint her transmitter was by shutting off the power in each of the surrounding houses so that her transmission could be isolated to her address. Although Foote described Rosy as 'a very indifferent worker'[102] and no great loss to the network, her transmitter, top secret call sign and cipher material were also captured, enabling the authorities to decrypt her messages too.

Foote was sitting in a cafe drinking his morning cup of coffee when he found out about the events in Geneva. He read a small story in the *Tribune de Genève* which said that a shortwave transmitter had been found in Geneva and its owner had been arrested. That night he heard Moscow plaintively tapping out the call sign for the Hamels' transmitter without getting any response. The next morning he received a telephone call from Radó who said: 'You will be sorry to hear that Edmond is much worse and the doctor has been called in. He decided after consultation that the only thing to do was to take him to hospital.' For 'doctor' read police. And for 'hospital' read prison.

Radó himself had had a narrow escape from arrest. He was about to enter the Hamels' address while the police were still searching the place. But at the last moment he noticed that a clock was placed in the front window with its hands set in a position which indicated danger. So he composed himself and carried on walking.

In his 1949 autobiography Foote said:

We never understood why the Swiss, having held their hands so long, acted in the end with such precipitancy. They had not kept the buildings under observation; but if they had they could have scooped the whole gang, including Radó.[103]

In 1967 Accoce and Quet offered an explanation for the fell swoop with which the Swiss closed down Radó's network. They theorised that as the Germans were honing in on the espionage network operating out of Switzerland, the possibility was opened up of them uncovering the fact that the Swiss had been tolerating their activity for some time. They might even discover the identity of Rössler's sources in Germany which would cut off their own source of intelligence about German intentions towards Switzerland. But this was not the worst of it. Knowingly allowing intelligence to be transmitted to Russia from Geneva and Lausanne might tip military thinking in Germany in favour of invasion; it would put the 'hawks' in Berlin into an ascendant position. Accoce and Quet reasoned that the Swiss saw their best option as being to 'cut the feet' from under the German investigation by arresting the *Rote Drei* operators and placing them beyond the torture chambers of the Gestapo. German nerves would in this way also be calmed by the complete and verifiable cessation of transmissions from Switzerland.

Otto Pünter, alias Pakbo, advanced a less melodramatic and worked-out explanation of these events. In his book *Guerre secrète en pays neutre* (Secret War in a Neutral Country) (with added notes and comments by the Swiss wartime cryptologist Marc Payot), he said that the Swiss had no idea who the broadcasts were coming from. For all they knew it could be coming from one of the many Nazi sympathisers in the Swiss German population. So when a broadcast was picked up it was quickly passed into the hands of the federal police who could not ignore the implications. In one of the notes accompanying Pünter's text, Marc Payot, who was in on the raids searching for the transmitters, takes Pakbo to task for this statement. He says that the Swiss armed forces were so worried about a German intervention after the collapse of the Italians that fear stimulated the renewed interest in finding the transmitters. It was politico-military events In Italy which set the ball rolling. Payot also said that nobody knew about Foote's broadcasts until 17 September.

With two out of three transmitters out of action, Radó was by now frantic with worry. He had, according to Foote, 'broken practically every security precaution in the espionage code'. These events now meant that Foote's was the only physical link with the Centre, and his was the only code book and call sign they could use. All the others had been cracked.

Foote's final meeting with Radó in Switzerland came to an unsuccessful yet dramatic end. They arranged to meet after dark in a Geneva park in October 1943. From his rendezvous point Foote observed Radó arrive in a taxi. As soon as he got out, the taxi driver ran directly to a telephone box. This was enough to panic both of them. They parted company immediately. Foote later learned that the police had circulated pictures of Radó to the city's taxi drivers telling them to call their headquarters should they see him. This was the last time Foote saw Radó in Switzerland, and the last time Radó emerged in public until he escaped to Paris one year later.

At this point Foote and Radó's accounts begin to differ significantly. In *Codename Dora*, Radó says that the Centre advised them to 'contact their friends' in Geneva for help. Any contact with the Swiss Communist Party, itself an illegal organisation, was strictly forbidden to Soviet agents for obvious security reasons so it was unlikely, it was thought, that the Centre meant them. Instead, Radó said that Foote came up with the suggestion that they might have meant the British or other Western Allies. But according to Foote, when he began to transmit again it was to carry a proposal about a British approach which was devised by Sándor Radó. Foote contended that to save the network and continue their broadcasts they proposed to adopt the radical solution of applying to the British legation for asylum. Informal contacts were made through Pakbo and his agent Salter, who had contact with British intelligence. Salter had sounded out the British on the asylum proposal and in principle they were not against the idea of taking in Radó's team and allowing them to broadcast to their ally, the USSR, the vital information they required. How this was to work, given the Swiss constraints on foreign diplomatic services sending encrypted messages outlined in Keith Jeffery's history of MI6 (see Chapter Eleven) is not at all clear.

Presciently, Foote communicated the request for Moscow's permission to get cosy with the British using Radó's call sign. This would save him considerable grief later on, as we shall see. The response of the Director in Moscow to this idea was unequivocal: Radó was under no circumstances to involve the British. The tone of Soviet outrage was clear from subsequent telegrams:

November 5, 1943. Director to Dora.
2. You must take immediate steps to undo this unpleasant action and to hush it up. Simultaneously take care of Jim's [Foote's] security so that part of the most important information from Lucy can be dispatched through him. Send immediately an explanation of your incomprehensible actions...'

Radó stood his ground:

November 11, 1943. Dora to Director.
Only from a building that enjoys diplomatic immunity could I continue work ... I believed I was acting in your spirit when I turned to the British through Salter ... the organisation is unable to continue work because of lack of funds ... Lucy's group will not continue if payments stop. Working from the British embassy would also solve the financial question, since you could send me money there.

The response from Moscow revealed just how far they were from understanding how serious was the situation facing their most important espionage group:

November 14, 1943. Director to Dora
We are inclined to think that the whole story [of the network's jeopardy], was built up by a few members of the British intelligence service in Switzerland ... We think that neither you nor the others

are seriously endangered at present ... You must arrange for immediate despatch of the most important information from Lucy through Jim. Besides, new stations must be set up without delay.

The Centre's instructions were that Radó was to go underground and Foote was to move to a different location elsewhere in Switzerland. This suggestion was easier said than done in wartime, to say the very least. Even for a Swiss citizen a change of address had to be registered with the police. Foote had only obtained his current flat due to some impressive bending of the rules. Finding somewhere else when half the intelligence services of Europe were on his tail would be impossible.

Radó and his wife Hélène, in the meantime, were hiding at different and invariably uncomfortable addresses courtesy of sympathisers in the Swiss Communist Party. On 5 November he was informed that Moscow had awarded him the Order of Lenin for his services, which may have made his privations somewhat easier to bear. At least, for the short time he was to hold it.

Meanwhile in Lausanne, Foote carried on transmitting what material he had from Lucy, as instructed by the Director at the Centre. The Hamels, although in prison, had kept up a communication with the residue of the network through the offices of a prison warder who was, in secret, a member of the Swiss Communist Party. In this way the network could be told what the police knew about them. Under interrogation by the BUPO, Hamel had been shown a picture of Foote, presumably the one taken by Laura. He was also told that the detector vans were on their way to Lausanne because they knew a transmitter was hard at work there.

On 17 November 1943 the Centre sent a message to Radó in his own code for him to instruct Foote to go underground too. But by this time the Swiss police could read all of Radó's messages as his code book had been captured. Realising that Foote was about to disappear the BUPO prepared for his arrest. The police located the source of the transmissions by shutting off the electricity in all the houses in Foote's street until they managed to shut off his transmitter. Foote's flat was raided at 01.15 on 20 November 1943, while he was in the middle of a broadcast. Present at the kill were Inspectors Pasche and Knecht. Their team entered his flat brandishing automatic pistols and shouting *'Hande Hoch!'* [Hands up!] Also in attendance was a 'genial and bearded' cryptographer, Marc Payot. As the police were trying to break down the heavy door to Foote's flat, he managed to destroy his coding materials and unsent messages before the police gained entrance. He also partially smashed up his transmitter. The police attempted to resume the transmission using Radó's call sign, but Moscow Centre knew that finally, Radó's team had been comprehensively compromised. The network was down.

The *Gazette de Lausanne* flatly contradicted this account of events. In a note attached to the 1949 serialisation of Foote's book in the paper they added:

> Here we go! British humour in action! There was no bottle of lighter fluid! Nobody was pointing revolvers! And above all there was no 'Hands Up'! In addition, even if he burned some of his papers, his transmitter remained intact! … The broadcast resumed after a couple of minutes and carried on for the rest of the night and for the next couple of days.[104]

In a footnote to its splash of the serialisation of Foote's book on 9 March 1949, the *Gazette de Lausanne* added their own detail to his account of the interviews conducted by Inspectors Pasche and Knecht:

> In his interrogation Foote seemed to have decided to say nothing. 'Just to warn you in advance. Everything I say in response to your official questions will be a lie.' During the course of his interrogations by the Swiss police he gave replies which were absurd. He said that he used to tap on his Morse key at night because he was an insomniac. When asked if he knew he was broadcasting he said he did not, because nobody ever replied

to him. He also said that he was an agent of the Republic of Guatemala.[105]

Foote was kept in police custody for ten months in the Bois-Mermet prison, Lausanne. This was not as bad a fate as it might seem. He no longer had to look over his shoulder for people trailing him, stay up late on his transmitter or fear abduction and/or assassination. His remand status allowed him to have his own meals sent in. He could rest, read and recuperate. The burden of arranging finances for the network was now somebody else's job. He spent the next ten months, in his words, 'working my way through the prison library'.

The police offered Foote a deal. If he told them everything he knew about Radó's network he would be immediately released. Foote pointed out that if he were to be released so soon after his arrest, the Russians would assume that he had given up his comrades under interrogation. If he *was* a Russian spy, this would be a serious breach of their stringently applied rules: 'Then the interrogation that I would get at a later stage from the Russians would be infinitely worse than anything the Swiss could do.'

Given this, Foote could only consider one objective: 'Therefore I demanded that I remain locked up and, what was more, for a longer period than all the other arrested persons, as the charges against me appeared to be graver.'[106]

In a note to their serialisation of Foote's memoir, the *Gazette de Lausanne* let the air out of this dramatic balloon too. Knecht could not have made this offer to Foote, they argued, because such a gift was not in Knecht's power to give.

So Foote spent his ten months in prison on remand and in relative comfort and relaxation. He was allowed to bring in one meal a day. His captors were broadly sympathetic and he entertained them with the occasional glass of Schnapps. Towards the end of his captivity he was visited by the legal branch of the Swiss army. Captain Blazer interviewed him, said he had not harmed Swiss interests during the war and expressed how sorry he was that he had been imprisoned when all he had done was to help Switzerland's real enemy, Germany. All Foote had to do was to sign a statement saying that he had worked for the USSR and he could go free. Foote refused. It was a cast iron law of the Centre, that on no account was an agent ever to admit working for them. In the end a compromise was fudged. Foote agreed that he had been working for 'a member of the United Nations'.

In May and June 1944 the rest of the Sissy network were rounded up and put on remand in prison. This meant that Radó's network had been severely and possibly terminally damaged. The only sources of his intelligence still viable were the Pakbo and the Long groups. Unfunded and without a transmitter they could do little to resume their work. Radó regarded his network as being smashed beyond repair but Foote was more optimistic.

By 1944 it was clear to the Swiss authorities that Germany was going to lose the war and therefore the fear of their retribution abated – but was by no means eliminated. By early September 1944 all of the Sissy team had been released from remand and were out on bail. Radio operatives Rosy and the Hamels had also been released. On 8 September 1944 Foote was released on a bail payment of 2,000 Swiss Francs (approximately £4,400 in 2010 prices). He was told that at some time in the future he would have to stand trial and that he should not leave Switzerland. Bizarrely, they also gave him a six-week permit to leave the country.[107] Pakbo asserted in 1967 that a judge actually advised him to *'disparaître de Suisse le plus rapidement possible'* (Disappear as quickly as possible).[108] He did not stay in Switzerland long and absconded, leaving behind everything he owned in storage at the Hotel Central, Lausanne. By 7 November 1944 he was in Paris, courtesy of the French resistance, and was presenting himself to the Soviet embassy. He was not the only one in town. Radó and his wife had fled to Paris three weeks earlier to avoid arrest in Switzerland, again courtesy of the French resistance grouping in the area called the Maquis.

Now released from remand and before he went to France, Foote made contact with Pakbo, who told him that his branch of the network was still intact and was still keen to pass on intelligence. He also met up with Rachel Dübendorfer (Sissy), who said that she had been receiving information from Lucy and that she had kept her documents in a safe owned by someone with diplomatic cover in the International Labour Organisation. She said that Lucy was aware contact with Moscow was lost and he wanted some of the materials in the safe to be given to the British. Against her better judgement she complied, but wished that Moscow could hear her side of this event as soon as possible.

Around this time Foote met Rössler, who had recently been released from his three-month stretch in prison. He showed Foote a document which more or less absolved him of any risk of prosecution in view of his service to the Swiss general staff during the war. He also assured Foote that his sources were ready to resume their activities when required. He gave Foote a bulging dossier of material to take with him to the Russian legation in Paris. Foote considered that Moscow should be apprised of this information as soon as possible.[109]

In October 1947 the trials of the Soviet spies came up in Switzerland. Edmond Hamel received a sentence of one year, his wife Olga seven months. Margaret Bolli (Rosy) got ten months. In absentia, Radó and Foote were sentenced to thirty months. These were heavier sentences in partial recognition of the fact that they did not show up to their trials. But while the wheels of justice in Switzerland had been turning slowly, Radó and Foote had been facing a more menacing tribunal in the USSR.

Chapter Seven

Paris

Arrival: 7 November 1944

Before Foote arrived in Paris Radó had communicated a pessimistic estimation of the possibility of restarting work to his Soviet handlers. The Swiss knew everything. The leading network cadres had been rumbled. Their espionage techniques had all been exposed. The transmitters had been broken up or captured. He himself had scarcely recovered from the physical and psychological effects of his close confinement in a tiny room while in hiding. Geopress had been abandoned.

But a few weeks after Radó's arrival, Foote also presented himself to the Soviet military mission in Paris. He requested to speak to a member of the senior personnel and was put in touch with a Lieutenant Colonel Novikov. In accordance with Russian intelligence service protocol, he requested to be allowed to send a telegraph to Moscow. In this communication he gave his call sign and the codenames of his colleagues in Switzerland. When his identity had been confirmed he was asked to return to the mission the following night. When he returned he was asked several questions about the Swiss network which had obviously emanated from the Centre. After these formalities had been observed his news for the Centre was that at least part of the team were ready to start up again away from the Swiss detectors and over the border in Annemasse, France, in a region which was then governed by the French Communist Party. The Pakbo and the Long groups had been unaffected by the events in Geneva and Lausanne. They were keen to continue, and Lucy was by now almost immune from any further interference from the authorities. The Centre seemed impressed by this proposal and told Foote to go ahead with its organisation while they would construct the paperwork he required to claim that he was a displaced Dutchman in France. Foote also handed over the 'voluminous' files of information he had brought from Switzerland that had come from Pakbo and Lucy.

Foote asked Novikov if he had seen Radó. He was told that he had not yet arrived in Paris, a 'terminological inexactitude' as Churchill once described a lie. Then, two weeks after this query, Radó appeared in the waiting room of the Soviet legation. He had been in Paris for weeks. Unable to shake off their espionage habits they ignored each other completely until they were in Novikov's office. They were both invited to a huge banquet at the mission that same evening. At the meal Radó looked ill at ease to say the least. Foote later described his conversation with Radó as being 'convivial but with rather sinister undercurrents' and said that Radó acted 'rather as the skeleton at the feast'.[110]

Seen through the lens of Stalinist paranoia about British intelligence, and in the light of Radó's proposal to take refuge with the British, warning lights of betrayal must have been blinking in Moscow. Moscow had always taken an attitude to their British allies which was, to say the least, uncomradely. On one occasion, Radó had come into the possession of material which would have been useless to the Eastern Front, but very useful on the Western Front. He was given strict instructions to burn it and under no circumstances to hand it to the British. Foote was shocked by this.

To Moscow's already paranoid suspicion of the Resident Director had to be added Foote's criticism of his boss, the poor accounting methods used to fund the network's spies and the unexplained evaporation of cash. Foote in turn was becoming more and more suspicious of the military attaché's behaviour. Novikov had known that Foote wanted to see Radó, but they had both apparently been kept apart deliberately. Now there was more to worry about. Foote's proposed mission to Annemasse was dropped by the Centre. Both of these by now senior officers of Soviet military intelligence, Radó a colonel and Foote a major, were called to Moscow for 'consultations', where 'they could cross examine us at leisure and compare one story with another'. No wonder Foote said he regarded his upcoming trip to the fatherland of the working class with 'mixed feelings'. Whether he thought this in 1944 or by the time he wrote his 1949 autobiography is unclear. By 1949 Foote's attitude to these invitations had hardened:

> Frequently these sudden recalls to Moscow are not dictated by necessity but from a desire by the Centre to ascertain the reactions of the person to such a summons. If he expresses immediate willingness to return the instructions are, as often as not, cancelled at the last minute. If, however, he hesitates ... [he] then becomes suspected by the Centre of 'Trotskyist sympathies' or some other crime.[111]

It is at this point of departure from Paris that Radó's autobiography goes very quiet and he gives no details as to his subsequent fate.

As for Foote, what possessed him to accept the invitation to Moscow? By this time he was thoroughly disillusioned by the Russians and the means by which they managed the people risking all to help them. In his autobiography he described them as the worst of employers: demanding, ungracious, making impossible demands and taking no responsibility for their own mistakes no matter how stupid. He had a half-hearted hope that he would be sent back to Switzerland to revive the network. But he had a more realistic expectation that once he arrived in Moscow he would never see Western Europe again. Turning these matters over in his mind it was plain to him that, should he present himself to the British embassy, he could be in London the same day. But the war was still on, anti-fascists were still being killed and the information he had was still vital to the venal and corrupt regime that had done so much damage to Nazism. To leave, he reasoned, would be to abandon his post when so many others had stuck to theirs. So he decided to go.

In 1949 British intelligence agent Courtenay Young wrote on Foote's behalf about Radó in *Handbook for Spies*:

I prefer to remember him [Radó] at the height of his powers as the genial cartographer to the world at large, and the successful spymaster to the favoured few, rather than as the hunted rat of his last Swiss days or the frightened, broken man of Paris and Cairo.

Whatever Foote would prefer, by 1949 Radó was in a Soviet prison camp and would not emerge until 1955. When he was released he went back to Hungary where he took up an academic career once again. In the fullness of time he would become a fellow of the Royal Geographical Society in London.

Chapter Eight

Moscow

Arrival: 16 January 1945

The plane that brought Maurice Thorez, the leader of the French Communist Party, back from exile in Moscow, took Foote and Radó to Russia via numerous stopovers, including one in Cairo. They were given Soviet passports and Foote travelled under the name Alfred Lapidus, while Radó was named Koulichev. Fellow passengers on the plane included a man called Miasnikov who entertained fellow passengers with the claim that he had authorised the execution of some of the Tsar's Romanov family during the revolution. This was an order, he said, which infuriated Lenin. Miasnikov was an all-round revolutionary loose-cannon. He had led a general strike against the Bolshevik government in 1920. Trotsky wanted him shot at that point, but Lenin packed him off to Siberia from whence he escaped to Turkey and subsequently went to Western Europe. This trip to Moscow was to be his homecoming.

During the flight to Cairo, Radó became more and more nervous. He was aware that to be told by one person that the Swiss network was destroyed, and by another that it was still up and running might suggest – in suspicious Stalinist minds – that the network had been penetrated by a Western intelligence agency. In a statement made to British intelligence in 1947 Foote described the scene during the stopover at the Hotel Luna Park in Cairo, where he and Radó were sharing a room:

> Radó remarked that we would probably both be shot for loosing [sic] what was considered vital sources of information. I replied that we could not be blamed for what had happened and in any case the sources of information still existed and it was only a case

of re-establishing the communications etc. I also informed him that I had telegraphed a considerable amount of information from the old sources to Moscow from Paris. This appeared to trouble Radó very much, and although he did not say so, I gathered that his report to Moscow must have announced the liquidation of these sources.[112]

Radó knew that minds who had successfully adapted to the horrors of the pre-war purges might regard the men on board the plane not as heroes who had risked everything to save the homeland of the socialist revolution, but as double agents bent on slowing the progress of the Red Army in destroying German fascism. Radó's anxiety here was not as far-fetched as it might sound. At that very moment Rudi Hamburger, Agent Sonya's first husband who was divorced on the basis of Foote's perjured evidence of adultery, was in the harshest of Soviet prison camps. He had been arrested in Tehran by the British for spying for the USSR but had managed to escape from his British and American captors. In 1943 he presented himself at the border of the USSR claiming asylum. He had spent ten years in faithful Soviet service, had spent time in prison in China with an amount of torture on their behalf, and yet he was imprisoned as a spy and held captive until 1955. The Russians considered his escape to be suspiciously easy and therefore thought he had been 'turned'.[113]

To be fair to the Russians for a moment, the Radó group were the only members of the Red Orchestra who had not been threatened/bribed/tortured into becoming double agents by the Nazis. There was the theoretical possibility that the same had happened to Radó's group. Although if this possibility were true, nobody in their right minds would go to Stalin's Russia.

Radó left the joint room he shared with Foote and disappeared into the Cairo night leaving his luggage and belongings behind him. 'Mute evidence,' as Foote put it, 'of a spy who has lost his nerve.' At some point Radó made contact with the British while in Egypt. A note signed by

British secret services agent 'H. Shillito' in Foote's MI5 dossier suggested that 'a good deal more might be got out of Radó'. One strategy for his interrogation, he mused, might be that they could 'insinuate, without saying in so many words' that Foote had turned informer and that they knew everything about his network.[114]

When he arrived in Moscow, Foote was met by one of the officers who had been his contact over the radio, Maria Poliakova (Vera). Both her father and her brother had been shot during Stalin's purge of 1937. Foote was given a place to stay at 29 Iznostvya Ulitsa in a flat occupied by Olga Pugachova, her daughter Ludmilla, and Ivan the interpreter. Nothing formal was said but Ivan gave Foote the impression he had been an NKVD officer at one point. His hostess was the widow of an Air Force colonel. The area in which he was placed was a part of the city where many of the country's military elite were housed. Because of the number of losses at the front, there was no shortage of widows who would be pleased to supplement their incomes by taking in a lodger. Each day he was visited by the woman called Vera, who he described as 'high ranking'. In his MI5 dossier, notes at the side of his 'homework' indicate that Poliakova was known to the British. Vera was extremely knowledgeable about the set up in Switzerland. Every telegram from Switzerland had passed through her hands, she said. She knew more about the personal lives of many of his agents than Foote.

Interrogation One: Moscow

I arrived in Moscow about January 16 ... Although all the individuals who visited me in the following days were friendly and never said it in actual words it was obvious from the questionnaires that I received that I was under suspicion. It was obvious to me that the Russians believed that my object in coming to Paris was at the instigation of the BIS (British Intelligence Service) in order to provide information calculated to retard the advance of the Red

Army. It seemed that they believed that Radó had been arrested by the British in Cairo to prevent him exposing me.[115]

The only first-hand account of his interrogation by Soviet intelligence comes from Foote himself. On his first night there he was handed a list of questions he would be expected to answer; after studying them, according to Foote he was 'to say the least, far from happy'. The tone of the questions revealed to Foote that the Russians suspected him of acting for the British (see p.160). The Swiss, according to the Centre, had released him on the understanding that he would set up a network and feed Moscow information given to him by British intelligence. This explained to the Soviets the degree of Foote's optimism about the state of the Swiss networks; they believed that British intelligence had set up a shadow network which Foote was to head up.

> The whole conception could only have been bred in brains to whom treachery, double-crossing, and betrayal were second nature. It was, in the abstract, high farce; but like so much farce, in the concrete it bordered on high tragedy as far as I was concerned ... unless I could clear myself I ... might only too easily find myself against a wall as a British spy.[116]

The same suspicion was applied years later to Guy Burgess and Donald Maclean when they arrived in the USSR. The first instinct of the Russians was to regard them as potential British spies:

> Burgess told foreign correspondent John Miller they were 'put in a small house guarded night and day by KGB troops. To all intents and purposes, they were under house arrest. The debriefing became an interrogation. This went on for several months and it quickly dawned on the two runaway diplomats that their hosts suspected they were in fact double agents. So they had to be

broken …' It's a view confirmed by Sergei Humaryan, then in his early twenties, who guarded them and was later director of the KGB museum in Samara.[117]

Foote was informed that the monthly sum of 25,000 French francs (£3,500 at 2010 prices) paid to Radó's wife in Paris had been stopped and she was told that she would receive nothing more from the Russians until she came to Moscow. This she prudently refused to do. In fact she divorced Radó to make her case for a residence permit in France stronger. They were only reunited when Radó was released from the gulag after Stalin's death. Their reunion was to be short lived, however, because she was already suffering from cancer when she joined him in Hungary. She was dead within three years.

Aware of the fearful predicament he was in, with a clear conscience (as he put it) Foote answered the reams of questions put to him in questionnaire form as truthfully as he could. Many of the questions, he came to realise, were intended to cross check and verify responses he had made elsewhere. Between these interrogation sessions Foote was allowed out to travel around Moscow, albeit with his 'interpreter, escort, guard all in one', as Foote drily called Ivan the interpreter.

Six weeks after his arrival in Moscow the Director came to see him. Charming, urbane, intelligent and intellectual, he spoke flawless English with a slight tendency to an American accent. Over dinner and drinks he interrogated Foote from six in the evening until two the next morning. They were especially interested in Lucy and Pakbo. They asked him who Lucy's sources were and how he got his information so quickly to Switzerland. 'On this point I was of course as ignorant as they were.'

The Director pulled out a telegram from a dossier and told Foote it came from his transmitter. The information on it was incorrect and had led Soviet troops into a trap and the loss of 100,000 men. This led to the Russians ignoring Lucy's messages until they could be certain that the mistaken message was an aberration. 'Perhaps, dear Jim, you could shed some light on this?' Foote could not. He transmitted what he was given.

After six hours of this the Director sent Foote to his bedroom as his dinner partners 'had some things to discuss'. After thirty minutes the Director came into his room and jovially slapped him on the back: 'There was nothing with which I could be reproached and as far as the Swiss debacle was concerned I was entirely exonerated.'

He continued:

> It was quite clever of the British not to approach me [after his release from prison] as it was not likely that I would put myself into the 'Bear's embrace' if I had a guilty conscience and had accepted a British offer to double cross.[118]

Accoce and Quet argue in their book that Foote was told at this stage that Radó had been executed. In his 1949 book Foote asserted that Radó was dead. It is not clear that he ever found out about his true fate. Radó was not as lucky as Foote. He was extradited from Cairo to Russia in August 1945 on a Russian charge of embezzlement. Foote says:

> About six months after my arrival in Moscow I was told that Radó had arrived there and that enquiries in Switzerland had shown that he had misappropriated a minimum of fifty thousand dollars and had been selling information to the British via Pakbo and Salter. Also, that the report he made from Paris contained numerous falsehoods.

In a secret military hearing Radó was sentenced to ten years in prison on a charge of espionage for the British, and embezzlement. After the death of Stalin he was released from prison on 25 November 1954 and allowed to live in Hungary. He was rehabilitated by the supreme court of the USSR and had his Order of Lenin reinstated. His commitment to Communism was undimmed. His autobiography ends with him saying that when his wife died three years after they were reunited, he marked her grave with a stone that read 'FOUNDATION MEMBER OF THE GERMAN COMMUNIST PARTY'.

After the interviews with his Soviet interrogators Foote considered himself to have a clean slate and requested that he be released from the Red Army to go back to England. This request was refused on the grounds that the British authorities would persecute him. Instead, further missions abroad were proposed. After a confusing set of potential missions, which turned out to be non-starters, the idea of travelling to Argentina to infiltrate Nazi émigrés who were reforming in that country was put to him (see Chapter Eleven).

During his stay in Moscow Foote's medical problems started to flare up again, largely due to the anxiety the precariousness of his position had caused him. He had suffered from duodenal ulcers for many years and these caused him intense pain, made worse by his dietary imprudence, smoking and alcohol, all of which figured highly in his lifestyle. He was treated in one of Moscow's top military hospitals and was very pleased with his treatment. After the acute phase had settled he was rested in a sanatorium until he was ready to resume normal life.

While in Russia, Foote was given extra training in radio construction and transmission and in microphotography. He was told that he would be sent on a fresh mission to China, or maybe to Mexico, or maybe to Argentina, where it was feared that the Nazis may have been regrouping. In order for him to build up a backstory for the Argentinian assignment, construct a paperwork trail and to improve his German, Foote was sent to Berlin.

In the end Foote spent some two years in Russia and he gave an unusual and unflattering portrait of the place. He described the rationing system imposed on the public; food was plentiful and high quality until the defeat of Japan, when the Lend-Lease arrangements with the USA ended abruptly. After that the quality of the food declined rapidly. And even where the food was of high quality he became 'heartily sick' of pickled cabbage. Soldiers were allowed to bring home booty from Germany and the higher the rank of the soldier, the more booty was allowed. His neighbourhood became noticeably wealthier while he was there.

He described the peasant free markets and the housing shortages. He described a gang-based crime wave that blighted Moscow in the years after the war. A whole division of Azerbaijani troops deserted and terrorised Moscow until they were all rounded up. The most brutal of the criminals were known as the 'Polish Gang', as they were most likely to kill the people they robbed. Armed robberies were commonplace in Moscow, he said. These were often sophisticated affairs where the robbers would be provided with covering fire from colleagues in order to ward off any local police militia unwise enough to 'have a go'. Crime stories did not appear in the Soviet press and so he only ever got an impression of the crime in his local area. He was advised by his neighbours not to intervene if he saw anybody being robbed. He was also strongly advised not to resist robbers if threatened, and to cooperate even if this meant the loss of his shoes and clothes.

He described the lives of those living without official papers in localities which were almost no-go areas for the authorities. These were often people who had managed to escape from the trains carrying people to the Soviet far east, destined for the camps. He said that one entire train had overwhelmed their guards and escaped. They terrorised the local countryside until they were rounded up. The population of undocumented citizens also included army deserters.

Foote and his interpreter Ivan were advised to always stick to back streets while out walking. This was because enthusiastic militia men might see a well dressed foreigner and jump to unwarranted conclusions about spying. In these circumstances, and it happened on one occasion, they were to refuse to answer any questions, particularly about names and addresses, and instead insist on making a telephone call to a number they should not reveal to the local constabulary. A car would be sent.

Foote's thoughts started to turn to getting out of the USSR as fast as possible. The comparison with pre-war Munich and post-war Moscow did not flatter the USSR:

> My first six weeks in Moscow had convinced me that Nazi Germany as I had known it was a paradise of freedom as compared with Soviet Russia. I was determined to get out of it as soon as possible and return to a world where freedom was more than a propaganda phrase.[119]

One is entitled to wonder what Foote would have made of post-war Munich. Bombed, starving and short of homes, Munich was a short distance from the Dachau extermination camp. The final days of the war also saw Gestapo lynchings of supposed traitors and backsliders in the streets of many cities.[120]

He attempted to persuade the Centre of his belief that Britain was entering a revolutionary phase and that his best option would be to return home to help build the Party, particularly if he was not being used for espionage work. His zeal impressed the director, but nothing came of this rush of revolutionary blood to the head.

After six months in Moscow he was told by the Director that Radó was in town and in all likelihood he was to be shot. He was accused of allowing his code to fall into the hands of the Swiss police, for falsely informing the Centre that the Swiss network had been 'liquidated', and for embezzling some $50,000. The Director also quizzed Foote about his opinion on the best way to lure Sissy to Moscow. She had plenty of questions to answer about the events in Canada, and there was a realistic prospect that she might have to, in Foote's words, endure 'the living death of an NKVD labour camp'. It would be hard to exaggerate the danger that Sissy was now in. She was blamed for the collapse of the entire espionage network in Canada and much of the USA at a time when the USSR was desperate to get its hands on American atomic secrets. The collapse of the Canadian set up had led to the sudden disappearance from the scene of Vera and the Director, who were replaced by people who could not be induced to say what happened to their predecessors. 'I never saw them again and they were never mentioned. The Centre has only one penalty for failure.'[121]

In fact, Major Vera survived this episode. She was interviewed for a film documentary of her life, *Alone Among Strangers*, in 2015. The film is on the internet but the links, in August 2023, are not working.[122] And besides that, it is in Russian with no subtitles.

Foote, still in Moscow and bored stiff, was sent to a training facility at Sehjodnya for extra instruction but this was all an exercise in keeping him busy. Books and periodicals were brought to him so that he could get up to speed with the current affairs of the countries he was supposed to go to. China was mentioned. Canada was mentioned. Mexico was mentioned as a base to work against the USA. But eventually Germany was chosen for his next mission.

This was the plan: he was to be Albert Müller, a German born in Riga in Latvia. In 1919 his English mother and German father took him to live in Spain. They both died when he was young. Having spent some time in the Far East, he was supposed to have travelled back to East Prussia in 1940 via the Trans-Siberian Railway. With the war now underway and with him (in theory at least) a German citizen, he was called up to the army to serve in the transport command on the Eastern Front. He was captured immediately and spent the war in Siberia. He had been returned to Germany because of ill health. His English accent was explained with reference to his English mother and him mixing with the English in the Far East.

With this background and the documents to support it, he was to go to Berlin. He was to stay out of active politics, but in private he was to express extreme right-wing and pro-Nazi sentiments. In this way he was to sniff out any escape routes being used by those Nazis left high and dry by the war, to get to Argentina. For six months he was to do nothing except to blend in and become as German as he could. Everything, he was assured, would be in place when he arrived.

Thoroughly disabused of any positive inclination towards the USSR, he left for east Berlin on 1 March 1947. Foote's estimation of the efficiency of the Soviet secret services did not improve when he found that all the promises he had been made about preparations for his arrival came to nothing. The famed rigour of Soviet espionage, he theorised, was due far more to the ideological commitment of the local Communist Parties who serviced the cranky Russian machine than anything Moscow did. Nobody in Berlin knew how to establish Foote as Albert Müller. All his paperwork was supposed to dovetail seamlessly in preparation for his arrival. Berlin was, theoretically, under German civilian management. Nothing was supposed to mark Müller out as being in any way connected with the USSR, yet here he was – faced by a clearly out-of-his-depth Captain Smirnov with no papers or anything else that would allow him to 'blend in'. So initially, Foote – AKA Müller – spent his days in a flat given to him by the Soviets at Grellenstrasse 12. His name was now to be Major Granatoff.

It was left to Foote himself to arrange his own paperwork: 'For anyone trying to do the same thing in Berlin I can give the only two infallible ingredients for success: endless patience and an inexhaustible supply of cigarettes.'

In *Aftermath: Life in the fallout of the Third Reich*, Harald Jähner described how scarce liveable accommodation was in Berlin, and how the cigarette became a negotiable unit of currency. An inexhaustible supply will have signalled that Foote was either very well off, or involved in the omnipresent black market, or both.[123] In the end, and after a seemingly infinite number of interviews with confused and inexperienced officials, Foote was placed with Frau Weber, at Wisbyer Strasse 41, in Pankow, a suburb of Berlin.

Foote was given a means of the Centre contacting him: someone would approach him in the street and ask 'When does the last train go?' He was to reply 'Since tomorrow at ten pm.' If he wanted to contact the Centre he was to leave a note on a local noticeboard which said: 'Wanted, a child's bicycle'. The next day they would meet at Prenzlauer station. When his German paperwork was finally in order, Major Granatoff was laid to rest. From April to August he stayed with Frau Weber. Then Müller disappeared too.

Chapter Nine

Berlin

Alone in Berlin: 7 March 1947

By the end of 1946, everybody seemed to be on the lookout for Foote. On 25 November 1946, a Mr Marriott of MI5 received a letter from Kim Philby. He asked whether a visit to Foote's sister Margaret might be in order to inquire about the whereabouts of her brother. The following month, in a note to Roger Hollis marked '13/12/1946', Winstone M. Scott at the American embassy asked: 'Our representative in Germany has asked whether or not you had an opportunity to question one of Radó's W/T operators ... Although the agent in question was not definitively identified we presume it was either Edmond Hamel or Alexander Allan Foote.' Michael Serpell responded 'I cannot find that we or MI6 have had any opportunity to question one of Radó's W/T operators, certainly not Hamel or Foote. I can say, however, that there is nothing we would like to do more!'[124] In 1947 Serpell's wish came true.

While he was in Berlin, Foote took the opportunity to present himself to British intelligence. On 1 July 1947, a summary of his personal details and an outline of his history was taken by Intelligence Team 147 and marked Top Secret in red. He was interviewed under the supervision of one 'Mr Steel' of (B) I.S. (British Intelligence Service) where Foote made an offer. For the return of his passport and a ticket home, he would reveal to the British authorities everything that he knew about the Soviet secret services. His offer was enthusiastically taken up. He was interrogated in Germany over three days where he was forensically debriefed.

The British secret service had been looking for Foote as early as February 1944, as a letter to Roger Hollis from Colonel Vivian[125] revealed.[126] Rumours of a connection with Russian intelligence had alerted the attention of the British secret services. From this point on they were on the lookout. They knew that he had left Switzerland in June 1945 and had gone to France, but enquiries after that with the *Service des Etrangers* in Paris had drawn a blank. It was even suggested by MI6, in the person of H.A.R. (Kim) Philby, that enquiries might be made at the address of Foote's sister, Margaret Powell, in East Grinstead to see if she had heard from him.[127] There are six letters from Philby enquiring about Foote's whereabouts in the records. When Foote eventually came back to Britain, he first went to live with his sister, so presumably by then the Russians knew where he was.

Behind the scenes arrangements were made with the RAF to prevent any arrest over the matter of his desertion in 1936. In his MI5 file there is a Discharge Certificate dated 23 December 1936 which states: 'Services no longer required – at own request.' He had only been with the RAF for one year of a six-year stint. There is an accompanying note in his file from Squadron Leader W.G. Parry. Dated 14 October 1947, it is marked Top Secret and says: 'I am now enclosing, as arranged, certificate of service and discharge in respect of the above-named, for onward transmission. When this is done, Foote's signature on page one is necessary.' Neat and tidy, the question of Foote's desertion in 1936 was closed.

From Berlin, Foote was quickly transferred by plane to Hanover, presumably to get him away from the long arm of Soviet retribution. Arriving in Hanover, Foote revealed everything he could about his experiences in Switzerland, including the systems by which the Russians coded their messages, and their rules concerning clandestine work. He made himself available to view photographs of Soviet agents for the purposes of naming or clearing suspected spies. Philby's interest in Foote's whereabouts suggests that from the outset, as the British secret services were finding out about the Russian secret service, they were being observed from Moscow. The information about Sonya that Foote revealed was channelled to, among others, Roger Hollis. In the 1980s, the book *Spycatcher* by Peter Wright had to be published in Australia because it was banned by the Thatcher government. Wright had made (repeatedly debunked) allegations that Hollis blocked any serious investigation into her spying activities. Hollis, by now the head of MI5, was accused by Wright (and others!) of being the 'Fifth Man' after Philby, Burgess, Maclean and Blunt. Later on, there is an appearance of Guy Liddell in the correspondence.[128] His friendship with the Cambridge spies led to him facing his own questions after their defections.

Chapter Ten

Hanover – The MI5 files

As with everything else in the history of Alexander Foote, caution must be exercised when considering his interrogations. He was comprehensively interrogated in Moscow when he arrived there in 1944, but the content of those episodes have only one first-hand witness and that is Foote himself. There is no reason to suspect his account of those events, but intelligence work is based on dissembling and deceit – none more so than in his own case, so maintaining a healthy scepticism about his accounts is prudent.

His interrogations by the British secret service commenced after he arrived in Berlin and presented himself to the British authorities there in 1947. In contrast to his Moscow interrogation we only have MI5's version of events on paper. His autobiography ends abruptly in Berlin where he 'walked to freedom'. Beyond this point the only voices to be heard were those of his interrogators and their back-up teams. His freedom did not extend to describing his handling by MI5.

His first interview was conducted by Sergeant Bodinger of the 147 Intelligence team, under the instructions of a 'Mr Steel'. Foote's case number was 270, and he was first interviewed on 30 June 1947. In his summary of Foote's interview Bodinger wrote: 'His object in contacting the British authorities he stated is to obtain permission to return to England or to work for the British as he dislikes continuing to work for the Russians.'[129]

Although the first of his interviews is dated 30 June, in Foote's book he gives the date of his leaving the Russian sector as being in August 1947, one month later: 'on August 2, 1947, I left the Russian sector and walked into the British zone and freedom.'

Subsequent interrogations were undertaken by MI5 officers Joan Paine and Michael Serpell. Serpell composed extensive summaries of Foote's interviews.

The files containing his interviews were made public in the National Archive in 2004 and even a cursory examination undermines many of the claims made about Foote in the more sensationalised accounts of his work. For instance, Read and Fisher claim in their 1980 book *Operation Lucy* that Foote had been recruited to British intelligence before his trip to Spain by Colonel Dansey, senior officer of a shady outfit called 'Department Z', and was a British agent throughout his time in Switzerland. There is little in The National Archives' files to support this view.

His initial records are composed of information of the following types. There are first-person statements he wrote about his history and the various stages of his career in espionage. These are referred to as his 'homework'. Then there are third-person accounts given by intelligence officer Michael Serpell, who was assessing the information as Foote was delivering it. It is perhaps a measure of the importance given to Foote's appearance that Serpell was flown out to Hanover to examine him. Serpell gives highly impressionistic accounts of his meetings and they frequently contain value judgements and comments about Foote's character. Sometimes it is hard to match the comments of Serpell with comments made elsewhere by other colleagues and friends; Foote is mostly described elsewhere as intelligent and resourceful. But Serpell reveals that he believes him to be an idiot. Who is one to believe? Could it have been that Foote was deliberately 'acting soft', to use a Liverpool expression, to influence the thinking of British security? Was he using the ingrained snobbery of the British service to shield him from too close an examination of his activities?

To read the interview transcripts, one is struck by the disrespect that Foote's interrogators had for him. At a professional spy-to-spy level they might have admired his achievements in dangerous and demanding circumstances as he conveyed information filched from under the noses of the enemy to assist Britain's greatest ally. But instead, the comments made about him drip with contempt:

> I asked Foote what he gathered ... was the extent of Swiss knowledge of the network. Either Foote was too stupid to sort [two words obscured] out in his own mind or he was unwilling to talk about it but he always turned the conversation around to points which were, anyway, of interest to me.[130]

A summary of Foote's case compiled and signed by Roger Hollis on 30 October 1947 echoes and amplifies the picture of Foote being a simpleton: 'On all his interrogators Foote left the impression of remarkable simplicity and to such an extent did this characteristic affect his career that the present article might be subtitled "An Innocent Abroad".'

The irony in this statement is profound. While Foote spent the war assisting an ally who faced an existential threat, dodging the Abwehr, the Swiss authorities and eventually his Soviet managers, Hollis was working in an organisation penetrated to its highest level by Soviet spies. The charge of 'remarkable simplicity' reveals a lack of self awareness which would only be partially corrected by the later revelations about the Cambridge spies. Hollis himself could perhaps accurately be described as an 'innocent at home'.[131]

Foote's appearance in Berlin created something of a dilemma for MI5. Was this person who he claimed to be? Was he a genuinely recanting Soviet agent? Or was he playing the British along? In an internal note Michael Serpell reflected on the prospect of interrogating him. He said that Roger Hollis had suggested Foote created two possibilities.[132] The first was that if he could be established as a truly converted individual, he might yet be sent to South America as a double agent for the SIS (otherwise known as MI6). The second was that, in either case, he should be interrogated in Hanover for his background knowledge of the *Rote Drei* and the Red Orchestra in general. All of this, concluded

Otto Pünter (Agent Pakbo) with microdot camera.

11 Clifton Gardens, formerly the Worsley House Hotel. Foote's post-war home.

Mrs Churchill's 'Aid to Russia Fund' posters.

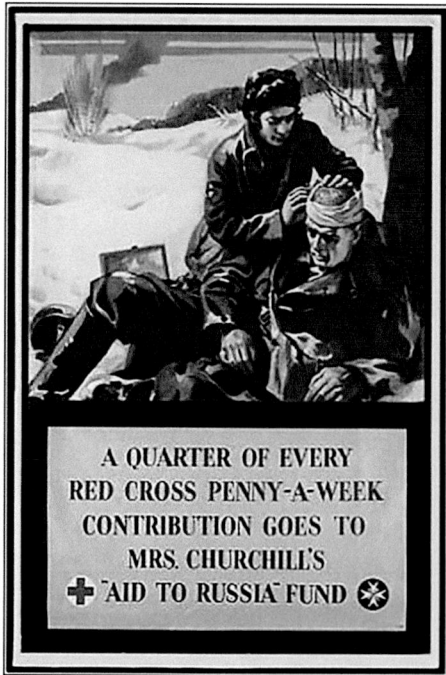

Foote's press reception for his autobiography.

Picture of Foote in 1954.

Picture of Foote circa 1940.

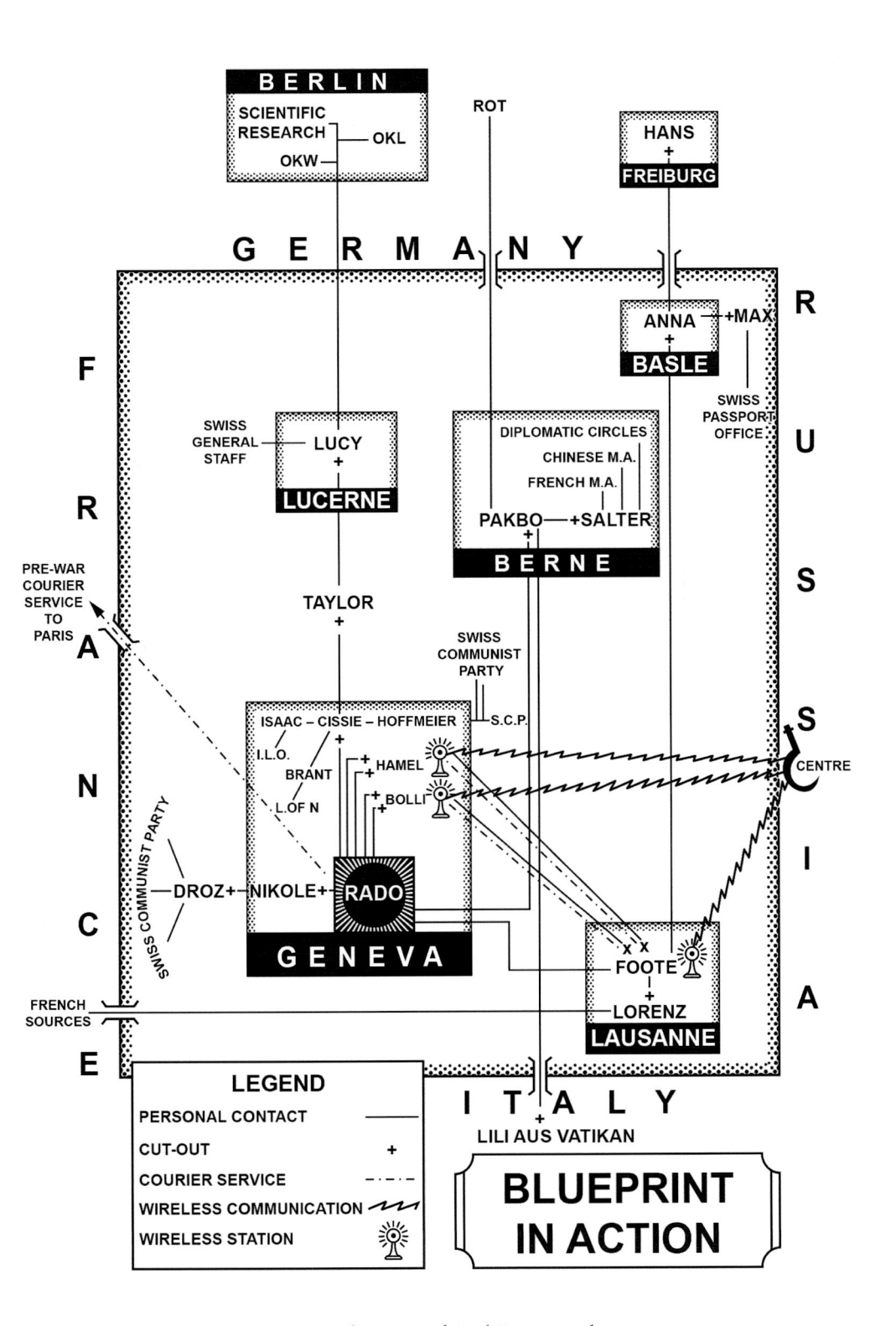

Foote's diagram of Radó's network.

Chemin de Longeraie, Foote's address in Lausanne.

German wartime radio finder van.

Foote's wardrobe. X marks where his transmitter was hidden. *(Arsenijevic archive)*

Cover, *Handbook For Spies*.

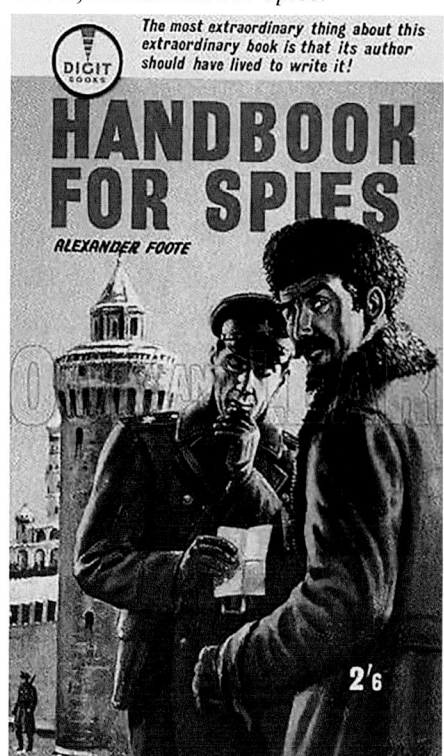

Hidden cupboard in Foote's wardrobe where the transmitter was hidden. *(Arsenijevic archive)*

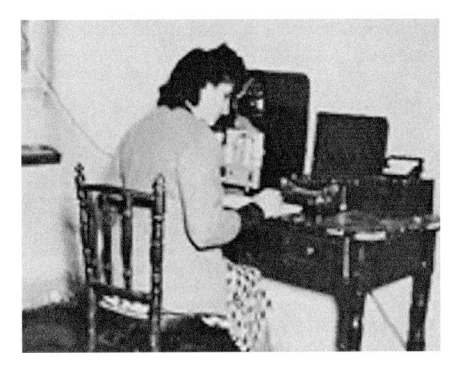

Olga Hamel at her shortwave radio.

Sandor and Hélène Radó.

Rudolf Rössler, 1950s.

Rugby Mansions; Foote's first address in London, an MI5 safe house.

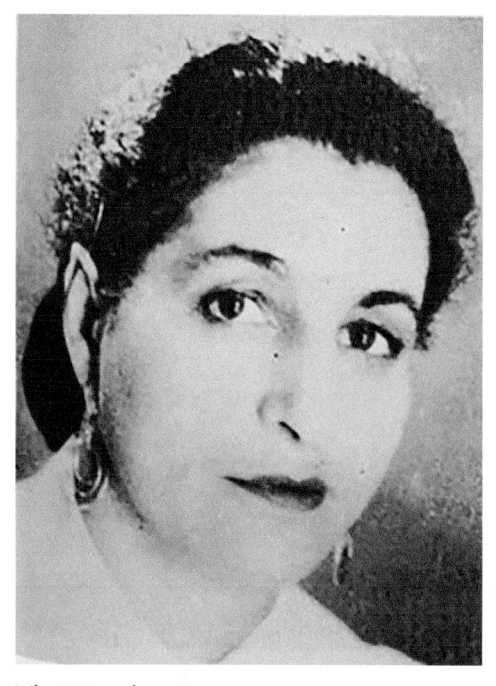

The Hamels.

Local news coverage in Lausanne of Foote's revelations.

NEWS REVIEW, March 9, 1950

PEOPLE BEHIND THE HEADLINE

Who Are the Reds in M.I.5?

LIKE most people in Britain last week, we wondered what a Russian spy looks like. So we invited one to come into the office for a chat. Apart from an alert glint in his eye and a suggestion of devil-may-care in his attitude, there was nothing to distinguish him outwardly from any fellow-traveller (British Railways variety).

But we were not disappointed. Alexander Foote, a 44-year-old North countryman, is now retired from the business. An 18-month stay in Moscow, whence he was recalled at the end of the war to prepare for a new assignment, finally made up his mind that the dreary Red city was not his spiritual home.

Foote started on the road to Soviet spydom when he went to Spain in 1936 to fight in the International Brigade. When that was over he was sent to

he pointed that one of the Communist Party's most useful functions was "the organising of study and discussion groups among young students and intellectuals.

"From among the members of these groups it is possible to discover potential spy material—people who, though not members of the Party, are likely to be amenable to the espionage approach, and people who are either in, or likely one day to be in, posts where they could obtain information of value to Russia.

"Such promising candidates would be discouraged from openly joining the Party or openly expressing Communist or Leftwing views."

Foote pooh-poohs the idea that Rus-

numbers of secret Communist [illegible] tions of trust in America [illegible]

He does not envy M.I.5 [illegible] rooting out Russian agents [illegible] was interrogated on quitting [illegible] sians in Berlin, he found [illegible] had a pretty scanty knowledge [illegible] Russian system. And from [illegible] experience he knows that [illegible] ment Department is [illegible] of the ideological [illegible] Party before country.

Says he: "During the war I [illegible] contacts in Berlin—I never knew [illegible] they were—who used to bring [illegible] formation out of the German [illegible] Command itself. It was much [illegible] difficult to spy in a country like [illegible] Germany than it would be [illegible] God knows what's happening [illegible] must be getting away with [illegible]

Others versed in the Soviet [illegible]

International coverage of Foote's revelations.

Gazette de Lausanne
ET JOURNAL SUISSE

LES RÉVÉLATIONS SENSATIONNELLES
d'un agent soviétique installé en Suisse pendant la guerre

Nouveaux aspects de la politique allemande

'Sensational Revelations'. How Foote's story was received in the Swiss press.

Pour ne rien manquer des

révélations sensationnelles

d'un agent soviétique en Suisse

que la

Gazette de Lausanne

publiera au cours des semaines à venir

abonnez-vous pour deux mois dès aujourd'hui

et profitez de notre prix spécial en envoyant le bulletin ci-contre à notre administration.

BULLETIN D'ABONNEMENT à prix spécial

(à découper et à envoyer à la « Gazette de Lausanne », rue de Genève 7, Lausanne, sous pli ouvert (5 cts)

Le soussigné s'abonne à la

Gazette de Lausanne

pour une durée de deux mois à partir de la parution du premier article concernant les révélations d'Alexander Foote, agent soviétique en Suisse durant la guerre, et pour le prix spécial de Fr. 6.50*

Nom : . . . .

Rue : . . . .

Ville : . . . .

* Je verse la somme de Fr. 6.50 au compte de chèques « Gazette de Lausanne », II 2.
* Je vous prie de prendre la somme de Fr. 6.50 en remboursement, plus frais.
* (Biffer ce qui ne convient pas)

Signature : . . . .

'SPY' TRIAL OPENS

Briton Accused

Lausanne, Friday.—Charges of using clandestine transmitters during the war to send vital military information to Moscow were made at the opening of the trial here in their absence of a Hungarian named Hamel, and a British subject, described as Alexander Allan Foote. The woman in the case is a beautiful blonde named Bolli, from whose apartment it is alleged messages were sent until they were tracked down by the Swiss Intelligence Service. Hamel was employed by another Hungarian, named Rado, who spent £16,000 in a few weeks on espionage for the Russians. He was chief agent in Switzerland for the Comintern. Foote, who seemed to have played a subordinate in the affair, escaped from Switzerland last year after being held by the police for several months.—*Evening News Correspondent.*

Evening News
31.10.47

LAUSANNE

UN PROCÈS D'ESPIONNAGE

Le Tribunal militaire de division 1-A jugera à Lausanne, le 30 octobre, sous la présidence du lieutenant-colonel Roger Corbaz, une importante affaire d'espionnage militaire au préjudice d'un Etat étranger.

Les inculpés sont Alexander Rado, de nationalité hongroise, domicilié en dernier lieu à Genève, actuellement sans domicile connu, sa femme, Hélène Rado, née Jansen, et Alexander Allan Foote, sujet britannique, domicilié en dernier lieu à Lausanne, également sans domicile connu à l'heure actuelle. Tous trois seront jugés par contumace.

Ils sont accusés d'espionnage militaire au préjudice d'un Etat étranger, de contravention à l'interdiction d'installations radiophoniques émettrices ou d'instigation à cette infraction, d'infraction aux prescriptions sur le maintien de la neutralité, de violation de secrets intéressant la défense nationale et de franchissement clandestin de la frontière.

Gazette de Lausanne,
15. 10. 47

Newspaper reports of Foote's trial.

Brigitte Kuczynski's flat in the Isokon building; the scene of Foote's recruitment.

Hollis, depended on clearing up a few things about Foote. The first thing was that Scotland Yard were aware of Foote leaving for Spain in 1936 after deserting from the RAF. They were also aware of him re-entering the country in 1938. Why, Serpell asked, was he not picked up and charged with desertion? Furthermore, enquiries at RAF records in Gloucester for 1936 showed no records of any deserters.

Serpell recommended a 'velvet glove' approach to his interrogation. He was to be encouraged in a friendly way to talk about his past so MI5 could check his story against what was known about his biography. By 1945 the interrogation of German counter intelligence officers had given the British a pretty accurate idea of what Foote's team had been up to during the war. The veracity and accuracy of Foote's words could be measured against this limited background. Foote was also to be asked to start writing his autobiography by hand so that his handwriting could be compared with his passport application.

There was one thing on which Serpell was emphatic: Foote should not be allowed back into the UK until he had been thoroughly interrogated in Germany, and he was the man to do the interrogation:

> I believed it would be best to hold up our admission of his British citizenship as long as possible. If the story of his desertion from the RAF turned out to be a mare's nest [an apparently huge discovery that turns out to be worthless] we should have little we could hold over Foote for the purposes of questioning him in this country, and it was imperative that we get everything out of him before releasing him in the UK.

In his autobiography Foote describes how he managed to avoid the worst of fates on his arrival in Moscow when he was being interrogated: he told them exactly what, in his estimation, he thought they would like to hear. Examples of this might include: the perfidy of the British ruling class and their determination to undermine the USSR at all costs, the cunning of the Foreign Office in London and the ever-present tentacles of British intelligence and secret services and so on. David Dallin interviewed Foote and recorded his technique:

> Soon I conceived how to answer their queries: it was reasonable to interpret every move by the Allies as inimical to the Soviet Union. When a British car, for instance, was made a gift to Stalin, I commented: the intention is to make Stalin's car easily recognisable and then, if necessary, to blow him to pieces etc ... Gradually I acquired the techniques of pretending.[133]

This was the approach that Foote advanced to his erstwhile Soviet colleagues to convince them that he was a true believer who was, like them, ever faithful to the cause. There is little evidence from the record of his British interviews that his interrogators suspected him of pulling the same trick on them. Defecting to Britain after years of service to the USSR, Foote emerged in Berlin anti-Soviet, antisemitic, pro-German, anti-communist, pro-conservative, and possibly intending to vote for a fascist party. Nobody in his notes seems to consider this volte face a little too ... complete. It is all too easy to imagine Foote's recantation after his time in Moscow, but the wholesale ideological conversion in his interviews seems a bit too convenient. Also, the gallery that he was performing to resembled the intelligence service that Foote may have last known when he left Britain for Spain in 1936: public school, conservative, sympathetic to Mosley, anti-Semitic and profoundly anti-communist. During his interrogation in Germany, his interrogator noticed his anachronistic take on world affairs: 'He showed himself to be very much out of date ... his main worry was that he would find a "1938" atmosphere in this country, referring to arm chairs, day dreamers and all the rest of the apparatus.'[134]

Continuing in a convivial vein, Foote was allowed to reminisce about his time in the International Brigade, which he did with gusto. A man described by his interrogator as his 'keeper' had also engaged Foote on this subject while he was out of the interrogation room, without revealing that he too had been in the brigade. The parallel here with Ivan the interpreter is hard to ignore. Foote gave thumbnail estimations of the character of people and politicians he had met in Spain. He was rude about Harry Pollitt and Dave Springhall. He did not rate Tom Wintringham as a soldier, but he did rate Malcolm Dunbar as a soldier – though not as a politician. He spoke highly of Giles Romilly, Churchill's nephew, who Foote claimed to have prevented from deserting.

In winding up his summary of the day's interview with Foote, Serpell added that he seemed very proud of the fact that he had saved himself a lot of grief from the Russians by insisting they respond directly to Radó (using the codename Albert) regarding Radó's proposal to take refuge in the British legation. This, Foote said, saved him a lot of explaining when he was in Russia.

In assessing his interrogation it is worthwhile remembering that Foote was at no point under caution in his interviews or in his statements. It is not clear that he was guilty of any offence in British law, apart from going missing from the RAF in 1936. Serpell pointed out to him that he might possibly have been technically committing a crime in spying for the USSR when Britain was at war with Germany and the Russians were supplying them with war materials under the Nazi-Soviet pact. But he was never accused of spying against the interests of Britain directly, and at interview – after some prevarication – denied that he would ever have done so. In fact, it would be easy to imagine him receiving a medal for the assistance he rendered Britain's most valued ally when everything was in the balance, especially when this assistance came at some considerable risk to himself.

What British intelligence had over Foote in 1947 was the threat, the real threat, of sending him back to the Russian sector of Berlin. When Foote had originally gone to Moscow from Paris, he did so with a Russian passport. That could be used to send him back. If he was handed over to the comrades, Foote's life – instead of petering out in boredom at the Ministry of Agriculture and Fisheries – might have had quite a different outcome. His initial interrogator in Hanover muses at one point: 'He fears (apparently) nothing from the British and indeed we have perhaps no direct espionage against him. So why not at least try this line with a possibility that we might send him out.'[135]

The first formal interview that Foote underwent at the hands of British intelligence was held in Hanover on 19 July 1947. The interviews began on a Saturday morning and went on until Monday morning.

Interrogation One: Saturday morning, 19 July 1947

The interviews that started on the Saturday morning and were reported by Michael Serpell (who gave his name to Foote as Mr Saville) have a meandering, conversational quality that jump around from date to date without following a strict timeline. When asked why he had defected from Russia, Foote stated that he had planned to escape soon after his arrival in the USSR. He wasted no time in saying that he was not a Marxist and had never been a member of the Communist Party.[136] His current aim, he said, was to 'expose Russian wickedness', and to save Britain from 'centralised socialised destruction'. This destruction he perceived developing in Attlee's post-war Labour government. His disquiet over this had gone so far that he was considering voting Conservative at the next election. This led Serpell to make the note that 'I doubt if Foote has any political principles whatsoever.'[137] This impression was strengthened by Foote's declaration that he was not bothered by the Nazi-Soviet pact of 1939. In fact, his refusal to work towards promotion in the International Brigade, he told Serpell, was because 'he didn't think his Marxism would stand up to the test'.

Nevertheless, he was comfortable among the communist leadership of the brigades. He indicated that he believed Peter Kerrigan had recommended him for courier work, while he thought that Dave Springhall had recommended him for the 'dangerous mission' abroad which kick-started his career in espionage. He denied doing any secret work in Spain and described the only Russian he met there as being a 'detestable nark'.

He described how he was sent for a meeting in London, at 4 Lawn Road, Belsize Park, to meet Brigitte Lewis of the Kuczynski family of left-wing academics and activists. He described his relations with Brigitte but denied that he ever knew her husband. Serpell clearly believed that this was important evidence regarding Brigitte. He said in his notes that Foote's remarks were 'completing the evidence against Brigitte', although it is not clear at this stage what she is supposed to have done. It suggests that Serpell was already suspicious about the Kuczynskis.

Saturday morning with Serpell continued with his account of how he had been assessed and recruited for secret work.

He described his meetings with Brigitte Kuczynski and his first meetings with Agent Sonya, Brigitte's sister, in Switzerland. He gave to Serpell the complicated rituals the Soviet secret service used when agents met each other for the first time. Then he went on to describe the circumstances in which he came to recommend Len Beurton for service alongside himself and Sonya. He said that Beurton, who had worked under him in transport while in Spain, was the only person he could think of to do the sort of work they had in mind. Now living in Munich and commuting to Switzerland for meetings with Sonya, Foote revealed that, at that stage, Beurton did not know he was working for the Russians. When he found out he became very annoyed, said Foote. He had seen the Russians at work in Spain. Foote said that Sonya 'had to plead with him' to stay on board.[138]

Foote described to Serpell the vague plans the three cooked up in Switzerland: to set fire to a Zeppelin in Frankfurt and/or to assassinate Hitler. Any future plans were forbidden by Moscow after the signing of the Molotov-Ribbentrop pact. Foote declared that neither he nor Beurton did any serious work for the Russians after this agreement was signed and that the reason they were there was rather baffling to them. They were supposed to try to contact staff at the BMW and IG Farben factories in Munich and Frankfurt respectively, but neither did. Apart from reading books about wirelesses, all Foote did in Munich was 'get around'. This did not impress him with the efficiency of Russian intelligence.

From here the conversation jumped to his experiences in Russia again. When asked why he agreed to go to Russia in 1945, he made the curious remark that he thought that 'the British would like him to go there'. This enigmatic remark has fed the imaginations of countless conspiracists ever since. Without accepting any of these theories, one would have to admit that it was an intriguing statement to come out with.

At first Foote told Serpell that he went to Russia with a clear conscience about his activities and that his record of espionage for them in Switzerland was sound, by their lights. But when Serpell pressed him further it became clear that Russian paranoia about British infiltration of their intelligence services was so profound that he 'went in fear of his life'. The Russians, he said, were in the habit of liquidating the innocent as well as the guilty. This fear was exacerbated when Radó went missing in Cairo and he felt that the anxiety induced by this episode contributed to the development of stomach ulcers in Moscow.

When asked directly if he would, at that time, have spied against Britain between 1938 and 1945, he replied 'I would really rather you hadn't asked me that question but yes, if they had asked me at the beginning I might have done.' But he did not, in retrospect, consider that he had ever compromised British intelligence.

Interrogation Two: Saturday afternoon, 19 July 1947

At the start of Saturday afternoon's interrogation, Serpell described Foote as being 'slightly chastened' by the contents of the morning's interviews and set about correcting some minor points he wished to clarify regarding technical details about whose call signs were used for their early broadcasts.

Much of the afternoon session was taken up with Foote providing thumbnail descriptions of the personalities behind the codenames of the people in his circle. Serpell made one note which was of relevance to the claims made by later authors that Foote had been a British agent: 'Questioned about anyone he thought might have been working for the British, F said he knew of no one except Farrell whom "everyone knew was connected with the British I.S. or was a channel for conveying information to it".'

Foote also revealed that Beurton had given Farrell some information concerning a Chinese diplomat in Geneva who was posing as a press attaché. In return, Farrell helped Beurton with his passport application and return to the UK. Foote knew about Eleanor Rathbone's intervention on Beurton's behalf from a wire that Moscow Centre had sent him.

Later, Foote revealed Radó had confided in him that he had some sixty people on his payroll. He also revealed the distribution of wireless sets between Beurton, himself, the Hamels (Edouard and Maude)[139] and Margaret Bolli (Rosy). He gave an account of Radó's wife enciphering and carrying reports to the radio operators.

One interesting feature of the Saturday afternoon interviews was that Foote revealed he had asked Moscow to find out what had happened to his old friend and sometime fiancée Agnes Zimmerman. The Centre subsequently told him that her house in Munich had been bombed. Foote did not believe that they had made any enquiries at all. Perceptively, Serpell made a special note that he thought Foote was especially fond of Agnes, and that Foote had not told him the full story regarding their relationship.

Foote also expanded on a theme to which he returned repeatedly: the incompetence of the Centre in Moscow in providing for their network's finances. He said they could not understand the realities of work in Switzerland.

He revealed that he had met the person he had known only as 'The Director' once, soon after he arrived in Moscow. This was later in his stay. First he met the woman in Moscow who had handled his radio traffic. Her codename was Vera, and it was this woman who had handed the network over to Sonya in 1939. He met her about twice a week until April 1946, when Vera and her boss were suddenly removed from their jobs. Foote met the new director who was of 'Mongol' appearance and could only speak German to Foote.

Interrogation Three: Sunday morning, 20 July 1947

The Sunday morning session began with Foote sheepishly seeking to take back his remarks about being prepared to spy against Britain. Michael Serpell seems rather sympathetic to him on this point. He said that he interpreted Foote's attitude in 1939 as being anti-Chamberlain rather than being anti-British: 'In so far as Foote had any genuine political convictions in 1938–1939 I think it may be said that he had a strong dislike for the Chamberlain government and what he described as their "policy of appeasement".'[140]

By 1945, of course, these attitudes to appeasement had become the consensus view of the Chamberlain years.

Serpell asked Foote what he thought the attitude of the British government would be to his defection from Russia. Foote declared that he had little to fear from returning as he had done valuable work in the interests of the Allies. Serpell deliberately poured cold water on this idea by suggesting that a British court might not see assisting the Russians when they were allies to Germany in 1939 in the same light. After this Foote returned to his theme of not being, and never having been, fully communist, and that his activities for the Russians had been motivated by internationalism. Foote responded to the charge that in 1939 he was helping an ally of Germany by stating that he was inactive in 1939, that he had done 'damn all' for them at this time.

Serpell changed the subject at this point and turned to events subsequent to 1945. He prodded Foote on the subject of 'ratting' on Len Beurton. Why, Serpell asked him, did this bother his conscience when Beurton had done nothing more than Foote had, in leaving the service of the Soviets? Foote argued that it was one thing to desert his post in the services of the USSR, and another to inform on a colleague. Such things were very poorly tolerated by Moscow.

Serpell returned to the question of Foote's time in Munich in 1939. Foote had very pleasant memories of his stay there. He was given generous 'expenses' in order that he might 'circulate'. He liked the Germans and thought they had a lot in common with the English. He had an English teacher who was in the SS, but who confessed to Foote that he was in the Nazi Party for reasons of professional advancement. All in all Munich had been a very pleasant interlude and, Foote thought, many anti-Nazis would have found the lifestyle there very acceptable. Serpell suggested that Foote might have considered working for the Germans. To his surprise, Foote said that he and Beurton had considered it. When he saw Serpell's reaction, Foote declared that he meant working for them with a view to double crossing them.

There followed considerable discussion about Agent Sonya and Len Beurton. When Sonya had travelled to Britain, Foote said he had had to tell the lovesick bridegroom to stop sending her 'stupid telegrams' written in plain English. This was especially the case because they included poorly disguised criticism of Sándor Radó in them.

The rest of the Kuczynski family came in for some discussion after that. Jürgen was singled out for his activities in compiling economic reports about Britain which he took to the Russian embassy.

Foote was asked what he knew about Rudolf Hamburger. Most of what he knew, Foote said, he gathered from the nurse Olga Muth. She had an inkling about Sonya's activities and had helped in one mission for Sonya. He described how upset Olga had been at Sonya's marriage of convenience.

Serpell was interested in exploring whether Beurton was still in contact with the Russians, indicating that their efforts on his behalf with Eleanor Rathbone, to facilitate a passage back to Britain, might suggest he was still of value to them. Foote replied that Beurton hated Radó and was highly critical of the Russians. After he had trained the Hamels, Beurton effectively stopped work altogether, even though Moscow ordered him to resume work.

The conversation then turned to the subject of Agent Lucy. Foote said that Radó had Lucy information 'before June 1941', but that the

Russians were not interested in it because they could not independently verify the sources Werther, Teddy and Olga – Lucy's agents in Germany. These three sources were prolific in their output. In 1967 the CIA published a research paper about the activities of the Red Orchestra in general and the *Rote Drei* in particular, where they analysed the volume of messages sent by each of these sources. They estimated that Werther contributed 21 per cent of the group's output of messages while Teddy and Olga contributed 10 per cent and 8 per cent respectively.[141] Together, these three sources therefore contributed 39 per cent of the total output of Radó's network. When Radó saw how accurately the information predicted German military activity he put it forward to Moscow again, but by Autumn of 1941 they began to receive the information 'with enthusiasm'. Foote described Lucy's cut out Schneider (Taylor) as working entirely for the money he received. Lucy himself, Foote said, was given 7,000 francs per month (approximately £11,600). Foote was given $150 (£1,068) per month rising to $200 (£1,424). This was not enough to live on, he said. But the Russians were generous with expenses, which they never quibbled about. Foote was supposed to send in his accounts yearly, but he did this more often as was required.

Serpell put to him that with a generous expense account he could lead a very comfortable life. Foote replied that he was often at work for twenty hours a day, and that he had little time for recreation. This was made worse by the obsessive security procedures he always had to observe when he was out. Although he had many rewarding, if platonic, relationships with married women, his job meant that he 'lived the life of a monk'. Serpell asked him about the couriers who carried communications between Radó and himself. Foote mentioned Olga Hamel and Margaret Bolli. Serpell added as a side note that Bolli's name was interesting in this regard as a high-ranking German radio counterintelligence official named Flicke[142] had mentioned under interrogation that the Abwehr had penetrated Radó's network via a female courier.

Serpell said he asked Foote to give him details of the flight from Paris to Moscow. He started by asking him about a man known to Foote as Ivanov. Described by Foote as 'plump, pink complexioned, medium build, fair hair, blue eyes', he spoke French fluently but with a funny accent. Serpell showed Foote a photograph of Leopold Trepper, the Resident Director of the espionage team operating out of Belgium. Without hesitation Foote said he was prepared to swear that this was the man known to him as Ivanov. Foote made disparaging remarks about Ivanov to Serpell, saying his contribution had been minimal because he had spent most of the war in hiding. Foote confessed that on the plane he made some rude remarks about Jews; Miasnikov, one of the other passengers, told Foote to tone down his remarks as Ivanov was a Jew, which Foote had not realised. Despite this, Ivanov was a good companion to Foote on the flight. When they eventually arrived in Moscow, because of some bureaucratic mix up, no car was there to greet them. Ivanov took matters into his own hands and telephoned the Foreign Ministry to arrange transport. In the car Ivanov expressed some fond sentiments about his wife in Moscow and said he was looking forward to giving her a hat he had bought for her in Cairo.

Foote was asked about Ivanov during his interrogation by 'the woman major' (Vera). Foote told her that Ivanov was of the opinion that Himmler might seize power in Germany and seek to make contact with the Russians to make a separate peace with them. When his interrogator heard this she described Ivanov as a 'stupid idiot'. Ivanov was arrested soon after his arrival in Moscow and was sentenced to ten years' imprisonment. A biographical article published in a declassified CIA document quoted Trepper (Ivanov) as saying:

In Switzerland he [Radó] had contributed substantially to the victory [of the USSR] but because of his profound understanding of the facts, and his realism as a man of learning, he felt in spite of victory nothing had changed in the kingdom of OGPU (KGB). He foresaw the fate that awaited him in Moscow. He did not care for the prospect of ending his life in one of Stalin's jails, hence he disappeared in Cairo after making sure his wife and children were safe in Paris ... The truth Radó perceived did not strike me with its blinding light until later. I was too naïve.[143]

Another passenger on the plane was Vladimir – a 'Hero of the Soviet Union' who had led a group of partisans in France called the Vladimir Group. Serpell theorised that this might be someone known to British intelligence as V.A. Malyguine. Foote described his travelling partner Vladimir as a 'complete savage'.

After giving the false names used by those on the flight (Foote was Alfred Lapidus), Serpell was told about Mr Miasnikov.[144] Serpell said: 'I had to disguise my ignorance of this name', because Foote told him Miasnikov was famous in the USSR, at one time second only to Lenin in fame. Ivanov told Serpell the story about Miasnikov ordering the Tsar's family to be shot (see Chapter Eight). Foote had asked him if this was true and Miasnikov confirmed it was and that Lenin had been livid about it. Foote was very impressed by him personally. He said that Miasnikov was very nervous in Cairo, then under the control of the British, because in his heyday he had had numerous Englishmen shot in Russia. Foote said that he gave the impression he was going back to Russia to 'put Stalin in his place'. He carried on him a book he had written which was critical of Stalin. When asked by Serpell if Miasnikov was involved in intelligence work, Foote 'roared with laughter' and said that such work was below his dignity. Miasnikov was shot in Moscow in 1945. He was posthumously rehabilitated in 2000.

Interrogation Four: Sunday afternoon, 20 July 1947

The session on Sunday afternoon started with Michael Serpell asking Foote to identify the three photographs he had on him when he approached the British in Berlin. One photo was of Agnes Zimmerman (Mikki), his one time fiancée from Munich. The second was of Frau Weber, his landlady in Berlin. The third was a picture of an Alsatian dog he had picked up in Moscow.

Serpell confirmed the details of the Agnes Zimmerman episode (see p.21). Frau Weber was a woman Foote had become close with while staying at her home. He had become fond of her as she had been kind to him when he was sick. Her husband, an ex-policeman, was in a Russian prison camp. Foote had felt close enough to her to reveal that he was a Russian agent. He was boarding with Frau Weber after a protracted wrangle with the occupation authorities about his rights of residence. This was only resolved when the Russian Kommandantur intervened on Foote's behalf. The stress of this confusion, mused Serpell the interrogator, may have been one of the reasons why Foote decided to jump ship.

After describing his life in Berlin, Foote was asked again about his time in Moscow. He gave details of his 'interpreter'. This man, who Foote believed had been an NKVD officer at some time, had poor English at first, but he accompanied him whenever he went out. As a 'hobby', Foote undertook to sharpen up his language. As they got to know each other better the interpreter began to open up about the difficulties of his life in the USSR: the inequalities and the 'evil conditions'. He became very lax about his duties, partly, Foote thought, because he was not used to the high life that Foote had introduced him to. This had gone as far as him forming 'a liaison' with Foote's landlady. They were given a number to ring if ever Foote was arrested by the police. The interpreter was instructed to insist that he alone ring, without revealing the number to the police. On one occasion they actually were arrested by police, who were under the impression that Foote was a foreign spy. When the interpreter rang the number a car came to take them away. No names or addresses were divulged in this exchange.

Foote went on to describe his interrogation by the Russian secret services. Naturally, they were interested in exploring the discrepancies between Foote's account of events revealed in Paris and that of Radó. It became clear to him very quickly that he was the object of Soviet suspicion. The fact that he had never been a Communist Party member they thought was very significant. Over ten days he wrote an autobiography in which he embellished parts of his story in a way that he thought might appeal to their sensibilities. He told the comrades that he had, in fact, been a secret party member and that he had been engaged in forming a cell within that RAF on the instructions of George Brown, the organiser of the Communist Party in Manchester. He felt on safe ground with this claim because he knew that Brown had been killed in Spain and was not therefore in a position to contradict him. He said George Aitken[145] was the *'éminence grise'* behind this initiative, and he believed that Aitken knew the wife of his old RAF friend Corporal Barnes 'very, very well', and that he suspected Barnes was also a member of the secret party outfit in the RAF.

The 'woman major' who interrogated Foote revealed in June 1945 that Radó had 'turned up'. She described him as a criminal who had embezzled intelligence funds in Switzerland. At this point Foote said that he felt he could relax, as Radó would now be taking the heat. He revealed to Serpell that he thought Radó was indeed guilty of the embezzlement with which he was charged.

In the autumn of 1945 Foote became very ill with duodenal ulcers. He was taken to a hospital in Moscow where he was given privileged treatment. His true identity was disguised from everyone caring for him and his lack of Russian was covered by the story that he was a hero from the Spanish Civil War. When he returned from the sanatorium he had been sent to for rehabilitation, discussions about his next mission started. There was a disagreement within the Russian service as to whether the American or the Far Eastern service should have first option on him. Foote himself requested to be sent to Britain but this idea was quickly scotched. The Red Army did not encourage agents to spy against their own country, and certainly not while on that country's territory.

Serpell indicated in his notes that Foote should be interrogated further about the sequence of events around the disappearance of the major (Vera) who had been interrogating him. As noted in Interrogation Two on Saturday morning, she had 'gone off sick' in April 1946, the same time as the Director (who was apparently of Jewish origin and a 'desk type') had also gone off sick. The reason Serpell was interested in these dates was that a spy ring had been broken up in Canada, largely as the result of a breakdown in security caused by Sissy in Switzerland. This breakdown in turn was caused by the lax provision of funds from Moscow. Serpell was attempting to link their removal to what he called in his notes, the 'Ottawa debacle'.[146]

While Radó was missing in Cairo, Vera said there would be little difficulty in finding him and bringing him to Russia. She told Foote that soon the Russians would be able to bring anyone to Russia they felt necessary. Foote took this to be a threat, should he ever consider desertion.

During his interrogation in Moscow he was visited by a succession of technicians who were particularly interested in him, describing how he thought the Swiss authorities had managed to detect his transmitter. He told Serpell he thought the Russians did not know how it was done.

For the months of January to September 1946 Foote stayed at a dacha which doubled as a training facility. He was required to write reports and proposals. He was also asked to write about life in England, despite the fact he had not been in England since 1938. He was given further training in spy photography and radio technique, though he was of the opinion that he knew more about radios than the technician sent to train him.

One of the items Foote said was exercising the minds of his intelligence colleagues in the USSR was the collapse of the extensive intelligence network that the Russians had built up in Canada. The defection of a minor embassy official called Igor Gouzenko with a pile of secret documents relating to espionage had had a domino effect on Soviet espionage activity in North America. The Russians had supplied many of their agents with phoney passports supplied from their contacts in Canada. Now all these passports were suspect and this mandated the rapid evacuation of agents. Prior to this an inspection of the secret services in Canada by the Soviet intelligence hierarchy had given the local apparat a clean bill of health. Now it was in collapse. In this context the Swiss network's own breach of security involving Canada took on a new and, for Foote, a potentially menacing aspect. The 'admission' by Sissy under interrogation by the Swiss that she was a British agent shone a queasy light on Foote's own status. As Foote put it to Serpell, the Russians were 'out for her blood'.

Interrogation Five: Monday morning, 21 July 1947

By Monday morning the main outline of Foote's activities had been gathered. The interrogator sought to broaden out his enquiries. What, he asked, had prompted Foote's disillusionment with the USSR? In reply Foote referred to several conversations he had had with the 'interpreter' with whom he had shared his Moscow flat, and who had been his constant companion. Foote indicated that he thought the man would have liked to leave Russia. When pressed, Foote summed up his own objections to life in the USSR under the following headings: 1. The lack of personal freedom; 2. The unequal distribution of goods; 3. The lack of enthusiasm among the Russian people for internationalism; 4. The popularity of nationalism.

When asked about his future plans Foote made vague noises about owning a farm. When the inquisitor put to him that he must be fed up with intelligence work, Foote sparked up and heavily hinted that he would like to do intelligence work for Britain. He was adamant that he wanted to work against the interests of Russia and that he may even decide to join 'some fascist organisation'. Again, the contempt for Foote – one of Europe's most successful spies – comes across all too clearly in his MI5 files. Serpell's immodesty here is striking. In professional terms Foote was much more accomplished than Serpell. In comparison to Foote, Serpell was a minor civil servant: 'Despite the strong evidence of F's innocence and incompetence as an intelligence agent ... it must be emphasised that he considers himself a first-class operative.'[147]

It is worth noting at this point that by now Foote was a major in the Red Army and had been decorated three times, including the award of the Order of the Red Banner, the third highest award anybody could receive. It was vanishingly rare for a British person to be awarded it. His Red Banner award was for inventing a simplified form of sending Morse numbers which 'cut transmitting time by a third'. One of the very few other British recipients of the honour was Clementine Churchill for her work in the Aid To Russia charity. Needless to say, by 1949 and the release of his book, Foote was not keen to go Moscow to receive his award.

Foote's interrogator was especially impressed by his almost complete lack of nerves about his defection. Foote had a low estimation of the quality of the Russian secret services and scoffed at the idea that they might plan to assassinate him. This is despite the fact that, in 1937, a prominent Polish communist NKVD defector called Ignatz Reiss, an acquaintance of Radó, who lived in Lausanne, had been gunned to death by Stalin's agents.[148]

It was put to Foote that he may have to spend some time incommunicado in London on his return. When the duration of this period was estimated at two weeks he visibly cheered up because he thought it would be months. Asked if there was anyone he wanted to be contacted by the service he was lukewarm. He stated that his father was 'queer like me' and had a single-minded passion for chicken farming. He expressed no interest in contacting his sister immediately. He did, however, express a strong interest in retrieving his personal baggage back from Switzerland. They contained, he said, some correspondence between himself and Agnes Zimmerman.

This interaction was described by his interrogator as 'cordial'.

Chapter Eleven

London

Arrival: 7 August 1947

On 25 July 1947, a meeting was held in the office of Roger Hollis to make arrangements for Foote's return to Britain. He was given a cover identity and identity card and was brought back in a military plane, posing as a non-commissioned officer called Corporal Forde. A Secret Intelligence Service (SIS) driver was to accompany him for the trip. On arrival at Northcote he was to be handed over to another SIS escort. In September, Hollis made it clear that his official return was to be credited to 'one of the south coast ports' and emphatically not Northcote. This in itself gave rise to a flurry of bureaucratic correspondence. He could not be registered as passing through Folkestone, because he did not have the right stamp on his papers – stamps being scarce at Folkestone.

It was emphasised at the meeting that his clothing, provided by the Russians, was to be closely examined in case this information might be useful following the arrest of yet unsuspected Russian spies in Britain. Foote arrived in Britain on 7 August and was kept incommunicado in a flat at Rugby Mansions in West Kensington.

On 7 August, Roger Hollis wrote to a Mr Poston of the Air Ministry: 'We are anxious that no legal action should be taken against FOOTE on account of his desertion from the RAF in 1936.'[149] Matters were arranged that no charge was ever brought against him subsequently. Elsewhere and unbidden, Serpell was keen to assure the Air Ministry that, to the British, Foote was 'in no way a hero'.

On 30 August, an order was signed by 'One of His Majesty's Principal Secretaries of State' that any mail addressed to Foote and sent to his sister's house in East Grinstead be opened for inspection. Foote had given this address, Oak Trees on Lewes Road, East Grinstead, as his postal address while he was in Switzerland. MI5 drafted a letter to his sister asking her to forward his mail 'urgently' to Marshall House, Milk Street, EC2. Foote added to it: 'Don't let anybody know that I am around again until I see you. Has anybody been asking for me?'

There was one mail exchange that Foote had with his lawyer in Geneva which contained some intriguing and enigmatic sentences. In a letter to Herzel Sviattsky, which was mainly about his 2,000 francs (£4,800) and personal belongings languishing in the Hotel Central, Lausanne, Foote said: 'If you have any connection with my old employees please do not inform them of this letter until you hear further from me. They are very probably annoyed with me.'

Who might these old employees be? Sviattsky was just as enigmatic in his response. He said (translated from the French): 'In Geneva there is nothing new, and your old employees are still at work on their own in a completely independent manner.'

Somebody in MI5 marked the side of the page next to this sentence, though there is no specific comment made about it.

Reading the documents of the secret service of this period, they veer from discussions of matters of the highest international importance to dreary matters of minor civil service detail. In one exchange of memos there is a discussion about what to do with a twenty dollar note Foote had arrived in Germany with. The note itself was taken from him and it had to go to the Americans in case analysis revealed anything. The discussion then concerned deciding how much twenty dollars was in sterling, and from whose budget the sum to pay Foote was to come. In his files there is a receipt, signed and dated by Foote, for the cash he received.

The analysis of the note's origins was no academic point. There was an extensive network of spies in North America and the journey of the note might reveal some interesting insights into how and where the Soviet networks were working.

The first in a series of requests that would become a feature of Foote's life in the following years was made on 16 August 1947. This involved him looking at photographs of people, most of whom he had never seen, in the hope that he might recognise someone. In March 1949 he was approached by MI5 to answer a questionnaire supplied by the Swiss authorities which sought information about the *Rote Drei*, but which was clearly, in reality, seeking information intended to discredit the communist father and son team of Léon and Pierre Nicole of the Swiss Parti Du Travail. One MI5 memo suggested that Foote might be induced to give full-throated cooperation with the Swiss if he were told that this would help the sales of his forthcoming book.

On 12 September 1947 Foote was visited by his sister Margaret Powell. In Foote's dossier Serpell had filed a telegram he had sent to Mrs Powell on Foote's behalf. It read 'Got letter can you meet me outside Cameo theatre Friday 3.15 for tea. Allan.' The subsequent meeting was bugged by MI5 and a transcript and summary of the conversation was made. Read and Fisher say that the meeting took place in a dingy room behind Victoria station. Presumably, though not stated as such, from conversations with Margaret Powell, Foote told his sister that their conversation was being listened to. She recalled 'a stilted, nightmarish conversation' according to Read and Fisher.[150] This atmosphere may have influenced what he subsequently said in this rendezvous. Perhaps at this point he said what he felt his MI5 handlers would find most politically convenient to hear. Foote was under as much suspicion in London as he had been in Moscow.

It is obvious that Mrs Powell still had a considerable amount of admiration for her brother, but one can possibly also hear a faint note of resentment in her opening conversational gambit:

P. Haven't you lived a most wonderful life?
F. You think so?
P. Well don't you think you have? All those cream cakes you have been eating all through the war when we were starving, and still are!

In his meeting with his sister he said that he thought that the British occupation of Germany was more brutal than the German occupation of their subjugated nations. Margaret told Foote that his other sister Anne had married a Czech man called Stiassny, who was half Jewish. He had lost his sister and her children during the Holocaust. Foote made the extraordinary response that he thought that the Nazi's genocide of their Jewish populations had been 'exaggerated'.

By November 1947 Foote was offering MI5 and MI6 detailed analysis of the Royal Commission report about the espionage ring which had been exposed in Canada. In these comments Foote argued that the set up in Canada was not typical of similar outfits. For instance, he pointed out that it was highly unusual for a Soviet diplomatic address to be used for espionage. It was always the case in his experience that a Resident Director had a parallel line of communication with the Centre in Moscow that specifically excluded embassies and legations, except in the direst of emergencies. Also, the identities of Resident Directors were kept entirely unknown to couriers and agents. The reason Foote gave for this was illuminating. He said that agents frequently felt their remuneration was inadequate and 'a denunciation from a dissatisfied one could unveil the whole network'.[151] Foote also argued that the practice of local branches of national communist parties delivering intelligence to embassies and legations was wholly unknown to him. Their intelligence was restricted to the parallel communication systems administered by the Resident Directors.

British attitudes to Foote

When everyone was settled back in London, Serpell became generous with Foote's time. He made an offer to the 'chief of the liaison section' at the American embassy, Winston M. Scott, that he could interview Foote should he wish, advising him that he should make any decision on this as a matter of urgency as he did not think he would be able to hold on to Foote much longer.

In the end Michael Serpell held on to Foote for six weeks of genteel incarceration during which, in addition to the information he had already given, he had marked Foote out as a human 'reference book' (Serpell's term) for future analyses of Soviet espionage.

In late August 1947, a new MI5 agent called R.V. Hemblys-Scales[152] asked Foote, who was at that point living in a cheap hotel at 11 Clifton Gardens, Maida Vale, what he intended to do now that he was back in Britain. 'The idea of doing anything beyond writing his book came as a bit of a shock to him.' The officer pointed out that 'writing a book' would hardly be enough for him to count as a job at the labour exchange. Foote seemed at a loss to know what to do. He had been a car salesman, and he had sold corn as poultry feed. He felt that with a background knowledge of French, German and Spanish he might be able to find a role in the field of commerce. He could even try his hand at joining the estate agency owned by his sister and brother-in-law.

Hemblys-Scales told Foote that should he want to proceed with the book of his experiences then the service would put him in touch with a publisher, but that it would be up to him to make a commercial case to proceed. An interesting observation made by Foote to his interviewer was that he wished to go back to Switzerland on a visit. He had several motives for this. First, he wished to consult with his lawyer there, one Maître Herzel Sviattsky, about events that took place after he had left. He said he thought the police might also be a useful source of anecdotes for his book. Second, he wanted to stand trial in the Swiss courts on the outstanding charge against him of espionage. The advantages of this for Foote were obvious. He was flat broke in Britain and yet there was 3,000 Swiss francs (£4,100) waiting for him in a bank account and a further 2,000 francs (£2,700) bail money just waiting to be claimed should he stand trial. It might also, he considered, give his book a little extra bite. In either case, he considered that by 1947 he would be unlikely to be given a very long sentence, given that he had already served ten months.

The intelligence services knew he had obtained a British passport and had assumed he was going to leave the country against Serpell's strongly expressed advice. Incidentally, Foote described his occupation as 'representative' on his passport application. It was never made clear what he was the representative of! In the end Foote did not go to Switzerland, concerned that Swiss justice might prove unexpectedly stringent. This concern turned out to be wholly justified.

Unable to prevent him going to Switzerland all the secret services could do was to stand back and observe. Then the MI5 press office picked up a report published in a lunch time special edition of the *Evening News* which said that a spy trial was underway in Switzerland which mentioned Foote by name in the indictment. MI6 made contact to say that he had not shown up at the trial. Mr Vesey of Robert Hale, the London publishers, had been in touch with Foote who told him that he had 'cold feet' at the possibility of ending up back in a Swiss jail and had stayed home.

Before changing his mind about going, Foote had applied for a passport; the reason he gave for being unable to produce his old one was that 'it had been retained by the general staff of the Red Army in Moscow'. He argued with the officer on the desk of the passport office that he needed a new passport in a hurry 'to appeal before a military tribunal in Lausanne in October 1947'.

The passport officer, Mr Tear, made a statement about Foote's application, which had been made in person at the passport office. He said that in a chatty, conversational style, Foote had outlined his work for the Soviet Union, his difficulties in Moscow and the fact that his case was 'well known in Whitehall'. Tear concluded his statement with the words: 'This type of rambling talk is not altogether new to examiners on the main Counter.'

It may have come as some relief to Foote that an announcement was made in the *Gazette de Lausanne* on 1 November 1947. A military court had sentenced him in absentia to a prison term of two-and-a-half years and the loss of all his remaining property. Foote viewed this sentence with wry humour; the judge in the case, Lieutenant Colonel R. Corbaz, was the lawyer facilitating the transfer of black-market funds from the

USA at the time of Foote's arrest. However, Foote was now entirely without funds and was 'in a state of great distress', as Hemblys-Scales commented.

Foote's prospects

Hemblys-Scales was left wondering if anybody had considered the psychological effects on Foote should his book not become the bestseller that Foote anticipated, and he be obliged to take a humdrum and poorly paid job.[153] Foote himself thought that he was unsuited to any normal job and, should the book not work out, he might find the lack of adventure so difficult to handle he could end up on the wrong side of the law:

> He also made it clear that he considers his story to be his trump card and he is obviously expecting a generous advance from his publisher to ease his immediate difficulties. He anticipates that by far the larger part of the profits will come to him and not to the ghostwriter and he imagines that the American rights to his book will keep him comfortable for the rest of his life.[154]

Apart from this, Foote made some half-baked suggestions about emigrating to one of the colonies, possibly South Africa. In case the Russians were after him seeking revenge for his desertion, he also made vague enquiries to Michael Serpell about obtaining a passport under a false name. Serpell made a theatrical show of being shocked that Foote should suggest such a thing, or that he thought that a crown employee might be able to do it.

On 16 September 1947, Foote's younger sister, Anne Stiassny, wrote to him:

> With everyone in the family I am very thrilled to hear that you are back in England. As far as I can remember I was 14 when I last saw you and now I am an old married woman of 36. So don't you think we could start getting to know each other again? ... I'm

taking mother down to Forest Row on Sunday where Margaret is expecting you for the weekend.

But maybe you would ring me first here – early (but not too early!) is the best time – before then and maybe come over here – or maybe we could meet somewhere for a drink and a talk ... If you can't manage to meet me do ring up to say hello and be sure to come to Margaret's at the weekend. I'm dying to meet this fabulous and almost mythical brother of mine.
Auf Baldiges Wiedersehen
Anne[155]

Foote's future plans were a constant worry to him and he was permanently short of both money and of prospects. His choice of employment was hampered by the blank years in his curriculum vitae and his complete lack of any references which might account for his years in Switzerland and Russia. MI5 opened and filed some of the letters he wrote to companies looking for work. One was to Rio Tinto, the mining company. But another intriguing one was a handwritten note dated 20 November 1947, which he sent to Mr Saville (Serpell). When he had received disappointing news about the prospects of his book being written he said:

It occurs to me that the possibility should exist that my services could be of value to the organisation with which you are connected. I would be more than prepared to work in any capacity in any country where the need may arise. Also to live under another name if necessary as I have no family ties. I would also point out that my recent activities have completely compromised me with my former employers and that any misfortunes which might befall them are also to my own advantage.[156]

One of his old friends from Switzerland, possibly one of the 'shadier' friends that Foote referred to in his book when discussing his connections with the 'black bourse', wrote to Foote with a heavy hint that he might participate in entering the world of wine importation. The friend was Osborne S. Reggio-Browne, of Monaco. On Boxing Day 1947, he let Foote know by letter that he had written on his behalf to ten wine and spirits companies recommending Foote, and who may contact him directly as he had given the companies Foote's home address. Browne was emphatic that he considered the prospects of securing Foote a position very seriously, but in what capacity he does not make clear: 'I really do hope that we can get a nice little business going in some line or another.'

Subsequent pages drift on to oblique discussion about the politics of 1947:

> I was very interested to hear what you say about Mosley but for the moment I should advise sitting on the fence as you say. At the moment the thing to do is to try and make some cash ... as we have lost six years of our lives during the war for ideals which have not come true and have completely disillusioned us.[157]

Reggio-Browne also has a presence in Foote's MI5 records. Born of an Irish father and an American mother, he may have lived on the Côte d'Azur but he was perpetually short of money. An MI5 note suggests that before the war he was the secretary of the Genoa branch of the British Union of Fascists. Another note signed by H.A.R. Philby in 1944 asked whether it would be possible for an intelligence operative to interview Reggio-Browne about the whereabouts of Foote, 'as we are concerned about the unexplained disappearance of a British national'.[158] At that point, the British national in question was living in Moscow.

One of the bright spots for Foote in 1947 was the return of his baggage from the Hotel Central in Lausanne. J.H. Marriott of MI5 wrote to the customs authorities to insist on a thorough search of their contents, which was duly conducted in Newhaven when they arrived. Despite this delay, at least his trunk was on its way to Margaret's house in East Grinstead. There was considerable interest in the contents of his trunk, most of which contained little more than the scraps of his previous life. Much of the correspondence they found was from or about Agnes Zimmerman: 'I was unable to discover any direct intelligence interest' in these letters, as Michael Serpell unsentimentally put it. He also noted that the trunk's contents had previously been rifled by the Swiss police. The letters were all tested for invisible ink. Among his baggage there was a notebook of handwritten entries. A specific entry in this handbook will be discussed in chapter twelve of this book.

The early months of 1948 went badly for Foote. None of his attempts to find a new career was bearing fruit. He attempted the life of an insurance salesman with little success. While he was supposed to be out selling insurance policies he was actually sitting in various cinemas. He applied for a post of tyre salesman and also as a copywriter at an advertising agency. His friend Reggio-Browne sent him numerous letters suggesting some sort of job in wine merchanting, all to no avail. Foote even went to the Swiss embassy to offer for sale his knowledge of Soviet espionage on their soil. The offer was politely declined.[159]

Foote's duodenal ulcers were causing him a lot of pain again, he was in penury and was uncharacteristically very depressed. London life had ceased to amuse him and he was later to live for a while with Margaret in East Grinstead. All his hopes were pinned on his book, now being ghosted by MI5 man Courtenay Young who, from his correspondence, clearly had little sympathy for his subject. Courtenay Young was not the first choice for this job. First up was another MI5 man, John Gwyer, who was reported to be most unwilling to take this job on as he was convalescing from an unnamed medical condition. Gwyer could possibly be the Major J.M.A. Gwyer, who was sent a note from Kim Philby on 4 April 1946, temporarily closing the file on Foote's unexplained disappearance.

By August of 1948 Courtenay Young reported that Foote had found a job working for the Ministry of Agriculture and Fisheries. In a typed minute, he added to his charges of stupidity and illiteracy a third: laziness.

> He regards this [job] as temporary as he is convinced that his book will make his fortune. Vesey attempted to dispel these rather roseate hopes pointing out that even the best bestseller is hardly sufficient to keep anybody in comfort for the rest of their lives without any further effort, but Foote still remained firmly of the opinion that once it is published he need never do another hand's turn in his life.[160]

What of his Russian ex-comrades? Did they have any plans for Foote? There is a curious collection of documents in his MI5 file concerning repeated invites to Foote for him to visit Paris. Jean Pierre Vigier, the son-in-law of Rachel Dübendorfer (Sissy), made several attempts to get Foote to visit him on an all expenses paid visit to the French capital. As flat broke as he was, Foote was not inclined to accept this offer. He was never particularly close to Dübendorfer, and certainly not to Vigier. Foote's attitude to these invites indicated that he was not, in his words, prepared to 'stick his neck out'. There is considerable contemplation in the Foote dossier about what the motive behind these invites might be. These ranged from the suspicion that Dübendorfer wanted to sound Foote out on what the Russians were thinking about her role in the *Rote Drei* and in the Ottawa debacle. Alternatively, he suspected that Vigier might be acting on behalf of the Soviets to lure Foote into a trap.

In a different spirit, on 28 April 1948 there arrived a letter from the Hamels. Conveying warm and generous sentiments, they were anxious to discover news of their old comrade. Life for them was good. They had paid the price for their conduct following their trial by serving short prison sentences. Although they had lost their licence to run their business, they were confident of a successful appeal against this decision. Unnamed 'friends' sent their good wishes and they said that they had no regrets and would 'go down the same road' if they had their time again.

Throughout the next few years Foote was badgered for information about his experiences in the Soviet secret services. No mention was made of any payment for these services nor any threats to him if he did not comply with requests. Mostly he was asked to look at photographs of suspects, but in September 1950 he was asked to draw a picture of the training camp he had attended outside of Moscow.

In one interview Foote gave in May 1950, he mentioned that he had met Brigitte Lewis in the street by accident in 1947 or 1948. She seemed surprised to see him as she had no idea that he was in the country. She confided in him that Sonya had been visited by two policemen at her home and that she was so terrified that she missed 'a most important rendezvous the following day'. It is tempting to speculate whether this rendezvous was related to her espionage activity. It is also a distinct possibility that one of the people who knocked on Sonya's door was Michael Serpell, who became very involved in her surveillance.

The constant demands of the Americans for information from Foote eventually came to try the patience of even their British intelligence allies. The note of irritation in their memoranda became clear through the early fifties:

> You will see that the FBI have written to ask us if we will interview FOOTE for information about someone called STEFANSSON ... For the life of me I cannot see that FOOTE has ever mentioned this man and I cannot believe that he would know him. Do you know any reason why FOOTE should be thought to know STEFANSSON?[161]

By April 1952 the irritation of the British with the Americans, in the person of a Mr Cimperman, was becoming more and more pronounced. Cimperman's letters to MI5 are written on headed notepaper bearing the name of the Foreign Service of the US government and came from the US embassy in London. On 28 April 1952 an internal memo from the Director General of MI5 clearly indicates the rising impatience:

> During the past year or two we have received a large number of photographs, mainly through Cimperman, which he has requested

that we show to FOOTE and there are some cases where it stretches the imagination to an enormous extent to expect that FOOTE will ever have seen these people in his life. It gets very boring for FOOTE and for us to go on showing him photographs of people he could not possibly have known, so do try to keep the numbers down to a minimum.

Handbook For Spies

On 4 May 1948 Mr Saville (Michael Serpell) contacted the publishers Robert Hale Ltd. with a book proposal. There is further allusion to this book from Hemblys-Scales[162] on 28 August 1947.

One of the interesting features about Foote's case is the degree to which the British secret services helped him publish his book. It was Michael Serpell who first approached the publisher Robert Hale. John Gwyer[163] was Serpell's first choice as a ghost-writer but was out of the running being in convalescence. Serpell (still known to Foote as Saville) asked Foote for a synopsis of the work, but on reading it was pessimistic about its appeal. He wrote to Desmond Vesey of the Hale publishing house, a personal friend of Serpell, on 19 September 1947: 'I am afraid it is a very unsatisfactory effort and may indicate the amount of work your ghost is going to have on his hands.'[164]

Serpell saw the publication of Foote's book as cutting the 'umbilical cord' joining Foote and MI5: 'We have now wished the author goodbye and sent him out into the world.' He further said that he was not in the least concerned by what Foote should say about his previous life, as long as his autobiography stopped short at the point he left the Russian service. Comments about his reception home were emphatically not to be the subject of the work.

On 25 September 1947, Michael Serpell had lunch with Desmond Vesey, who 'was struck by Foote's humility and didn't think he would be a difficult customer to handle'. But what worried Vesey was how Foote was to live until the book came out. It would be nine months at the earliest before the book was written, and eighteen months before there was any financial return. There was a possibility that a small advance could be made, depending on how successful Robert Hale Ltd. was in selling the work to an American publisher. Vesey indicated, to a wry smile from Serpell, that Foote (ever the fixer) had offered him access to a 3,000 francs (£4,100) bank account, should he wish to take a holiday in Switzerland.

In his note marked 5 November 1947, Serpell described some very dispiriting communications about Foote's proposed book. Vesey now estimated the chances of the project ever coming to fruition as about 50/50, particularly if he could not get the Americans interested. This would mean that Foote's hoped-for publishing salvation would come to nothing. Serpell wondered if the service's current approach of cutting Foote adrift with no support was altogether wise. He might come in handy, it was reasoned, if there were defections from the Soviet service. However, Serpell's own view was that: 'The chances of further profit in this direction are slender and I am convinced that Foote is an untrustworthy contact for this office.'

Things did not improve for Foote. True, he was given a contract from Robert Hale for a book to be 'not less than 80,000 words and not more than 100,000 words'. He was even given an advance of £50 divided into weekly payments of £2 10s. The secret service records surrounding this £50 reveal a lot about the service culture of the time. There is an enormous bureaucratic exchange of memoranda about who agreed to what and whose contractual obligation the payment should be made under. The records also reveal that the operational file under which Foote's payment was made was named 'SNEAK'. Again and again interspersed between 'TOP SECRET' communications between Washington, Ottawa, Paris and Whitehall are memoranda concerning the fate of Foote's £50 and who should pay it.

More bad news for Foote came in the shape of reports that the American contacts of Robert Hale were showing little interest in promoting the work of a Soviet agent at a time of intense anti-communist feeling in the USA. The contempt with which Foote was regarded by some in MI5 was apparent in a minute of 1 December 1947 by ghost-writer Courtenay Young, in which he reviewed the book-proposal: 'Foote is himself, I gather, well-nigh illiterate and the original idea was that the book might be "ghosted" by John Gwyer.'

A ghost-writer called Bernard Willis had been suggested to Foote; Young suggested that Foote, 'not a man of acute intellect', might give things away to this trusted writer that he neglected to mention to his MI5 interrogators: 'The advantage of this work being done by Willis, who is of course myself, is that the office would have control of the book from the start.'[165]

The first typescript copy of *Handbook for Spies* was delivered to Foote in November 1948. MI5 had a draft of the book in their hands on 12 March 1949. On 10 March, Desmond Vesey wrote to MI5 that the Swiss were about to release some documents which corroborated Foote's version of events. One of these documents was a memoir written by a cryptographer named Marc Payot, who was present at Foote's arrest in Lausanne.

It was not only MI5 who wanted a peek at Foote's book. In a note marked 'personal', Mr R. Thistlethwaite of the British embassy in Washington wrote on 11 August 1948 that copies had been 'hawked around the Sunday newspapers'. At the start of 1949, when Foote's book was still in draft form, a serialised version of his life and career began appearing in the French paper *Le Figaro*.[166] Where they got this copy from is anybody's guess, but a note in Foote's MI5 file dated 5 February 1949 said that Foote himself had signed the articles for the newspaper. French intelligence contacted MI5 to ask how accurate the version was. The response of the British (and the least labour-intensive solution for them) was to tell the French that Foote's book would soon be out and available for their inspection. By 26 January, the *Gazette de Lausanne* was splashing 'Sensational Revelations' on their front page (see p.146). Their source was *Le Figaro*.

In a minute dated 16 February 1949 an intelligence officer recorded an interview he had had with Fred Copeman, the Invergordon mutineer, ex-International Brigade commander and ex-executive committee member of the Communist Party, now an enthusiastic promoter of the Catholic Moral Rearmament movement. He said that Foote had telephoned him to ask his advice about a dilemma he had regarding his book. Writer and journalist Charlotte Haldane[167] had been in touch looking for permission to use the draft of *Handbook For Spies* as the basis of a BBC documentary she was making. Foote was at a loss to know how to respond. Copeman said that on no account should he let his draft leave his own hand, and especially not to Charlotte Haldane who, he said, would use his material at whatever cost to Foote.

There was better news in September 1949 when the American publishers Doubleday finally made up their minds about Foote's book. Desmond Vesey received a letter from them which was positively effusive: 'I hope that we can do a good job with this book because it's quite extraordinary. It's in a field that isn't selling too well in this country but we do think that it is so good that it must be published.'[168]

However impressed his publishers were by Foote's work, the sales in America were disappointing. In Foote's opinion this was due to the lethargy of his publishers in promoting the work and he was not shy in expressing this view to his intelligence contacts. There is correspondence which indicates that the British service made some desultory contacts within the American embassy to sell the film rights to the book, but nothing came of this initiative.

Vesey communicated with his contact in MI5, Mr R.T. Reed, to inform him that the current total of royalties for *Handbook For Spies* was running at £300–£400, and that the book had resulted in a number of articles written by Foote which had brought in more money. One of these articles was published in an American magazine called *News Review*. It alleged that Britain and America were full of Russian spies, some in very senior and unsuspected positions.

On 17 December 1950, a large article appeared in the *Sunday Sun* which profiled Foote and publicised his book.

In precisely the manner in which MI5 had insisted, Foote's book gave the impression that he had had free rein to express whatever sentiments he wished. That is to say, up to the events subsequent to his presentation in Berlin. All mention of the British secret services was forbidden. This was a condition of MI5 assisting him with finding a publisher and arranging a ghost-writer. To be fair, this does not seem to have been a condition he found too onerous.

Responses to *Handbook for Spies*

Despite it being an excellent read, Foote's book did not set the world on fire. For all that his observers in the intelligence world looked down on Foote and said unflattering things about him in private, there was a substantial traffic in correspondence between departments requesting an early viewing of the work with many requests for a copy signed by Foote the author.

Foote himself was less than entirely pleased about how his book was presented, or received. In an interview he gave to Professor David Dallin in 1955, he said that MI5 had mutilated his book. They left things out that he thought were the most interesting bits and inserted things without even informing him. But this was not the worst thing that was said about *Handbook for Spies*. Many of the worst things came from his former colleagues.

The bitterness with which Foote's recruiter Agent Sonya felt about his desertion to the British was still palpable when she wrote her 1977 autobiography *Sonya's Report*. Hers is a vituperative and embittered description of her ex-recruit. The word 'traitor' and 'betrayal' are liberally used about Foote. To have had profound doubts and disillusion about communism would be one thing, she said in the afterword to an English edition published in 1991, by that time she had doubts and disillusionment too, but to betray his comrades so comprehensively and to give away all of their secrets was something quite different. To be fair to Foote, his disillusion is all too easy to understand considering how close he came to serving time in NKVD prison camps like so many of his former comrades. It is not clear why he ought to have maintained a loyalty that was so clearly not reciprocated.

The other contemporary critique from a first-hand witness came, not surprisingly, from Sándor Radó. Throughout his autobiography he draws attention to sections of Foote's book in which he detects that his ex-comrade is being 'economical with the old actualité' – in Alan Clarke's memorable phrase. He frequently uses expressions such as 'Foote, for reasons of his own, says...' where he means to say that Foote had made something up. For the rest, Radó heavily suggested that Foote had presented the world with a romanticised and boastful account of the network's activities. He poured cold water on Foote's claims about how quickly intelligence could be transmitted to the USSR. He explicitly stated that Foote's aim in writing the book was to maximise his income, not to write a reliable history and certainly not to wave a Red banner. One wonders what he would have made of the fact that it was MI5 who had written Foote's book for him.

At the end of his autobiography Radó listed the most dispiriting published reviews of Foote's book. He quoted the words of Marc Payot, the cryptographer who was present at the raid on Foote's flat: 'Foote's book positively teems with inaccuracies and even untruths.'

Wilhelm von Schramm, German historian of the Second World War, was quoted by Radó as saying 'His book is a first person account and not a historical report. He wanted it to sell and so strove for a sensational effect.'

Radó continued in this line with a quote from Gert Buchheit, the historian of the German secret services: 'Foote's book is a mixture of reality and imagination.'

It is only at the end of these somewhat restrained reviews that Foote's old Resident Director Sándor Radó reveals his true feelings: 'He sank back into the swamp of petty bourgeois existence from which, fired by a momentous task, he had been able for a while to free himself. His character was marked by an inner contradiction that his betrayal finally sealed.'

Yet there is a symmetry between Foote and Radó's books. They both end at the point that each of them entered the jurisdiction of a hostile secret service: the Soviet one in Radó's case and MI5 in Foote's.

The reception of *Handbook for Spies* in Switzerland

However much Foote was disappointed by the reception for his book in Britain, in Switzerland it became the object of public fascination. With the threat of war now behind them, the Swiss could look on with curiosity at the strange events which were going on under their very noses, without any fear of unpleasant consequences. All Switzerland was fascinated by the activities of Radó's team, but in the local Lausanne press fascination turned to obsession.

It has often been said that the key to local journalism is to take a large story, the largest possible story, and to find a local angle. This publication of *Handbook for Spies* could hardly have been bettered for its local angle: international conflict, nations hanging on in desperation, waiting for help from their friends. Espionage, radio transmissions, beautiful blondes (Agent Rosy) and foreign spooks all feature. The story dropped straight into the lap of the editor of the *Gazette de Lausanne*. Originating from a small flat in an anonymous apartment block, his big story of 1949 presented itself to him with hardly any costs attached. Not only was this good fortune as a local interest story, he had to do very little to it, apart from translation, and he had himself a serial. Over several months of 1949 Foote's book was delivered to the Lausanne public, chapter by chapter. The serialisation was front and centre of the *Gazette*'s front page when it was announced: 'Sensational Revelations'. It was also the hook on which the *Gazette* ran a subscription campaign for the paper. For the first half of 1949 every edition of the paper ran a large, front page story 'Les Révélations d'un Agent Soviétique en Suisse,' where the *Figaro* version of the book was faithfully serialised. Not only this, but they would add notes to Foote's text, questioning his account of the events he described. Side stories would run. For example, they tracked down and interviewed one of Foote's Lausanne agents, the ex-leader of the Swiss Communist Party Jules Humbert-Droz. They offered him the right to respond to claims in Foote's book that he had been a key supplier of information emerging from Southern Germany and the insights of Swiss and German communists working there. He never knew anything about this mission, he said. Nor did he receive 200 francs (£330) a month to lay on this service. Whoever it was that had the duty to pass on money to him probably kept it for themselves, he added tartly. He also said that Foote had filled the gaps in his memory of those times from his imagination. This would not be the last time that this charge was laid against Foote.

Did Foote receive any royalties for this serialisation? There is nothing on record and this question will probably remain open.

Also, what did Foote think the effect of his revelations would be on his erstwhile colleagues in Switzerland? The Hamels sent Foote a charming note in April 1948, wishing him well for the future and conveying to him the good wishes of his Swiss friends. They had gone to prison for their activities and were still suffering the consequences. They had lost their business as a result of their conviction. But in 1949, on the release of *Handbook for Spies*, their lives could well have been turned over once again by press intrusion. Radó and Dübendorfer were beyond such cares, being tucked up tightly in the Soviet penal system. But what impact did his book have on Margaret Bolli (Rosy)? Foote had even made adverse comments about her love life in his book, hardly the action of a 'Parfait Gentleman'. Did that have consequences for her? The man who forged Swiss passports for the network, Agent Max, might also have come in for some unwanted attention. On 14 March 1949, the question of how information was gathered from the Hamels while they were in prison was raised in Switzerland's Cantonal parliament. During a stormy session in the Grand Conseil, in which one communist MP was expelled from the chamber for rowdiness, a right-wing MP, Monsieur

Deonna, laid out the case against Radó's network and the communist sympathisers who assisted him. At the end of his speech he asked a series of questions about the affair. First he quoted from Foote's book:

> The Communist Party of Geneva succeeded in making contact with the Hamels and Margaret Bolli while they were in prison, thanks to one of the prison warders. Hamel made it known that he had been shown a photograph of me saying that it was known that I was the chief of the network.

Deonna said that he had read in the *Gazette de Lausanne* that the prison guard in question had been '*éliminé*'. He asked:

> Does this mean he has been provisionally suspended, sacked, sent on holiday or transferred? In any case it would be wrong for such a functionary to avoid severe punishment for such a grave dereliction of his duty, in making himself the agent of communication between a prisoner and an espionage network.

But the main recipient of press hostility were the father and son team of Pierre and Léon Nicole of the Swiss Parti de Travail. They had been useful to Foote and his team again and again during Foote's stay. They had introduced the Hamels and Margaret Bolli to Radó's network and had repeatedly helped them with money and accommodation. On 3 February 1949, an article signed 'J. Ch. Vy.' in the *Gazette de Lausanne* said: 'Foote has called into question the Nicole family, father and son, especially the son who acted as a liaison agent and recruiter between the party and the Russians. This is an abscess that now needs to be drained.' In the normal course of things the Nicoles were beyond the reach of the Swiss civil authorities because of the statute of limitations. But the limitation did not apply to military matters so they remained in legal jeopardy. MI5 were sent a list of questions for Foote about the Nicoles and others. For example, they asked Foote to confirm the name of the doctor who accepted Radó into his home when he was on the run. In a document outlining this approach a note was added by the British which said that 'the chief idea is, of course, to discredit the Parti de Travail'. Mr R.T. Reed suggested that publisher Mr Vesey should 'tip off' Foote about the likely approach from the Swiss government. Cooperation with their enquiries might assist in the sales of the book due to the positive publicity. 'Mr Vesey said he felt sure that Foote's response would be to accede to the Swiss request.'

For the Swiss press the story of the Soviet spy ring on their soil became a hardy annual. Every new book about the Lucy ring was analysed and reanalysed. But none of the Geneva or the Lausanne newspapers reported the death of Foote in 1956. Sándor Radó's death on the other hand was duly reported.

Chapter Twelve

Controversies

'The simplest way to explain the behaviour of any bureaucratic organisation is to assume that it is controlled by a cabal of its enemies.'

Robert Conquest, Third Law of Politics

Foote, Agent Sonya and Roger Hollis

One reaction to Foote's book occurred many years after his death. *Handbook for Spies* became a key piece of evidence in a controversy which plagued MI5 for decades. This was the conspiracy theory that when Sonya returned to Britain, her tracks were covered up by a leading member of Britain's secret services. It is not the intention here to examine the truth or falsehood of these claims, but rather to bring out how the story of Alexander Foote intersected with these controversies.

In 1984 Chapman Pincher, the defence correspondent of the *Daily Express*, published a book entitled *Too Secret Too Long*. In the book, Pincher advanced an argument first developed in his book *Their Trade is Treachery* (1981), that Britain's secret services had been penetrated at the highest levels by Soviet intelligence and that much of their activity had continued even after the dramatic defections of Burgess, Maclean and Philby. In particular he argued that Roger (later Sir Roger) Hollis, 1905–1973, who had been the Director General of MI5 between the years 1956 and 1965, was in fact an active agent of the USSR. In this capacity he had obstructed investigations into the activities of Soviet agents that, as head of counter intelligence, he was supposed to be exposing. As part of his undercover work he shielded Ursula Kuczynski (Agent Sonya) when she came back to Britain from Switzerland and gave cover to Klaus Fuchs, the atomic spy, when he went to America to work on the Manhattan project.

The charge that the head of MI5 was a Soviet mole was investigated by the secret services and was repeatedly debunked. The notion is drily repudiated on MI5's own website: 'In 1981, allegations were published claiming that Sir Roger had been a Soviet secret agent. These were investigated and found to be groundless.'[169]

This unlikely sounding story had some interesting and undeniable facts to support it, though, and Pincher made the most of them in his telling of it. At the time of his writing, Pincher only had the confidential conversations of serving and previous MI5 agents to use as evidence. These were no doubt given in direct breach of the Official Secrets Act undertakings they had made upon taking office. But now MI5 files declassified in 2004 have revealed one crucial source of secret service evidence on the matter: the interrogations of Alexander Foote.

The background of Roger Hollis

A drop out from Oxford university in the 1920s, Hollis, like many people at the time, enjoyed a flirtation with left-wing politics. He was a friend of Claud Cockburn[170] who was a prominent left-wing journalist and communist and who, under the pen name Frank Pitcairn, was a regular correspondent for the *Daily Worker*. He was also a friend of left-wing labour MP Tom Driberg[171] (himself an ex-communist), and communist novelist Maurice Richardson.[172]

Out of university, Hollis worked briefly in a bank and then he transferred to the Far East hoping to work as a freelance journalist, mainly for the *Shanghai Post*. In 1928 he joined the British and American Tobacco company and lived the life of an expatriate Englishman in the vibrant social scene of that city. He became friendly with the left-wing American journalist Agnes Smedley. She in turn was a close associate of Richard Sorge, the most influential Soviet spy of his generation.

Whether or not Hollis knew that Agnes Smedley was acting on behalf of the Comintern in China is not known. In 1931 Hollis moved to Beijing, where he shared a flat with Captain Anthony Staples. Staples is said to have reported to MI5 that in 1931 Smedley visited Hollis' flat in Shanghai with someone called Arthur Ewart.[173] Owen Mathews repeated this assertion in his biography of Richard Sorge.[174] Arthur Ewart had been an MP for the German Communist Party before the Nazis came to power. In China he was a very highly placed Comintern agent.[175]

In 1932 Richard Sorge, who was the head of the Soviet espionage station in Shanghai, was transferred to Tokyo from where he would do most of his damage to the Japanese war effort. In Shanghai he was replaced by another spy, Karl Rimm. Ben Macintyre, the biographer of Agent Sonya, states that Hollis and Rimm's wife had an affair at this time. This is repeated by Owen Mathews, the biographer of Richard Sorge. Both Mathews and Macintyre say that there was 'evidence' of such an affair, without saying what this evidence consisted of. Karl Rimm was executed during Stalin's purges and Luisa Rimm was imprisoned in the gulag until 1957. Luisa was released from her prison camp and both her and her now dead husband Karl were 'rehabilitated'. Mathews also says that in 1932 Hollis was recruited to Soviet Military Intelligence, the GRU. Others place this date in 1927.[176] Whatever Hollis said about this period in his subsequent interrogations by MI5, no evidence was ever brought forward that led to a successful disciplinary charge.

In 1934 and also in 1936, Hollis visited Moscow. One source quotes Pincher when he asserted that while in Moscow Hollis continued his affair with Luisa Rimm in a grisly sounding 'GRU love nest'.[177]

In the summer of 1938 Hollis was recruited to MI5, and in 1939 he joined the team dedicated to hunting down Soviet spies in Britain. In 1940 Agent Sonya returned to Britain from Geneva. The circumstances of this return are at the heart of the allegations made by Chapman Pincher against Hollis. In Sonya's autobiography, published in German in 1977 and in English in 1991, her flight from Switzerland was retold as a young, Jewish, communist woman fleeing Europe with her children to escape the horrors of being caught by the Nazis. This was what motivated her marriage to Len Beurton, and explains the speed of her application for a British passport following their marriage. It is what explains her dragging her children across Europe from Geneva to Lisbon to board a steamer for Liverpool. Her biographer in 2020 endorsed this picture. Moscow Centre perceived the danger that she was in and concurred: escape was mandatory.

Foote's account of Sonya's escape in *Handbook for Spies* is curiously lacking in details. Foote says that Sonya badgered Moscow to let her escape, but it was only when transition arrangements with Sándor Radó had been established that she was given the green light. Foote then went on to say: 'I do not think that since that time she has had any connection with a Russian spy net. She had been too disillusioned by the Russo German pact to want to go on working and was only too thankful to sink back into respectable obscurity.' And that was about all he had to say on the subject.

However, despite what Foote said about Sonya giving up her old profession in his autobiography, Sonya told a different story in hers. She said that when she was safely settled in Oxfordshire and Foote was back in London following his defection, a curious incident occurred:

> In 1947 the Austrian comrade who had introduced us to Jim asked to see me urgently. He reported the following: the bell rang. He opened the door: in front of him stood an agitated individual he did not immediately recognise and took for a beggar or a sick man. It was Jim. He refused to come in, trembled and stammered incoherently: 'Len and Sonya, great danger, not to work, destroy everything.' Then he ran away.

If this story is true, it reveals that despite what he said in his autobiography, Foote knew that Sonya and Beurton would be up to their old tricks. In 1947 he would have known that MI5 were on to them because he was a grade-one eye witness to their activities in Geneva and had revealed all.

Sonya herself was at a loss as to why a 'traitor' like Foote should have put himself out to convey this message. She said: 'It would seem that with all the damage he had done, there remained a spark of the British sense of fair play. Having nothing against us personally, he risked a secret warning before the security officials could visit our house.'[178]

For Chapman Pincher a far more sinister sequence of events was unfolding. Sonya's move to Britain was not an escape, it was a redeployment. She was not instructed by Moscow to save her own skin. She was ordered to England on a new mission. In fact, her time in Switzerland had been just a warm-up exercise for the main event which was to take place back in Oxfordshire. Her disillusionment with the Ribbentrop-Molotov pact (which traumatised the communist world outside of the USSR) was a smokescreen for her single-minded Stalinist determination to get to Britain and start spying. 'Her claim that the Centre was allowing her to leave Switzerland because she was in extra danger through being Jewish was transparently false.'[179]

According to Pincher then, Roger Hollis was secretly working for an intelligence service of the USSR. Officially he was paid by MI5 to track Soviet spies operating in Britain. But in Agent Sonya's case he smoothed the passage into Britain of his old Shanghai connection and covered up for her when she set up shop in Oxfordshire. The ease with which she was able to get up to her old tricks came as something of a surprise to Sonya herself. In her autobiography *Sonya's Report*, Ursula Kuczynski said: 'Or was it possible that there was someone at MI5 who was, at the same time, working for the Soviet Union and had protected us?' Pincher's answer was 'Yes', and the protection came from Hollis. But disappointingly for Pincher, later on the same page Sonya wrote:

> I want to make it crystal clear that it is pure nonsense to proclaim that 'the master spy still hides her biggest secret' – this secret doesn't exist … I know no Fifth Man, and I must also spoil the speculation or, as some writers state 'the fact' that I had ever had anything to do with the one time director of MI5, Roger Hollis …

I resent the way journalists try to turn me into a sensation, simply to make money.[180]

If Hollis was indeed a Soviet spy, one can only imagine his feelings when, in 1947, Foote emerged in Berlin. To have a *Rote Drei* veteran come forward spilling details of the Swiss espionage setup could easily have raised questions about how a Soviet agent of Sonya's seniority happened to come into the country under their noses. Sonya's brother, Jürgen Kuczynski, had already been interned during the war as a possible subversive. Now here was another member of the Kuczynski family on British soil, with an established career in the service of the USSR exposed by an ex-comrade. And there was always the possibility that Foote would reveal that Sonya had a new mission.

Even before Foote defected in Berlin, he was on the radar of Roger Hollis, who had been looking for Foote since 1944. In a reply to Hollis' request for information regarding Foote's presence in Switzerland, the head of MI6, Colonel Vivian, wrote in February of that year of reports that Foote had been arrested by the Swiss on a charge of owning an illegal radio transmitter: 'The Swiss take a serious view of this incident and refuse to let him be seen by a consular lawyer. Rumour connects him with Russian activity ... Foote is not known to our organisation.'[181]

On the other hand, and assuming that Hollis was not a Soviet spy, an interest in Foote's story was highly appropriate for Hollis. His department was precisely designed to become familiar with Russian spies and how they operated in Britain. If not Hollis' department then who?

Most of the MI5 files relating to Foote were copied over to MI6 and straight into the hands of Kim Philby, who most certainly was a Soviet asset. From the earliest days of Foote's reappearance in the West, the Russians had – if not a ringside seat at his debriefing – then at least a prominent place on the mailing list.

From the outset in his interrogation Foote maintained that to his knowledge, Sonya had quit the Soviet service after the Ribbentrop-Molotov pact in 1939. However, he also said in conversation with Serpell that Sonya went, on Moscow's instructions, to meet Radó in 1940 in order to help him establish radio communication with the Centre, with Foote as the lead telegraphist; it is hard to reconcile these two statements. It is even harder to reconcile the address in a note revealed by Foote to MI5 in 1950 of a pub in Epping at which Sonya could be contacted by Soviet agents, with the dates and times she would be there. By 1950 Sonya was safely domiciled in the GDR so the usefulness of this information was limited.

In 2015 a well publicised meeting of the Institute of World Politics was held called 'British Patriot or Soviet Spy? Clarifying A Major Cold War Mystery: an analysis of Chapman Pincher's indictment of Sir Roger Hollis'. In their well referenced chronology of Hollis's life they say of Foote's re-emergence in Berlin:

> In July [1947], GRU agent Alexander Foote defects in Germany ... Hollis is put in effective control of his interrogation. He identifies SONIA [sic] as Ursula Beurton. He says she had been working for GRU while in Britain and gives details of her radio sets. Foote reveals her 1940-41 assignment to England and the Oxford area.

The claim that Foote exposed Sonya's new espionage role in Oxfordshire is repeated in David Burke's excellent book about Melita Norwood, but evidence for the claim is not specifically referenced.

If he did in fact reveal a specific mission, nobody in MI5 made a note of it in his file, apart from the rendezvous details in Foote's note described above. As far as what Foote wanted his early interrogators to know, Sonya's exploits ended on her leaving Switzerland. It stretches credibility somewhat to imagine Sonya packing for her escape with her two children and leaving her new husband, saying to Foote (of all people!) 'By the way, I am off to the Oxford area to set up a brand new operation.' Early on, Foote was insistent that the reason for Sonya's extraction from Switzerland was her own safety:

Towards the end of 1940 both Sonia [sic] and Beurton received permission to leave Switzerland and proceed to England, it being deemed unsafe for them to remain in the country in view of the rumors [sic] circulating by Sonia's children's nurse about their activities. Sonia and her two children left for England about the middle of December 1940, however Beurton stayed in the country a considerable time longer being unable to obtain the necessary visas etc.[182]

All very convincing. But then how did Foote get to know about the Wake Arms in Epping? What did he think was going on there? Interestingly, his interrogators do not seem unduly concerned by the inconsistency in Foote's account. But by the time the Beurtons had flown the coop, much of the urgency had gone from their case.

On 17 July, Serpell synthesised much of the information already known about the Kuczynskis with new material provided by Foote:

'Foote's account of Ursula Beurton and her first and second husbands matches in certain details with our own records and at present there seems to be no reason to doubt Foote's story of her espionage in Switzerland'. He went on to recommend that '1 ... We should develop Foote's information particularly against the Kuczynski family. 2. That we should consider extending the investigation of Ursula Beurton and her husband to cover other members of the Kuczynski family including Brigitte and Anthony Lewis.'[183]

The picture then is clear. Sonya escaped from Switzerland because of the threat of a German invasion, the threat of her exposure by Olli, and the imminent expiry of her official documents allowing her to stay put.

What sense then are we to make of the account in Sonya's report that Foote showed up at Uhlman's house to warn Sonya and Len to 'destroy everything'? Was this because, knowing Sonya, he thought that she would set up in business again wherever she was? Or did he know about some specific mission she was on?

Sonya most assuredly was on a mission soon after she established herself in Oxfordshire. The secret services had her under a sort of gentle surveillance. Sonya's biographer suggests that MI5 found it hard to believe that a busy housewife, living on her own with two small children, would have the time to engage in international espionage. Nevertheless, surveillance of Sonya's house was established. This was not by the usual means; MI5 officers would stand out in the small village where she lived. Instead the local constable was asked to keep a lookout. And indeed he did. In 1943 he reported that a large aerial had been positioned outside the home of Sonya.

Perhaps in the circumstances of 1943 it is easy to understand how the constable's observations were not followed up. The secret services had their hands full hunting down Nazi sympathisers who might have been tempted to stay in touch with Berlin. Investigating a woman with a known track record of anti-Nazi activity might have taken a low priority in 1943. If this was the attitude the services took, it would not be long before they would regret their decision. In September of 1943 she transmitted the Quebec agreement to Moscow Centre. This established the cooperation between the USA and Britain on the development of nuclear weapons. It also expressly left Stalin out of the loop. Incidentally, the British end of the agreement involved the Tube Alloys company – this was the cover name for the British research arm of the nuclear effort.[184] The top secret nature of the talks in Quebec were rather undermined by the fact that Tube Alloys had a Soviet mole right at its centre.[185] This was Melita Norwood, secretary to the boss of the British Non-Ferrous Metals (i.e. uranium) operation that the name 'Tube Alloys' was disguising. She became part of Sonya's team in addition to Klaus Fuchs and would furnish Sonya with information about the behaviour of uranium at differing high temperatures. Melita Norwood was exposed in 1999 but faced no prosecution because of her advanced years. She was portrayed by Judi Dench in the film *Red Joan* (2019).

On 13 September 1947, MI5 got around to interviewing Sonya at last. The interviewers went to Sonya and Len Beurton's house and, over tea and biscuits, they asked her about her life as a Soviet agent. An account of this meeting was written up by Sonya herself in her autobiography, although caution is required about taking her recollection at face value. The interviewers were Michael Serpell and Jim Skardon, an ex-police officer. Serpell was fresh from interrogating Foote, and Skardon from interrogating Fuchs. One of them opened the interview with: 'You were a Russian agent for a long time, until the Finnish war disillusioned you. We know that you haven't been active in England and we haven't come to arrest you, but to ask for your cooperation.'

It is not clear where the business about the Russo-Finnish war came from. It is not mentioned in any of Foote's MI5 files. Even Sonya was baffled: 'Had the traitor Foote really "protected" us and reported our "disappointment" about the Finnish war to MI5? (In his book, which at the time we had not seen, I seem to remember that he mentioned the non-aggression pact between the Soviet Union and fascist Germany as our disappointment).'[186] Perhaps they were checking the truth of Foote's account. Had the Beurtons agreed that it was the Finnish war that spooked them, this might have cast doubt on Foote's tale. In the end they 'no commented' every question relating to their time in Switzerland. MI5 did not bother the Beurtons again.

The visit from the British security services, however much Sonya laughed it off, must have come as a shock to the system. But not as much of a shock as when *Handbook for Spies* came out. Their activities in Switzerland were all now brought into daylight. No real names were used, to be sure. Len Beurton was given the name Bill Phillips and Sonya was called just Sonya. But even though they were protected from the gaze of the general public by this ruse, they must have known that professionally the game was up. Foote must have told the British everything.

In January 1950 Klaus Fuchs called Jim Skardon to his home and confessed that he had been spying for the USSR. Three days later he wrote a ten-page confession in a room in the War Office. In this confession he stated that he had been handing British and American atomic secrets over to 'a foreign woman with black hair in the Banbury area', as it was reported in the local press. For the Beurtons it was time to pack up. In February 1950, Sonya and the kids defected to the German Democratic Republic, and one month later, Fuchs pleaded guilty to espionage. Len Beurton could not go to the GDR immediately as he had broken his leg in a motorcycle accident, but he followed on later.

As far as the conspiracy theories about Roger Hollis went, this was the end of Foote's involvement.

Was Foote a double agent for the British?

> In recent years a number of articles and books have appeared in various countries dealing with my activities during the Second World War. The motive behind many of them was sensation seeking, and the culmination of this series of lies and distortions ... set out to prove that the Soviet Union owed its victory in the Second World War not to the military successes of the Red Army, but to the Swiss group of Soviet intelligence ... But the recent tidal wave of more or less mythological publications concerning the Swiss group and my part in it ... has forced me to break my silence.
>
> Sándor Radó, 1971[187]

Many authors have pointed to a central problem at the heart of the story of the *Rote Drei*. Leaving aside for the moment the contributions of the Pakbo and the Long groups, how did Rudolf Rössler manage the sheer volume of the materials he was offered? And given that the Germans were frantic to plug the leak that was delivering so much of their precious intelligence to a bitter enemy, why were there so few effective arrests? The odd anti-Nazi resistance group inside Germany would be rounded up now and again, but the flow of information from Lucy never seemed to falter.

The quality, timeliness and volume of the Lucy material, combined with Rössler's implacable silence on the subject of his sources, has led to innumerable outlandish theories attempting to explain his achievement. Each decade has produced claims attempting to outdo the last in unlikeliness. The best summary of these theories and the gaping logical holes they contain can be found in chapter four of Nigel West's book, *Unreliable Witness: Espionage Myths of the Second World War* (1984).

It was not just the volume of information which baffled even those people transmitting it to the USSR. It was the speed with which it arrived. According to Foote, Moscow should lose sight of a German division: 'an enquiry was put through Lucy and in a matter of days the answer would be provided, giving the composition, strength, and location of the unit in question.'[188]

All of this together placed the Soviet general staff in an unrivalled position. They could see for themselves the flags that the German OKW were putting on the maps of the USSR indicating where their troop deployments were situated. The very quality, speed and accuracy of the Lucy insights caused the Russians to mistrust their source. Initially, as we have seen, they ordered Radó to ignore them. But in what Foote described as 'one of his few independent gestures of the war', Radó continued to pay for – and deliver to Moscow – Lucy's insights. And 'as dripping water wears away the hardest stone', as Foote put it, Moscow came around to appreciate what they had in their hands.

Foote, even in 1949, was baffled by how this was achieved. He had a couple of tentative theories. The intelligence could not have been brought to Rössler on paper. There was, as he said, no question of a courier or safe route by land. The speed of delivery would not permit such a time-consuming route. It had to be, according to Foote, achieved over the air, by radio. This route struck him just as unlikely: 'his sources, whoever they were, must have gone almost hotfoot from the service teleprinters to their wireless transmitters to send the information off.'

This scenario is hard to imagine. German counter intelligence would surely notice if a secret transmitter was operating from Berlin – or anywhere in Germany. Other transmitters from the anti-Nazi resistance in Germany had been suppressed, with their associated teams rounded up with ruthless efficiency.[189]

In *Handbook for Spies*, Foote was keen to clear up one possible explanation, addressing the argument that the information was coming from official sources. In this scenario the Germans would give information which was true in order to slip in some information which was false and which would lead to catastrophic consequences for the enemy, in this case the Russians. The Germans called this *funkspiel*. He dismissed this 'double cross' idea out of hand, although as we have seen, the Russians themselves took the idea seriously. There was only one occasion when the information Foote transmitted turned out to be false. In this instance it led to a genuine catastrophe. Incorrect information about German troop deployments around the city of Kharkov led to the loss of 100,000 Soviet troops. As we have seen, when Foote went to Moscow serious questions would be asked about this debacle. One historian attributed these losses to last-minute changes in German military strategy caused by Hitler's micromanagement of the general staff's battle plans.

Sándor Radó for his part was just as baffled about Rössler's sources as was Foote, even with over thirty extra years to ponder the problem. But before he added his own insights Radó was keen to pour cold water over some of the claims made about his team. They did not get information to Moscow in ten hours (Accoce and Quet) nor in twenty-four (Foote). As best as he could calculate, their delivery time was about three to six days. In fact, said Radó, Moscow requested that Lucy put dates on his missives so that Moscow Centre could add the message's age into their calculations.

Even then, three to six days was still very impressive. But Radó was less impressed by many of the theories about how Rössler managed to get his information. The 'courier' hypothesis might just have worked for one or two missions per week, he argued. But this and other theories faced a big problem. Even if they could explain how the Lucy material was carried out of Germany, they failed to take account of the two-way nature of communications between the Centre and Lucy's sources. Carrying questions from Moscow into Germany and getting responses out in such volumes and at such speed would be next to impossible in wartime, even with the semi-porous border between Switzerland and Germany.

Illegal radio communications got a similar thumbs down; 'even less convincing', as Radó put it. Accoce and Quet put forward a theory that Rössler's friends in Germany had equipped him with a transmitter and with his own code book.[190] Tarrant was even more generous to Rössler. He said they supplied him with his own Enigma machine.[191] Radó dismissed this theory. The operation of a radio transmitter requires training and practice, neither of which Rössler had. And the problem of detection remained. Even if the Swiss were prepared to tolerate unauthorised transmissions from their territory, the Germans would not allow a neutral neighbour to tolerate such a (to them) hostile action.

Accoce and Quet raised the intriguing possibility that encoded messages were sent out of Germany via the vast, official military broadcasting service of the German armed forces. So many encoded messages were being sent out that to slip one into the in-tray of a military telegraphist would be straightforward. The person on the Morse key would have no idea what was being sent out; all they would see was a simple row of numbers. At the Swiss end of the operation, Rössler's co-conspirators brought him a shortwave radio composed of spare parts lifted surreptitiously from the German military supplies organisation. It was then reassembled in Lucerne. This is a very neat and tidy theory. It is also one which was eviscerated by Nigel West, a British doyen of non-fiction espionage history. In an unreferenced sentence, he laid the claims of Accoce and Quet to rest: 'In the face of mounting controversy about their version of events, Accoce and Quet admitted that they had made it all up.'[192] Where, when, and to whom this admission was made has not been easy to establish.

Radó had more sympathy with the idea that official lines of communication were being used to supply Rössler. He suggested two possible candidates for this information highway. The German vice-consul in Geneva, Hans Bernd Gisevius,[193] was anti-Nazi and was an 'active participant' (according to Radó) in the plot to kill Hitler. Perhaps he laid an official embassy transmitter and telegraphist at Rössler's disposal. Another 'official channel' theory that Radó examined was the possibility that the Swiss, through Buro Ha, were knowingly or unknowingly allowing their own facilities to be used by Rössler, one of their employees. He suggested that because of the close personal relations between the Swiss and the Germans, not least through a common language, Buro Ha might itself have been the source of Rössler's material. German speaking, flamboyantly neutral Swiss citizens with jobs and relations at all levels of German society would hear the unguarded remarks of people which could be passed back home. Snippets of information could be filed away by Swiss intelligence to form an overall impression about life in the Reich. Rössler had access to these files. It was important that the Swiss maintain active surveillance of information from Germany because of the ever-present risk of invasion. Rössler could help himself to the resources of Swiss intelligence, package them up into reports and hand them over to Radó.

What the truth was behind these musings, we will never know:

> Six months before his death, he [Rössler] had revealed to Schnieper's 18-year-old-son [Schnieper was a friend of Rössler] the names of his German informants from World War II: 'When you are a grown man and all those currently still alive are dead, you may name them publicly.' A year later, Schnieper Junior was killed in a car accident'.[194]

What does any of this have to do with Foote being a double agent?

In 1967 Malcolm Muggeridge wrote a review of Accoce and Quet's book *La guerre a été gagnée en Suisse* (The War Was Won in Switzerland), about the Lucy spy ring.[195] This was no ordinary book review. The *Observer* gave him a full page to air his opinions. Muggeridge had himself been in the secret services during the war and, what is more, after the war he came to know Foote personally and used to enjoy a drink with him when Foote was on his way home from his job at the Ministry of Agriculture and Fisheries. They used to laugh about the bureaucratic idiocies they had encountered in their respective intelligence organisations. In his review Muggeridge put forward a startling new theory; he argued the notion that Radó's spy ring in Switzerland could handle the volume of material from Germany was fanciful. The Lucy network in Switzerland was bringing in more information than Rössler could conceivably handle on his own. If it was not coming by radio, then how was it getting to him so quickly and in such volume?

Foote himself was at his transmitter sometimes all day and all night, according to Radó. At the peak of his activity he was 'living like a monk' he was so busy. Muggeridge was scathing about the idea that Rössler's fellow protestant mates from the First World War were Rössler's source:

> They suggest in all seriousness and, what is more remarkable, the suggestion has been taken seriously, that in the 1914–1918 war 10 Bavarian officers, all protestants, served with Roessler [sic] in the same company: that they all subsequently joined the Reichswehr, all became anti-Nazis but swore allegiance to Hitler, all reached eminent positions in the [armed forces] so eminent that they were able to send to Rössler in Geneva **by official [armed forces] channels** intelligence which covered in great detail all operations on the Eastern front.

For Muggeridge, the idea that the information flowing through Lucy's hands came from '10 evangelical worthies' was too ridiculous to take seriously. He called the idea 'unresisting imbecility'. Rössler died without revealing from whom he was getting the bulk of his most important information, but Muggeridge had a theory. He thought that it was all coming from British intelligence. They were decoding information from the Germans that the latter thought was entirely secure. The British facility at Bletchley Park (which in 1967 Muggeridge was still not allowed to name) could provide real-time insight into the thinking and planning of the German high command by intercepting coded messages. They could not use much of this information without revealing to the Germans that they had access to their communications. Much of the information in the decoded German communications referred to events on the Eastern Front. The British knew that the Russians would suspect any information that came from Imperialist Britain because they were devoted to the idea that Britain secretly wished to wear out the USSR with an unending war with Germany. The Russians had had British armies on their soil attempting to restore the Tsar, and this was still fresh in their mind.

The Muggeridge theory was thus: that Britain was supplying material from Bletchley, codenamed 'Ultra', to Rössler and the Lucy network. This was then being transmitted by Foote, unaware of its source, to Moscow. How this information was transported to Switzerland from Bletchley and so quickly, Muggeridge did not say.

Accoce and Quet did not take Muggeridge's stinging review lying down and replied to him with such vehemence that it occasioned a partial retreat. Muggeridge wrote on 29 January: 'May I again stress, as I did in my review, that my suggestion as to the source of Rössler's information is only a suggestion.'

Muggeridge was not the only person who was to put forward the view that Foote was acting (unwittingly in this case) for British intelligence. Others have developed the theme further and presented Foote in an altogether less innocent light than he might at first have appeared. The following is a non-exhaustive list of the hypotheses regarding Foote's possible role as a double agent.

1. <u>The null hypothesis.</u> This, the conventional view, states that Foote was an idealistic young man who went to fight in Spain and later worked for the *Rote Drei* as a dedicated anti-fascist. He tapped out his messages to the USSR in good faith without

knowing where, ultimately, they came from, but in the honest belief that he was helping the Soviet Union defeat the Nazis. His experiences after the war in Soviet Russia turned his mind against his former sympathies and he returned to Great Britain prepared to tell all he knew about Soviet intelligence to MI5 and MI6.

2. <u>The Muggeridge hypothesis.</u> Foote was an idealistic young man caught up in the same whirlwind which attracted many people to become sympathetic to communism and the USSR. He became, in Switzerland, an unwitting vehicle for British intelligence to send 'Ultra' material from Bletchley Park to the USSR. This would assist the Russians to fight Germany and buy Britain the time to prepare D-Day. How this information came to and from Britain is not known.

3. <u>The Dansey hypothesis.</u> Foote was a knowing agent of Department Z inside SIS/MI6 before he went to Spain and later, in Switzerland, fed material to the Russians from the British whether that information was true or false, according to requirements.[196] This is the hypothesis expressed in *Operation Lucy*, published in 1980.

4. <u>The Soviet hypothesis.</u> Foote was a knowing and willing agent of SIS passing on deliberately harmful material in order to slow down the Red Army in its progress in defeating the Nazis.

In 1980, some ten years after Radó's book *Codename Dora* was published in Hungary as *Dora Jelenti*, Anthony Read and David Fisher published *Operation Lucy*, a book which took the Muggeridge hypothesis further and set out the 'Dansey Hypothesis'. This is a very readable book and gives several valuable (if unreferenced) insights into the personal life of Foote, especially in its non-espionage aspects. In the foreword to the 1980 edition, they acknowledged numerous people for their help in preparing the account. And the list is very impressive: Fred Copeman,

Edmond Hamel, Margaret Powell, Otto Pünter and Sándor Radó are all there, as is the Communist Party of Great Britain. It is not possible to say from their work what these acknowledgements were for. Were they interviews? Were they refusals of an interview? It is impossible to say. The frustrating thing with the book is that conversations were presented as if they were verbatim but without any attempt to reference them or even to indicate the context in which they were collected. One is never certain if one is reading an actual conversation or whether, as they say in TV dramas, 'a scene has been added for dramatic effect'. In a biography of Alexander Foote such matters are important. Any account of espionage will be given to dramatisation and exaggeration and flights of fancy are not uncommon. Across the board in *Operation Lucy* the lack of verifiable references is woeful, but more of this later.

In *Operation Lucy*, the authors argue that Foote had been recruited by British intelligence before he went to Spain by a shadowy outfit called the 'Z Organisation', established in 1936 as a new and more secure wing of the secret intelligence service. It was an organisation kept apart from the rest of the Secret Intelligence Service in order that, should war break out, it could carry on functioning in the event of British collapse. It was an organisation that ran agents and was designed to obtain intelligence about Germany and Italy. The Z Organisation was led by Claude Dansey, described by Keith Jeffery as 'able but extremely irascible'. Jeffery went on to describe Dansey, using the words of one of his recruits: he was a 'copybook secret service man. Dapper, establishment, Boodles [club], poker playing expression, bitterly cynical, but with unlimited and illogical charm'.[197]

One of the apparent strengths of the case that Read and Fisher advanced is that in September 1939 most of the Z Organisation did in fact decamp to Zurich, using consular facilities as cover. At this moment Foote was establishing himself in Switzerland. The evidence put forward that Foote was recruited by the Z Organisation is, to say the least, thin. This is how *Operation Lucy* explains the recruitment to the Z Organisation of Alexander Foote. Before he went to Spain:

Controversies 169

> The organisation into which Foote had been recruited was not the British Secret Intelligence Service as such, then under the control of the legendary Admiral Hugh 'Quex' Sinclair, but a strange, semi-official, semi-private affair known by the melodramatic name of the 'Z Organisation' ... Most of its work is still a mystery, and there are no records of those who were employed by it. Our investigations show the SIS files have nothing in them concerning Allan Foote.

Perhaps this was why Read and Fisher offered no references. There were none to be given. Other writers might regard such a problem as insurmountable, but to *Operation Lucy* the lack of evidence was a challenge.

They hang their theory that Foote was a British agent on a reported remark that Foote made to his sister Margaret, decades after the words were supposed to be uttered. When Foote told her of his plan to desert from the RAF, Margaret was horrified:

> You can't just walk out of the air force ... You'll be a deserter. You'll never be free again. If you go abroad as a deserter you'll never be able to come back into the country again. They'll arrest you and put you in prison.

Read and Fisher's account went on:

> Foote smiled confidently. 'Don't worry. It's all been taken care of. I'm quite safe. They can't touch me or do anything to me.'[198]

When Foote emerged from the Soviet sector in Berlin in 1947, MI5 officers did indeed question why Foote had not been arrested for desertion from the RAF when he arrived back from Spain. As we know, Roger Hollis personally emphasised the need to bury any possible post-war prosecution for desertion. But these are thin threads on which to hang the theory that Foote was all along the creature of Claude Dansey.

The Dansey theory is given comprehensive amplification in the (very readable) work of Tony Percy.[199] In 1955, American historian David Dallin mentioned the suspicions emanating from other comrades in the Swiss network that Foote was working for the British: "'I have no documents to prove it", says a former member of the Radó network, "but I am certain that he was a British agent."'[200] Dallin himself poured cold water on the theory.

Sándor Radó gave many of these theories short shrift. In *Codename Dora*, first published in English in 1977, Radó put forward a number of different theories about his operation in order of their unlikeliness. Top of that hierarchy was Muggeridge's view. Radó died in 1981 and probably did not get to see Read and Fisher's elaboration of Muggeridge's ideas at his home in Hungary. But the Muggeridge theory boiled down to this: the war was not won from Switzerland; on that he agreed with Radó. But he disagreed with Radó that the war was won by the skill and determination of the Red Army. Instead, it was won in the Nissen huts of Bletchley Park and by extension, no doubt, the playing fields of Eton College and Winchester School. Muggeridge goes halfway to actually saying this in his *Observer* review:

> I had occasion, while serving as an intelligence officer, to visit the establishment in which, if my supposition is correct, the Lucy pabulum was being produced. It was a country house where the cypher breakers, for the most part dons, chess players and violinists ... lived together. In the lunch interval there was a game of rounders on the lawn. It is interesting to reflect that if the battle of Waterloo was won on the playing fields of Eton, the battle of Stalingrad was, if not won, at any rate appreciably influenced by that remote lawn.

In his book *The Red Orchestra* published in 1995, V.E. Tarrant joined in the assault on the Bletchley Park 'Ultra' theory of Rössler's sources. Without mentioning Muggeridge's 'suggestion' of events, he described

Read and Fisher's account as 'a complex conspiracy theory which is not only fantastic but totally untrue'.

The 'complex conspiracy theory' ran as follows: early in the war the British used the Pakbo ring to deliver Enigma-derived 'Ultra' material to Stalin via their agent Foote. But, when the volume of material became too much to pass through Foote without arousing questions among the ever-suspicious Moscow handlers, they called on another of their assets to launder the 'Ultra' material via Rössler to Radó. That asset was none other than Rachel Dübendorfer (Sissy), the communist employee at the International Labour Organisation, who offered this service to the British for money.

Tarrant responded to this by saying that there was 'no truth in this nonsense', and he quoted the words of the official of the secret services, Professor F.H. Hinsley: 'There is no truth in the much publicised claim that the British authorities made use of the "Lucy" ring, a Soviet espionage organisation which operated in Switzerland, to forward intelligence to Moscow.'[201]

Tarrant went on to offer point by point refutations of Read and Fisher's arguments. Dansey had no access to the 'Ultra' material. Even if he did have access, he could not have got the material to Foote with the speed that Foote was hammering it out. According to Tarrant, the cryptologists at Bletchley had their hands full with material of direct relevance to Britain. Tarrant argued that much of the German traffic to the Eastern Front was sent by teleprinter, beyond the eyes of Bletchley's enigma machines. Further, he said, Eastern Front material would always have a lower priority. On the other hand, and without wishing to play devil's advocate, this was not the picture presented by the spy John Cairncross in his autobiography *The Enigma Spy: The Story of the Man Who Changed the Course of World War Two*. He was at Bletchley Park at around the time of the Battle of Kursk and would therefore count as a first-hand witness to events. For him, passing Enigma material about the Eastern Front to his Soviet handler became almost a full-time job, there was so much of it:

As more and more of the German ultra decrypts passed through my hands, I saw that the signals contained a vast amount of precise information which would be of the utmost use to the Soviet armed forces in their struggle against the powerful German army. They would provide advance information of German intentions from which it would be possible to plan appropriate counter-moves. The ultra decrypts on the Luftwaffe details of the strength, unit numbers and location of the enemy's air force squadrons. Furthermore, this data was not just limited to the Luftwaffe, but was related to the army as well.[202]

But even if the Z Organisation had access to the 'Ultra' material, how was the two-way communication between Foote and Dansey's people transmitted? Communications between Britain and Switzerland were extremely poor. Keith Jeffery outlines the problems at length:

Another difficulty with the Swiss operation [of MI6] concerned communications. There was an SIS wireless set at Geneva, but it could be used only for receiving messages as the Swiss authorities did not permit foreign missions in the country to send enciphered messages except through the Swiss post office. Before the fall of France messages went in a diplomatic bag ... This ceased after the Germans occupied Vichy in November 1942, but it was thereafter found possible to bribe South American diplomats to carry the bags out. 'Two journeys and retire for life' was the saying.[203]

There was a third version of the 'Foote as British spy' theory which emerged from a most surprising source. For reasons known only to himself, Sándor Radó did not mention it in his denunciation of *more or less mythological* theories. The information coming from Rudolf Rössler's informants did not just travel east. It was also sent to the Western Allies where appropriate. There was, therefore, always some tenuous contact between Soviet and British intelligence throughout the war via the

Lucy ring: information from differing sources was being redirected west and east according to the requirements of each of the Allies. When the Swiss police were stamping out the Soviet espionage organisation, Foote's senior officer Sándor Radó suggested, as we have seen, that they take refuge in the British consulate and continue to transmit to Russia under diplomatic cover. How this would have worked with the British communications being so restricted is not known. But even the suggestion of involving the British must have caused panic in Moscow. They jumped to the paranoid conclusion that there was treachery afoot. As David Dallin put it:

> The 'British spy' obsession that affected the Soviet intelligence service during the war against Germany was part of the morbid mentality which, emanating as it did from the sanctum of the Kremlin, was a kind of order for all lesser agencies ... None of the agents working abroad was secure from being suspected of treason in favour of London, and this was particularly true of the leading people in the Swiss intelligence group.[204]

When Foote arrived in Moscow he was surprised to find that instead of a hero's welcome, he was at first subjected to an interrogation, the point of which was to discover whether his activities in Switzerland amounted to spying for the British. And the accusation was not, á la Muggeridge, that he was passing on information to assist the Russians, but that he was knowingly passing on information designed to hamper the Red Army in its progress towards Germany. The British motive for this, according to the Russians, was that the Germans and the Soviets would wear each other out before the opening of the second front in the west. In this way, the British and the Americans could come in and mop up the mess in Europe to their own advantage.

For Foote, the penny dropped that this was how the Russians were thinking on the first day. When he arrived in Moscow he was welcomed by Maria Poliakova (Vera). She had been the previous Resident in

Switzerland before Sándor Radó, and knew more about aspects of Foote's network than he did. After some formal welcome activities, Vera got down to business:

> [She] turned up again the next morning with a list of questions as long as my arm ... [She] left me with the list of questions, and after studying them I was, to say the least, far from happy. It was obvious from the tone of the questions that the Centre regarded me as an agent provocateur planted on them by the British.

This suspicion was not confined to Vera. It came from the top:

> In the view of the director, I had obviously been released by the Swiss police on British intervention, the British quid pro quo being that I would transmit to the Centre only such information as the British would supply, although attributing it to all the various sources known to Moscow. The British object in all this being, of course, to hinder the advance of the Red Army by feeding them false information. Equally, the director thought that Radó had been conveniently 'liquidated' in Cairo to prevent his giving a different story to Moscow ... Fantastic as the whole thing was, the Centre obviously believed quite seriously that the British would, in the middle of a war when all the allies were fighting for their lives, settle down to produce as complicated a plan as this, merely to deceive their allies.[205]

Foote managed to talk the Russians out of this way of thinking, at least as regards himself. Poor Sándor Radó was not so lucky (see Chapter Eight).

In an activity as shady and suspicious as espionage, madcap theories are bound to be generated – especially where, as in the case of Foote, the stakes were so high and so many loose ends were still left lying around. But if Foote had been a double agent for the British, would he have taken the risk of travelling to Moscow? What potential advantages would have justified that risk? But on the other hand, did the Soviet agents who peppered the personnel of British intelligence not inform Moscow that Foote was the genuine article and not a British cuckoo in Radó's espionage nest? If Foote was genuinely a British spy, it rather undermines the all-knowing picture of the Soviet penetration of British intelligence we have all been brought up with. Surely, by now, the British secret services would have let the world know that they had a mole inside Soviet intelligence. After suffering slings and arrows about the Cambridge Five and the rest of the intelligence leaks for decade after decade, the temptation to claim one back would have been irresistible. But despite interesting academic speculation there has been nothing official said about Foote as a British agent. Bletchley Park and its secrets have been revealed. Films have been made about Alan Turing. The Enigma machine and its capture is now a standard feature of spy fiction. But the secret services have kept from the world that they had a man at the heart of the Lucy ring? This does not sound too likely.

If Foote was in secret an employee of the British secret services from 1936 until at least 1946, then his British employers were even worse than his Soviet ones. Here he was, a hero of the most audacious piece of double agent work, first in Spain, then in Switzerland and then in Moscow. And he came home to a dog's life. Sick, poor and isolated – did he ever think that he might have been better off if he had taken the Soviet job in Argentina? This is how his ghost-writer Courtenay Young described his state in 1948. Note the cynicism in his remarks:

> You may be interested to know that FOOTE is in a state of extreme depression. His ulcers appear to have returned in full force and he is contemplating going to live with his sister ... He does not think that he can stand London life and wishes to live on a farm where he will be well and wholesomely fed for, as far as I can gather, about half an hour's work a day ... He ended rather depressingly saying that he was extremely ill, flat broke and that he would probably die. I fear that this last contingency is unlikely.

Anyway, with any reasonable luck, it should be unnecessary for me to see him more than two or three times, as by then the book will be finished and the rest of the negotiations can be conducted through Mr Vesey.

Tony Percy expressed the dilemma well for anyone trying to make sense of the conflicting stories about Foote and the rest of the Radó network:

It is a fruitless endeavour to try to depict accurately the web of relationships in the intelligence world of Switzerland in WWII. Which informants were working for whom, who out of ideology and who for pecuniary reasons, who were merely couriers and intermediaries, who was officially on a foreign payroll, what information was fresh, which invented, who in Swiss Intelligence connived at the activities of foreign networks, how they held off the Nazis, which way intelligence was passed.[206]

A double agent theory of my own

'There are no Kremlin objections to retirement from the service if circumstances permit and discretion is maintained.'

Handbook for Spies, p.46.

Imagine the scene. Alexander Foote was living in Moscow. He was no longer a young man and the shine had well and truly been rubbed off his initial idealism about communism and the USSR. Close up and personal, Stalin's Russia did not inspire him. After eighteen bleak months he began to pine for the shires of old England. The Russians were, according to him, not keen to send him on a spying mission against Britain while he was actually in his home country. They were not especially inclined to send him on a normal spying mission anywhere else in the world either. His cover had been comprehensively blown in Switzerland. What use is a secret agent who has spent ten months in a Swiss jail on a charge of espionage? The secret service jobs proposed to him in Moscow sounded like jokes. A 6-foot Liverpudlian spy in China? The penetration of a Nazi émigré nest in Argentina? With a Yorkshire accent? True, he would have been in Berlin for the grand total of six highly conspicuous months, perfecting his back story. But Foote, acting as a German among the deeply suspicious, hard-core Nazis in South America would have been as convincing as Dick Van Dyke being a cockney chimney sweep in *Mary Poppins*.

However, there was one potential way back to Britain which would give Foote a clean break with his past in Soviet intelligence. All of Foote's espionage experiences were by now in the past and were rapidly receding in his rear-view mirror. The overall shape of what he had been up to in Switzerland would already have been familiar to the British secret services. They had captured all the German cryptographers who had been hunting the *Rote Drei* and debriefed them extensively. He might have been able to add some colour to their picture of his network and the Swiss aspect of the work of the Red Orchestra, but what he added would only be interesting titbits to a general story with which they were already familiar.

For Moscow, Switzerland and the *Rote Drei* were in the past, too. A heroic past maybe, but the problems Radó's network addressed had by now all been solved with the defeat of Nazism. The new problem for the Soviet Union was the atom bomb. Here they were lucky. From the British countryside a constant flow of high-grade intelligence on this subject was being transmitted by Foote's old comrade Agent Sonya, ably informed by Comrades Melita Norwood[207] and atomic scientist Klaus Fuchs.

Perhaps the plan was this: if, in early 1947, Foote 'defected' in Berlin and went to British intelligence, he could tell them everything they wanted to know about his activities in Switzerland, at little cost to the USSR. Much of it was known already by the British and it was all in the past anyway. He could also lay out how the Soviets structured their spy networks and the basics of their spy craft. Much of this had come out after the Canadian spy network collapsed, and from the multiple defections of Soviet citizens. He could say whatever he wanted about his disillusionment and his dissatisfaction with the USSR, and he could exaggerate his pro-German, anti-Semitic, fascist-leaning new views all he wanted – the more the better. But all he had to do for his former Soviet bosses was the following: first, he was to maintain that when Sonya left Switzerland for Britain, she did not intend to continue spying. He should say that she longed for the life of a dutiful homemaker and mother. She was thoroughly disillusioned by her former employers and wanted nothing more to do with them. Second, he was to make a note of the questions that he was asked about her current activities. How much did the British know? What were their investigative priorities? What names did they ask him about?

Len Buerton was equally disillusioned. Even in Switzerland he had abandoned espionage and had only one ambition left: to be reunited with his bride. This apolitical picture of Beurton in Switzerland created by Foote was inconsistent with what actually happened when he arrived back in Britain. He immediately took out a Communist Party card and became an active member.

After a couple of months of well-mannered interrogation in Britain, Foote would be free to pursue whatever life he wanted, free from any concern that the Russians would try to bump him off. His career in intelligence would have ended, to be sure. This would be his final service to them. Perhaps this explains Foote's devil-may-care attitude to the possibility of Soviet reprisals, noted in one of Serpell's first interviews in Hanover:

> One interesting point which emerged this morning from my interrogation of Foote was his apparently complete lack of nerves. I had been given to understand that he was considerably worried in Berlin about the trips he had to make to the Soviet zone to arrange his affairs ... He denied any fear of the Russians whatever. I asked him if he had any fear of reprisals and he seemed genuinely unable to understand what I was talking about.[208]

When the Hamels were in prison, it will be recalled, they used their own interrogations as an intelligence-gathering exercise. They said as little as they could during their interrogations, but they made a great deal of use of their interrogators' line of questioning to estimate what they were up against. Perhaps this is an example of the same technique that Foote was to use. A sort of face-to-face *funkspiel*: give some true but trivial information to the opposition in order to conceal, or obtain, a greater truth.

This scenario makes sense of the bizarre, rain-soaked, doorstep warning given to the 'Austrian Comrade': tell Sonya and Len to stop working! Destroy all documents! Foote may have gathered from MI5 that Sonya was a 'person of interest' and sought to prevent her capture, hence the warning. Or at least he enabled her to take more serious precautions. On the other hand, that Foote uttered this warning at all comes from Sonya herself, and is at best third-hand hearsay from an unnamed source, so extreme caution is required in believing it.

But my theory also makes sense of the reckless plan he had of returning to Switzerland and possibly into the arms of a GRU hit squad. He felt safe enough to travel because he knew the Russians would behave themselves.

As a double agent for Moscow, this theory makes a lot more sense than the cockamamie Argentine mission he spoke about, if indeed this was ever actually mooted. When Foote was arrested in Switzerland, it should be remembered, he told the police officers who were interrogating him that he was not working for the Russians. He told them that he was an agent of the Republic of Guatemala. Perhaps the Argentina mission came from the same source in his fertile imagination as his Guatemalan posting.

When MI5 eventually got around to interviewing Sonya, Foote had already primed them with a story that she would easily be able to take advantage of: she had become disillusioned with the USSR over the Nazi-Soviet pact, or the Russian invasion of Finland, whatever. Her cover story had been pre-planted in Serpell and Skardon's heads by Foote. When they told her that they knew she had stopped being a spy at the time of the Russian invasion of Finland, she must have known that she was home and dry.

There we have it, my theory. Rich in speculation, thin on evidence – as is much of the commentary about Foote's career. Foote was not a double agent for the British. He was a double agent against the British for the Russians.

It makes as much sense as anything else.

Chapter Thirteen

Decline and Fall

After the drama of Foote's defection from the service of the USSR, he settled down to a somewhat humdrum existence as a low-grade civil servant in the Ministry of Agriculture and Fisheries. This position is frequently portrayed (by proponents of the Foote-as-a-double-agent hypothesis) as a sinecure, a cushy number arranged by his friends in the secret services. But in reality he seems to have lived a miserable existence on poor pay, existential disappointment and a chronic sense of grievance. Compared to his life in Lausanne there was little to stimulate his interest. His MI5 file contains little after about 1952 and the primary sources about his life dry up. Apart from reviews of his book, his name did not appear in any headline except once in 1953 where he was reported in his local newspaper, the *West London Observer*, to be addressing what is described as a Brains Trust style event on 29 May. He was reported as asserting that confidential decisions made in Whitehall were known about in Moscow in the same week. Two years on from the defections of Burgess and Maclean this could hardly have come as news to the meeting's attendees.

His MI5 file also indicated that he was in contact with, and did lectures for, Russian émigré organisations.

Little is known about how he lived his life in these times. He maintained contact with his sisters and occasionally visited Malcolm Muggeridge on his way home from the torpor of his desk job but apart from this, his life is opaque. He did not marry, that much is known. How he came to know Malcolm Muggeridge, is not known. Muggeridge summarised his existence:

He was working as a clerk in the Ministry of Agriculture and Fisheries, then located in Regents Park near where I was living. He used to drop in for a chat on his way home: a large stolid looking Yorkshireman, who could be very funny about his time in the USSR and the training in espionage methods he was given – no less fatuous I was relieved to learn than our own essays in the same field ... no one could have been less than the popular idea of a secret agent – he was much more like an insurance agent, or possibly a professional cricketer – but he had developed a taste for clandestinity, and found his overt life with Ag and Fish very tedious.[209]

In *Operation Lucy* Read and Fisher thank numerous people for their help in writing their book. What this help consisted of they do not say. One of the people they thank is Charles Knecht, one of the police officers who arrested Foote in his Lausanne flat. On a business trip in 1949 he looked Foote up in the Worsely House Hotel at 11 Clifton Gardens in Maida Vale, as old adversaries are wont to do. What he saw horrified him, according to Read and Fisher. His living conditions were so poor that Knecht invited him to stay in his hotel room for the duration of his one-week stay in London. Nevertheless: "'Foote was always good company" he told us "and he was at the top of his form".' Both men spent the week reminiscing about their common story and toasting each other with booze.

According to Read and Fisher, Foote was due to embark on a lecture tour of America. As the USA was in the grip of anti-communist spy-fever at the time this might have proven to be very profitable for him. But he was tormented for the rest of his life by the health problems which had dogged his time in Russia. His duodenal ulcers made his life miserable with constant and increasing pain. A picture of Foote taken in 1954 for the cover of *Der Spiegel* portrays a man who looks older than his 49 years.

Nevertheless, he stayed in contact with his sisters, making frequent visits to East Grinstead. He kept his rooms in Clifton Gardens, Maida

Vale, and was apparently well known in the Bridge-playing circles of West London. But his health deteriorated inexorably until, in 1956, he was operated on for his duodenal ulcers in University College Hospital. Things did not go well. He developed peritonitis as a complication of his surgery and in the final days of his life suffered intense pain that could not be controlled. He tore at the dressings on his wounds in his distress. He died on 1 August 1956, aged 51.

It has been suggested that Foote may have been poisoned by the Soviet secret services as a punishment for his defection and subsequent betrayal.[210] The substance used in this version of events was thallium. This, it is argued, causes painful abdominal symptoms which could be confused with peritonitis. This is a highly unlikely scenario. In the post-Skripal and Litvinenko era, poisoning by the Russian authorities of traitors cannot be ruled out, but in Foote's case a surgeon will have seen the consequences of his years of duodenal ulceration. The evidence of the surgeon's own eyes will have left little doubt as to the cause of Foote's demise. There was no inquest.

His death was recorded in the Pancras district of London. In 1957 a probate record was made which named Agnes May Clemetson as a 'linked person', but there is no information about her possible relationship with Foote.

No obituaries marked the passage of Alexander Allan Foote, which is perhaps appropriate for someone who, as one of the most notable spies of the twentieth century, lived his life in the shadow.

Epilogue: And in the end, a personal view

It was only a couple of years ago that I even came to know about Alexander Foote. He does not have a high profile in the town of both our births. The first I came to know about him was from reading V.E. Tarrant's book *The Red Orchestra*. I have always found the psychology of spying intriguing. The fact that you, as a spy, can go into work and live all day with the knowledge that everything your colleagues hold dear is being given away by you, somebody they trust. On the other hand, given the dire circumstances of 1943, when the world was on the brink of a 'Dark Age made more sinister, and perhaps more protracted, by the lights of perverted science', as Churchill put it, what would I have done? If, by telling someone something I knew, I could save the lives of Russians who were just about holding on against a fascist enemy that I myself had spent the last decade fighting on the streets ... what would I have done?

I was reading Tarrant's book and the name of 'Liverpool born' Foote came up. Born in Liverpool he is entirely unknown in the city, and I should know. I've asked around. The closest he comes to recognition as being connected with the city is his name on the list in the Casa of Liverpool men who went to fight in Spain.

Looking for more details about his life and times I had to discard some initial assumptions I made at an early stage. I rather expected to read the story of a classical Comintern-era Stalinist; dour, ascetic and his outlook on life determined by precepts derived from nineteenth-century German political philosophy. Foote's espionage, combined with his record of service in Spain, had led me to expect someone dedicated to a particular view of socialism, and a belief in the leading role of the Communist Party of the Soviet Union in carrying the hopes of humanity of a sunlit future. I expected him to be, in short, more like the woman who recruited him to the military intelligence service of the USSR, Agent Sonya. In her book she described how living in Switzerland had preyed on her conscience for being too easy. She and her children were enjoying themselves too much among the meadows and slopes of the Swiss. The life of a country lady suited her and her children loved it. The quiet period she and her recruits enjoyed before the outbreak of war came at a cost to her peace of mind. It troubled her. Too easy. Insufficient struggle. But then, she read that in his exile years Vladimir Ilyich Lenin, leader of the Bolshevik revolution, also enjoyed the countryside in Switzerland and the life he lived there. So it was OK. Conscience clear.

Did Foote mention Lenin in his book? I do not think so. Radó certainly did.

I do not imagine that such thoughts would have occurred to Allan Foote. This was not the horny-handed son of toil of Bolshevik imagination. First impressions of him by anyone he met (who wrote them down) conveyed the image of a bon viveur. This was a man who enjoyed life and who let people around him know that he did. Everyone in his circle of spies seems ascetic to one extent or another in comparison to him. Food, booze and company – especially of women – it comes as no surprise to read that he found himself a nice flat in a posh part of Lausanne and stocked up on scotch. He may have, in his words, lived the life of a monk, but his friends saw him as an Englishman half-way through a Grand Tour interrupted by a world war.

Eighty years after his death as a relatively young man, what emerges is a somewhat enigmatic character. He is so full of contradictions that it is always hard to work him out. Incidentally, it was not just the relative youth of his demise that gave his life a tragic note. It is that, today, the disease that killed him is eminently treatable. Whoever hears of people dying of duodenal ulcers these days?

He was a complex character and I wonder what his comrades made of him. The comrades in his circle were composed of three types of person.

The largest group, the Russophile Bolsheviks, were the kind of people who believed that in helping the USSR they were ushering in a new age for mankind. People in this group may well have spied for the USSR even if the Nazis had never existed.

The second group were not committed to communism and were in many instances enthusiastically opposed to communism and communists. But this group could see that should the Nazis win, all their hopes would be dashed. This group held their nose and worked for the Russians because, let us not forget, at one point the Russians were the only ones on mainland European soil fighting the Nazis. In this group I would put the Pakbo and the Long groups. I would also, tentatively, place Foote here. As the years went on his initial sympathy for communism drifted further and further into line with other social democrats involved in their network. Ideologically, this is how John Cairncross presented himself in his autobiography *The Enigma Spy* first published in 1997.

The third group were the people who spied for money. Well, they all spied for money to one degree and another, but this last group would have spied for anyone who paid them. Into this group fell the Martins: Lorenz and Laura. There have been some historians who have accused Rössler of being in this camp, including the Russians, as Foote found out when he was in Moscow. I do not buy it. I would place Rössler at the head of the second group.

It would have been interesting to read the accounts of every first-hand participant in the work of Radó's network. As it is, there are four primary sources: Foote, Radó, Sonya and Pünter. The first off the block was Foote's book. All the others who wrote books condemned Foote's. Inaccurate was the kindest thing that was said about it. Radó and Pünter insisted it was an overly glamourised and self-glorifying account of the period. Sonya seems to be of the view that he would have been better shot by Stalin than to publish that book. Radó took a more measured view of his work; he adopted the tone of a disappointed headmaster, assuring Foote that he had let the Comintern down, let the international working class down, but mostly, let himself down.

Radó published his version of events in 1977 and had the advantage of being able to comment harshly on the works of Pünter and Foote without them answering back. Mind you, however much the surviving members of the network may have cast unfriendly eyes on each other's work it is nothing compared to the scathing remarks they made about the work of Accoce and Quet. Again and again they give the French journalists a tongue lashing. I cannot imagine what they would have said about the fanciful theories which drove Read and Fisher in their book. Radó gave Malcolm Muggeridge a mauling, and Muggeridge did not propose half of what Read and Fisher came up with.

Whoever's account of these times one believes, and homing in on Allan Foote again, there are several things on which all the authors agree. As a spy Foote was gifted. He was the best at coding and transmission. He was cautious to a fault – he did not give himself away, he was given away by the failure of others to observe a 'few rules and simple' protocols. He was also quick on his large feet and adaptable to unfavourable new circumstances. He was selfless and paid a heavy price for his anti-Nazism as measured by his ill health, his disillusionment and the loss of his family life.

How seriously are we to take the recantation of his views, some eighty years on? My own view is that Muggeridge probably had it right when he said that Foote retained some leftish instincts of his youth, but in an unworked-out and reflex manner. Left or right, there is precious little nodding in his book to any political doctrine. Foote's was a meat-and-potatoes approach to politics. He probably had as little time for theorising at the end of his spying career as he had at the start. What Andrew Lownie, the biographer of Guy Burgess, had to say about Burgess could equally be said of Foote:

Burgess was a product of his generation. Born a few years earlier or later, his life would have taken a very different course, but he came from a generation politicised during the early 1930s that felt it needed to stop theorising and do something, even if this call to action took many forms and led few to beat a path to Moscow.[211]

Any lingering sympathies he had with the USSR would have been thoroughly quashed when he heard what had happened to his comrades in the Red Orchestra. On the other hand, Foote did not, as many did, rush headlong into another version of doctrinal thought. Many ex-communists and fellow travellers flocked into the arms of the Catholic Church after their experiences with *The God That Failed* (1949), a collection of essays edited by Richard Crossman which included the works of recanting communists. One of the essays was written by Radó's old friend Arthur Koestler. A few ex-comrades refashioned their beliefs by joining Trotskyist groups. Not Allan Foote. The year of Foote's death, many thousands of members would leave the Communist Party after the Soviet invasion of Hungary. Many more would do so when the barbarity of the Stalin years was exposed in Russia in Kruschev's so-called secret speech. The years between Stalin's death and the secret speech were the years that Radó, Dübendorfer, Hamburger and Trepper were sprung from the camps and allowed to enjoy the freedom they had worked so hard to save for everyone else. The field of ex-communists became a crowded one.

What can you say about Foote's reception back in Britain? Well, it was by some degrees less than a warm welcome. MI5 treated him with ill-disguised contempt. Eighty years on from the Second World War this does not raise so much as an eyebrow. The poisonous influence of the Cold War years blind us to the attitudes towards Russia during the war. Of course a Russian spy would be treated harshly by MI5! Treating Russian spies harshly was what MI5 was for. But viewed from the perspective of 1944 things were not so clear.

The Russians were gallant allies. Men went from Liverpool to Murmansk in the Baltic convoys to help them. Churchill shook hands with their leader. On the back of Russia's sacrifice and courage the

Communist Party of Great Britain got two MPs elected in the 1945 election and grew to 50,000 members. Foote did not harm British interests; on the contrary, he was vital to them – even if it was unwittingly. And his breaking of UK law was somewhat technical if you ignore the whole RAF desertion thing. The hostility to him which was personal, educational and social, was over the top. Foote was someone who could easily have been regarded as an international hero.

In the city of his birth there is nothing to commemorate him. There is no plaque on the wall, there is no wall on his birth address to put it on. It has all been knocked down.

Bibliography

Books

Accoce, P., Quet, P. and Sheridan Smith A.M. [Trans] (1968) *The Lucy Ring*. London: Panther Books.

Arsenijevic, D. (1969) *Genève Appelle Moscou*. Paris: Lafont. This book is particularly useful for its photographs.

Burke, D. (2008) *The Spy Who Came in from the Co-Op*. Woodbridge: The Boydell Press.

Cairncross, J. (2021) *The Enigma Spy* London: Lume Books.

Dallin, D. J. (1955) *Soviet Espionage*. New Haven: Yale University Press.

Foote, A. (2011) *Handbook for Spies*. Landisville, Penn: Coachwhip Publications. I have quoted extensively from the 1949 edition.

Jeffery, K. (2011) *MI6: The History of the Secret Intelligence Service*. London: Bloomsbury Press.

Kesaris, P. [ed] (1979) *The Rote Kapelle*. Lanham MD: University Press of America. Available as a searchable PDF from: https://ia800702.us.archive.org/3/items/rotekapelleci00unit/rotekapelleci00unit.pdf

Koestler, A. (2005) *The Invisible Writing*. London: Vintage.

Lownie, A. (2015) *Stalin's Englishman – The Lives of Guy Burgess*. London: Hodder and Stoughton.

Macintyre, B. (2020) *Agent Sonya*. London: Viking Books.

Mathews, O. (2019) *An Impeccable Spy: Richard Sorge*. London: Bloomsbury Press.

Muggeridge, M. (1981) *The Infernal Grove*. London: Fontana.

Pincher, C. (2014) *Their Trade is Treachery* London: Biteback.

Pincher, C. (2021) *Too Secret Too Long*. London: Lume Books.

Pünter, O. and Payot, M. [Commentary] (1967) *Guerre secrète en pays neutre*. Lausanne: Payot. (Yes, the publishing company owned by the family of cryptographer Marc Payot who was present at the police raid on Foote's flat in 1943).

Radó S. and Underwood J.A. [trans] (1990) *Codename Dora*. London: Abelard.

Rings, W. (1974) *Schweiz im Krieg*. Zürich: Ex Libris. I mainly consulted this book for photographs.
Tarrant V.E. (1995) *The Red Orchestra*. London: Arms and Armour.
Werner, R (1991) *Sonya's Report*. London: Chatto & Windus. Translated by Renate Simpson (née Kuczynski, her sister).
West, N. (1984) *Unreliable Witness*. London: Weidenfeld and Nicolson.

Press sources

With thanks to https://www.letempsarchives.ch for their excellent online archive of the following Swiss newspapers:
Gazette de Lausanne
Journal de Genève

Der Spiegel for the use of a front cover of their magazine.

Journal Articles

The Rote Drei: Getting Behind the 'Lucy' Myth by Mark A. Tittenhofer CIA HISTORICAL REVIEW PROGRAM. Available from : cia.gov.
Sándor Radó, the jovial and worldly spy by Anon. Studies in Intelligence. Volume 30, Spring 1986.

Websites

Institute of World Politics: Roger Hollis, British Patriot or Soviet Spy?
https://www.iwp.edu/press-releases/2015/04/21/was-roger-hollis-a-british-patriot-or-soviet-spy/
Coldspur. For the genuine espionage obsessives. This is a must-read website for those who like to take their espionage history neat and uncluttered. Well researched, well referenced and well written. Not that I agree with half of it! http://www.coldspur.com/sonias-radio/.

Endnotes

1. The National Archives KV 2/1615_1 p.5/84
2. The National Archives KV 2/1613_2 p.10/80
3. Gyory, R. *Communist Geography Instead of Nationalist Geography: The New Cadres and the Case of Sándor Radó.* Journal of the American Hungarian Educators Association Vol 8, 2016
4. Radó, S. *Codename Dora.* Time Life books, London 1990. p.276
5. Koestler, A. *The Invisible Writing.* Vintage Classics, London 1953. p.368
6. The National Archives KV 2/1611_3 p.31/80
7. Read, A. and Fisher, D. *Operation Lucy.* Stodder and Houghton, London 1980
8. Ibid.
9. The National Archives KV 2/1612_3 p.72/74
10. The National Archives KV 2/1611_2 p.9/64
11. https://blogs.brighton.ac.uk/sussexbrigaders/2022/01/24/alexander-foote-sussex-brigader/
12. Foote, A. *Handbook for Spies* (1949 ed). Coachwhip Publications 2011, Pennsylvania. p.11
13. Read, A, Fisher, D. *Operation Lucy.* Hodder and Staunton, London 1980, p.21
14. Macintyre, B. *Agent Sonya.* Penguin Random House, London 2020. p.147
15. Werner, R. *Sonya's Report.* Chatto and Windus, London 1991, p.193
16. Read, A. and Fisher, D. *Operation Lucy.* Hodder and Staunton, London 1980, p.31
17. Tarrant, V.E. *The Red Orchestra.* Arms and Armour, London 1995 p.173
18. Dallin, David J., *Soviet Intelligence.* Yale University Press, New Haven 1955 p.198
19. Accoce, P. and Quet, P. *The Lucy Ring.* Panther books, London 1967. p.94
20. The National Archives KV 2/1611_3 p.8/82
21. Foote, A. *Handbook for Spies* (1949 ed). Coachwhip Publications 2011, Pennsylvania. p.12
22. Werner, R. *Sonya's Report.* Chatto and Windus, London p.229
23. The National Archives KV 2/1611_2 p.8/64
24. Foote, A. *Handbook for Spies* (1949 ed). Coachwhip Publications 2011, Pennsylvania. p.15

25. Foote, A. *Handbook for Spies* (1949 ed). Coachwhip Publications 2011, Pennsylvania. p.17
26. Read, A. and Fisher, D, *Operation Lucy*. Stoddard and Houghton, London 1980. p.26
27. https://grahamstevenson.me.uk/2008/09/19/peter-kerrigan/
28. Foote, A. *Handbook for Spies* (1949 ed). Coachwhip Publications 2011, Pennsylvania. p.194
29. https://en.wikipedia.org/wiki/Malcolm_Dunbar
30. Foote, A. *Handbook for Spies* (1949 ed). Coachwhip Publications 2011, Pennsylvania. p.19
31. Read, A. and Fisher, D. *Operation Lucy*. Hodder and Staughton, London 1980. Chapter One
32. https://grahamstevenson.me.uk/2008/09/19/fred-copeman/
33. Foote, A. *Handbook for Spies* (1949 ed). Coachwhip Publications 2011, Pennsylvania. p.21
34. https://grahamstevenson.me.uk/2008/09/20/dave-springhall/
35. Foote, A. *Handbook for Spies* (1949 ed). Coachwhip Publications 2011, Pennsylvania. p.20
36. Radó, S. *Codename Dora*. Time Life books, London 1990 p.46
37. McDermott, K. (1995). *Stalinist Terror in the Comintern: New Perspectives*. Journal of Contemporary History, *30*(1), 111–130. http://www.jstor.org/stable/260924
38. Foote, A. *Handbook for Spies* (1949 ed). Coachwhip Publications, Pennsylvania 2011. p.21
39. Read, A. and Fisher, D. *Operation Lucy*. Hodder and Staughton, London 1980. p.160
40. The National Archives KV 2/1611-2 p.53/64
41. A cut out is defined as 'a mutually trusted intermediary, method or channel of communication between agents. Cut outs usually know only the source and destination of the information to be transmitted, not the identities of any other persons involved in the espionage process ... The cut out also isolates the source from the destination, so neither necessarily knows each other.'
42. The National Archives KV 2/1616_1 p.14/82
43. The National Archives KV 2/1613_1 p.25/74
44. Matthews, O. *'An Impeccable Spy: Richard Sorge, Stalin's master agent.'* Bloomsbury, London 2019
45. https://de.wikipedia.org/wiki/Franz_Obermanns
46. Foote, A. *Handbook for Spies* (1949 ed). Coachwhip Publications, Pennsylvania 2011. p.40

47. Werner, R. *Sonya's Report*. Chatto and Windus, London 1991, p.219
48. The National Archives KV 2/1611_2 Saturday morning interview. p.10/60
49. The National Archives KV 2/1611_2. p.40/60
50. Macintyre, B. *Agent Sonya*. Penguin Random House UK, 2020
51. The National Archives KV 2/1616_2 p.32/60
52. Werner, R. *Sonya's Report*. Chatto and Windus, London 1991, p.224
53. Foote, A. *Handbook for Spies* (1949 ed). Coachwhip Publishing 2011 Pennsylvania, p.42
54. Macintyre, B. *Agent Sonya*. Penguin Random House UK, 2020 pp.194–5
55. Ibid., p.180
56. https://en.wikipedia.org/wiki/Léon_Nicole
57. Thomas, L. *Alexander Radó*. Studies in Intelligence Vol 12, No 3 1968
58. The National Archives KV 2/1616_1 p.79/82
59. The National Archives KV 2/1615_2 p.7/133
60. Dallin, D. *Soviet Espionage*. Yale University Press, London 1955. p.182
61. Ibid., p.85
62. https://blog.nationalmuseum.ch/en/2022/01/master-spy-rudolf-roessler/
63. https://en.wikipedia.org/wiki/Rudolf_Roessler
64. https://en.wikipedia.org/wiki/Anatoly_Gurevich Agent Kent was sentenced in 1945 to fifteen years' detention in the USSR. He was rehabilitated in 1990
65. Dallin, D. *Soviet Espionage*. Yale University Press, London 1955. pp.167-81
66. Foote, A. *Handbook for Spies* (1949 ed). Coachwhip Publishing 2011 Pennsylvania, p.47
67. Macintyre, B. *Agent Sonya*. Penguin Random House UK, 2020 p.213
68. https://en.wikipedia.org/wiki/Margrit_Bolli
69. Foote's statement to British intelligence, 1947. The National Archives KV 2/1611_2. p.18/64
70. There is a fascinating interview (in French) with Pünter which was made in the 1970s here: https://www.rts.ch/archives/tv/culture/personnalites-suisses/3468883-punter-alias-pakbo.html
71. Radó, S. *Codename Dora*. Time Life books, London 1990 p.101
72. Foote, A. *Handbook for Spies* (1949 ed). Coachwhip Publishing 2011, Pennsylvania. p.79
73. https://en.wikipedia.org/wiki/Hans_Hausamann
74. Radó, S. *Codename Dora*. Time Life books, London 1990 p.135
75. An interesting account of the complex politics of the period is given in chapter seven of Accoca and Quets book *The Lucy Ring* (1967)

76. Lownie, Andrew. *Stalin's Englishman: The Lives of Guy Burgess*. Hodder & Stoughton London, 2015
77. Accoce, P., Quet, P. *The Lucy Ring*. Panther books, London, 1967 p.108
78. Dallin, D. *Soviet Espionage* Yale University Press, New Haven 1955. p.195
79. West, N. *Unreliable Witness. Espionage myths of the Second World War* Weidenfeld and Nicolson, London 1984. p.55
80. Dallin, D. *Soviet Intelligence* Yale University Press, New Haven 1955 p.202
81. Radó, S. *Codename Dora*. Time Life books, London 1990 p.64
82. Foote, A. *Handbook for Spies* (1949 ed). Coachwhip Publishing 2011, Pennsylvania. p.48
83. Dallin, D. *Soviet Intelligence* Yale University Press, New Haven 1955 p.200
84. https://en.wikipedia.org/wiki/Georgi_Dimitrov
85. Dallin, D. *Soviet Espionage*. Yale University Press, New Haven 1955, p.198
86. Foote, A. *Handbook for Spies* (1949 ed). Coachwhip Publishing 2011, Pennsylvania. p.51
87. https://fr.wikipedia.org/wiki/Pierre_Accoce
88. Accoce, P., Quet, P. *The Lucy Ring*. Fontana books, London, 1967. p.84
89. Foote, A. *Handbook for Spies* (1949 ed). Coachwhip Publishing 2011, Pennsylvania. p.88
90. Dallin, D. *Soviet Espionage*. Yale University Press, New Haven 1955, p.223
91. Ibid., p.186
92. Werner, R. *Sonya's Report*. Chatto and Windus, London 1991. p.219
93. The National Archives KV 2/1612_1. p.39/75
94. Foote, A. *Handbook for Spies* (1949 ed). Coachwhip Publishing 2011, Pennsylvania. p.84
95. Ibid., p.94
96. The National Archives KV 2/1612_4 p.64/71
97. Accoce, P., Quet, P. *The Lucy Ring*. Panther books, London 1967. p.138
98. https://en.wikipedia.org/wiki/Leopold_Trepper
99. https://en.wikipedia.org/wiki/Walter_Schellenberg
100. https://en.wikipedia.org/wiki/Reinhard_Heydrich
101. https://www.rts.ch/archives/tv/information/bonsoir-1969-1970/12396052-portrait-dun-espion-suisse.html
102. The National Archives KV 1612_1 p.26/75
103. Foote, A. *Handbook for Spies* (1949 ed). Coachwhip Press, Pennsylvania 2011. p.129
104. *Gazette de Lausanne* 7 March 1949
105. *Gazette de Lausanne* 9 March 1949

106. Foote, A. *Handbook for Spies* (1949 ed). Coachwhip Publishers, Pennsylvania 2011. p.138
107. The National Archives KV 2/1612_4 p.1/71
108. Pünter, O. *Guerre secrète en pays neutre.* Editions Payot, Lausanne 1967. p.170
109. The National Archives KV 2/1611_2. p.22/64
110. Foote, A. *Handbook for Spies* (1949 ed). Coachwhip Publishers, Pennsylvania 2011. p.152
111. Ibid., p.63
112. The National Archives KV 2/1611_2 p.23/64
113. Macintyre, B. *Agent Sonya* Viking books, London 2020 p.239
114. The National Archives KV 2/1611_3 p.73/82
115. The National Archives KV 2/1611_3 p.23/64
116. Foote, A. *Handbook for Spies* (1949 ed). Coachwhip Publishers, Pennsylvania 2011. p.162
117. Lownie, Andrew. *Stalin's Englishman: The Lives of Guy Burgess.* Hodder & Stoughton. Kindle Edition, Location 5208
118. Foote, A. *Handbook for Spies* (1949 ed). Coachwhip Press, Pennsylvania 2011. p.167
119. Ibid., p.180
120. McConnell, MP. 'The Situation is Once Again Quiet': Gestapo Crimes in the Rhineland, Fall 1944. Central European History. Vol 5, No 1. pp.27-49
121. Foote, A. *Handbook for Spies* (1949 ed). Coachwhip Publishers, Pennsylvania 2011. p.185
122. https://www.net-film.ru/en/film-100747/
123. Jähner, H. *Aftermath: Life in the fallout of the Third Reich.* Penguin Random House, London 2021. Chapter 6
124. The National Archives KV 2/1611_3 p.50/82
125. https://en.wikipedia.org/wiki/Valentine_Vivian
126. The National Archives KV 2/1611_3 p.79/82
127. Ibid., p.53/82
128. https://en.wikipedia.org/wiki/Guy_Liddell
129. The National Archives KV 2/1611_3 p.4/82
130. The National Archives KV 2/1611_2 p.4/64
131. The National Archives KV 2/1613_1. p.24/74
132. The National Archives KV 2/1611_3 p.35/82
133. Dallin, D. *Soviet Espionage.* Yale University Press, London 1955. p.231
134. The National Archives KV 2/1611_1 p.24/60

135. The National Archives KV 2/1611_3 p.6/82
136. The National Archives KV 2/1611_2 p.8/64
137. Ibid., p.9/64
138. Ibid., p.13/64
139. A video interview (in French) of Edmond Hamel in his shop can be found at: https://www.rts.ch/play/tv/redirect/detail/12396052
140. The National Archives KV 2/1611_1 p.41/60
141. Kesaris, P. *The Rote Kapelle*. University Publications of America, Washington, 1979 p.185
142. https://www.nsa.gov/portals/75/documents/news-features/declassified-documents/cryptologic-spectrum/german_intercept.pdf
143. Quoted in: (b)3(3)(c) (Author). *Sándor Radó The Jovial and Worldly Spy*. Studies In Intelligence, Vol 30, Spring 1986. Declassified 09/02/2014. p.9
144. https://en.wikipedia.org/wiki/Gavril_Myasnikov
145. https://grahamstevenson.me.uk/2009/03/08/george-aitken-sp-1533623727/
146. Dallin, D. *Soviet Espionage*. Yale University Press, New York 1955. pp.223-8
147. The National Archives KV 2/1611_1 p.22/60
148. https://en.wikipedia.org/wiki/Ignace_Reiss
149. The National Archives KV 2/1611_1 p.15/60
150. Read, A. Fisher, D. *Operation Lucy*. Hodder and Stoughton, London 1980. p.219
151. The National Archives KV 2/1612_4 p.62/71
152. https://heatholdboys.org.uk/obits/Hemblys-Scales_R.html
153. The National Archives KV 2/1612_4. p.47/71
154. Ibid., p.68/71
155. The National Archives KV 2/1613_3. p.20/80
156. The National Archives KV 2/1614. p.89/107
157. Ibid., p.16/107
158. The National Archives KV 2/1611_3 p.56/82
159. The National Archives KV 2/1615_2. p.9/133
160. The National Archives KV 2/1615_1. p.7/94
161. Ibid., p.11/82
162. https://heatholdboys.org.uk/obits/Hemblys-Scales_R.html
163. O'Reilly, D. *Interrogating the Gestapo: SS-Sturmbannführer Horst Kopkow, the Rote Kapelle and Post-war British Security Interests*, Journal of Intelligence History, 2023 22:2, 192-215
164. The National Archives KV 2/1613_2. p.7/80
165. The National Archives KV 2/1614. p.75/107

166. The National Archives KV 2/1615_1. p.16/94
167. https://en.wikipedia.org/wiki/Charlotte_Haldane
168. The National Archives KV 2/1615_1. p.51/94
169. https://www.mi5.gov.uk/sir-roger-hollis
170. https://en.wikipedia.org/wiki/Claud_Cockburn
171. https://en.wikipedia.org/wiki/Tom_Driberg
172. https://en.wikipedia.org/wiki/Maurice_Richardson
173. https://www.iwp.edu/wp-content/uploads/2015/04/20150417_ReportandChronologyHollis.pdf
174. Mathews, O. *An Impeccable Spy: Richard Sorge, Stalin's Master Agent.* Bloomsbury, London 2019 p.80
175. https://en.wikipedia.org/wiki/Arthur_Ewert
176. https://www.iwp.edu/wp-content/uploads/2015/04/20150417_ReportandChronologyHollis.pdf
177. https://fbistudies.com/wp-content/uploads/2015/04/20150417_ReportandChronologyHollis.pdf
178. Werner, R. *Sonya's Report.* Chatto and Windus, London 1977 p.229
179. Pincher, C. *Too Secret Too Long.* Lume Books. Kindle Edition p.62
180. Werner, R. *Sonya's Report.* Chatto and Windus, London 1977 p.289
181. The National Archives KV 2/1611 p.79/82
182. The National Archives KV 2/1611_2 p.17/24
183. The National Archives KV 2/1611_2 p.52/64
184. https://en.wikipedia.org/wiki/Tube_Alloys
185. Burke, D. *The Spy Who Came In From The Co-Op.* Boydell Press, Woodbridge, 2008
186. Werner, R. *Sonya's Report.* Chatto and Windus, London 1991 p.279
187. Radó, S, *Codename Dora. (Foreword)*, Time Life Books, 1990
188. Foote, A. *Handbook for Spies* (1949 ed.). Coachwhip Books, Pennsylvania 2011 p.79
189. Tarrant, V.E. *The Red Orchestra.* Arms and Armour, 1995.
190. Accoce, P., Quet, P. *The Lucy Ring.* Panther, London 1967 p.64
191. Tarrant, V.E. *The Red Orchestra.* Arms and Armour London 1995 p.159
192. West, N. *Unreliable Witness: Espionage Myths of the Second World War* Weidenfeld and Nicolson, London 1984 p.59
193. https://en.wikipedia.org/wiki/Hans_Bernd_Gisevius
194. https://blog.nationalmuseum.ch/en/2022/01/master-spy-rudolf-roessler/
195. Accoce, P., Quet, P. *The Lucy Ring.* Panther Books, London, 1967
196. Read, A, Fisher, D. *Operation Lucy.* Stodder and Houghton, London 1980

197. Jeffery, K. *MI6: The History of the Secret Intelligence Service.* Bloomsbury London, 2010 p.314
198. Read, A. Fisher, D. *Operation Lucy.* Stodder and Houghton, London 1980 p.22
199. http://www.coldspur.com/Sonyas-radio/
200. Dallin, D. *Soviet Espionage.* Yale University Press, London 1955. p.202
201. Tarrant, V.E. *The Red Orchestra.* Arms and Armour London 1995 p.170
202. Cairncross, John. *The Enigma Spy: The Story of the Man who Changed the Course of World War Two* Lume Books. Kindle Edition. p.127
203. Jeffery, K. *MI6: The History of the Secret Intelligence Service.* Bloomsbury London, 2010 p.380
204. Dallin, D. *Soviet Espionage.* Yale University Press, New York, 1955. p.226
205. Foote, A. *Handbook for Spies* (1949 ed.). Coachwhip Books, Pennsylvania 2011 p.162
206. http://www.coldspur.com/sonias-radio/ Section 4. *Foote's awareness of Lucy*
207. Burke, D. *The Spy Who Came In From The Co-Op.* Boydell Press, Cambridge 2008
208. The National Archives KV 2/1611_1 p.22/60
209. Muggeridge, M. *The Infernal Grove.* Fontana, London 1973. p.208
210. http://www.coldspur.com/sonias-radio/
211. Lownie, Andrew. *Stalin's Englishman: The Lives of Guy Burgess.* Hodder & Stoughton. Kindle Edition. Location 6000

Index

Abwehr, 74-81, 85, 120
Accoce P and Quet P, 8, 47, 65, 76, 77, 82, 99, 162, 163, 166, 187
   opinion of Foote, 8
Aitken, George, 124
Albert, Agent, *See* Radó, Sándor
Argentina, 100, 103, 175, 177, 179
Attlee, Clement, 10, 116
Avoceta, 41

Barbarossa, Operation, 49, 52, 65
Barber, Charles, 3
Barbie, Klaus, 2, 75
Barnes, Corporal, 12, 13, 124
Beurton, Len, 9, 18, 40
   arrival in Switzerland, 27-9
   as John Miller, 41
   evacuation from Switzerland 42
   "lovelorn newlywed", 41
   marriage to Sonya, 29-34
   zeppelin fire plot, 28
Bletchley Park, 166, 167, 170, 171, 175
Blunt, Anthony, 107
Bodinger, Sergeant, 108
Bolli, Margaret, 117, 120, 147, 148,
   See also Rosy, Agent
Brand-Roth, Madame, 21
British Union of Fascists, 136
BUPO, Bundespolizei, 79, 80, 81, 85
Burgess, Guy, 48, 97, 107, 150, 181, 187

Burke, David, 156
Buro Ha, 47, 64, 65, 164

Cairncross, John, 171, 186
Cambridge Five, 48, 49, 107, 110
Casa, The, 2, 184
Catholic Church, 143, 188
Centre, Moscow, 22, 39, 45, 49, 69, 71, 78, 83, 85, 88, 90, 92, 97, 102, 104, 131, 156, 158, 162
   and Lorenz and Laura, 73-5
   Sonya's evacuation from Switzerland, 34, 153
   Len Beurton's evacuation, 117
   and the Red Orchestra, 38
   suspicions of Lucy, 48
   suspicions of Foote, 174
   transmission schedules, 43, 53, 59, 60
Churchill, Clementine, 127
Churchill, Winston, 113, 184, 188
Cimperman, Mr
   requests for Foote's services, 139
Clemetson, Agnes May, 183
Clifton Gardens, 132, 182
Cockburn, Claude, 151
Codename Dora, 37, 38, 66, 83, 167, 170 *See also* Radó, Sándor, Autobiography
Comintern, 36, 59, 152
Communist Party, 9, 124, 188

Index

British, 9, 10, 13, 14, 17, 143, 168, 178, 189
British, Gosport area, 12
British, Portsmouth area, 12
French, 90, 94
Geneva, 148
German, 20, 80, 95, 100, 102, 152
Soviet Union, 184
Spanish, 9
Swiss, 40, 59, 67, 71, 72, 79, 80, 83, 85, 147
Copeman, Fred, 13-18, 143, 167

Daily Express, 150
Daily Worker, 13, 151
Dallin, David, 36, 37, 40, 54, 112, 144, 170, 173
  opinion of Foote, 8
Dansey, Colonel Claude, 109, 167, 168, 169, 171
Deonna, M, 148
Department Z (Also Z Organisation), 109, 167, 169, 172
Der Spiegel, 50, 182
Dimitrov, Georgi, 59
Director, The, 22, 45, 49, 62, 72, 74, 84, 85, 98, 99, 102, 117, 124, 174
Dora, Agent, 36, 84 *See also* Radó, Sándor
Dübendorfer, Rachel, 46, 48, 66, 171-3, 78, 89, 138, 147, 171, 188, *See also* Sissy, Agent
Dunbar, Malcolm, 15, 113

Edouard, Agent *See* Hamel, Edmond
Enigma machine, 163, 171, 175
Ewart, Arthur, 152

Farrell, Victor, 42, 117
Foote, Alexander Allan
  and Franz Obermanns arrest, 25-6
  and Agnes Zimmerman, 21-4
  and accusations against Roger Hollis
    See Pincher, Chapman
  anti semitic views, 10, 178
  apartment, Chemin de Longeraie, 51-2, 55
  arrest, 42, 71
  attempted abduction by Abwehr, 74-5
  autobiography, 14, 19, 41, 78, 81, 92, 108, 111, 124, 153, *See also Handbook for Spies*
  confession to the Swiss, 86, 87, 108
  disillusionment, 92, 179
  enigmatic figure to Swiss friends, 52, 56-8
  experience of Life in Moscow, 96-102, 126
  experiences in Spain, 17
  financing the Rote Drei, 67-73
  in Germany, 28-9
  Hitler assassination plot, 28
  home life, 1-7
  interrogation in Moscow, 97, 98, 121-5, 173-4
  Lorenz and Laura, suspicious of, 58-9, 73, 75, 85, 186
  marriage of convenience, 30-1
  medical problems, 100, 116, 124, 137, 175, 182, 183
  military rank and honours, 61, 91, 126, 127
  moves to Lausanne, 40
  personal qualities, 713-16
  political views, 9-13

post war career prospects, 113, 137, 165, 134-8, 181
prison sentence, 87
radio transmission schedule, 27, 53-4, 58
recruitment into espionage, 16-19
relations with police, 56, 132, 182
relationship with Radó, 42, 69, 78
Wake Arms, The, 34
Foote, William, Father, 3
Forde, Corporal, 128 See also Foote, Alexander Allan
Franco, General, 14
Fuchs, Klaus, 35, 151, 158-60, 177

Gazette de Lausanne, 7, 37, 56, 57, 86, 87, 133, 142, 146, 148
GDR, 31, 73, 156, 160
Geopress, 37, 39, 90, 111
Gisevius, Hans Bernd, 164
Gouzenko, Igor, 72, 125
Granatoff, Major, See Foote, Alexander Allan
Guatemala, Republic of, 87, 179
Guerre secrète en pays neutre, See Pünter, Otto
Guisan, General, 47, 65
Gwyer, John, 137, 142

Haldane, Charlotte, 143
Hamburger, Rudolph, 20, 30-2, 95, 119, 188
Hamel, Edmond, 40, 41, 42, 63, 79, 80, 85, 89, 105, 148, 168
Hamel, Olga, 40, 53, 120
Hamels, 40, 42, 43, 50, 54, 69, 79, 80, 81, 85, 88, 117, 119, 138, 147, 148, 179

Handbook for Spies, 46, 92, 140-53, 159, 162, 176
Hausamann, Major Hans, 47, 65
Hemblys-Scales, RV, 132, 134, 140
Hermann, Agent, See Obermanns, Franz
Heydrich, Reinhard, 77
Himmler, Heinrich, 77, 121
Hinsley, Professor F.H., 171
Hollis, Roger, 25, 105, 106, 107, 110, 111, 128, 150-60, 169
Hotel Central, Lausanne, 34, 88, 129, 136
Humbert-Droz, Jules, 59, 147

Independent Labour Party, 18, 28
Institute of World Politics, 156
International Brigade, 5, 10-16, 26, 28, 112, 114, 143
International Labour Organisation, 46, 68, 89, 171
Ivan the interpreter, 96, 98, 101, 113, 123, 126
Ivanov, 121, See also Trepper, Leopold

Jaquillard, Colonel, 76
Jeffery, Keith, 168, 172
Jim, Comrade, 1, 5, 6, 18, 19, 35, 55, 56, 66, 78, 85, 98, 153, See also Foote, Alexander Allan

Kent, Agent, 39, 69, 75
Kerrigan, Peter, 14, 114
King Street, 12, 17, 28, See also Communist Party, The
Kirkdale, See Liverpool
Knecht, Inspector, 86, 87, 182

Koestler, Arthur, 188
Kommunistische Partei Deutschland (KPD), 20, 25, 32, 36
Koulichev, *See* Radó, Sándor
Kuczynski, Jürgen, 20, 119, 155
Kuczynski, Ursula, *See* Sonya, Agent
Kursk, Battle of, 1, 50, 54, 61, 77, 171

La guerre a été gagnée en Suisse, 63, 164, *See also* Accoce P and Quet P
Lapidus, Alfred, 94, 122, *See also* Foote, Alexander Allan
Le Figaro, 142, 146
Lenin, 39, 85, 94, 99, 122, 185
Lewis, Brigitte née Kuczynski, 17-20, 115, 139, 157
Liddell, Guy, 107
Liverpool, 2-5, 41, 49, 109, 153, 184, 188
Long group, The, 45, 48, 50, 88, 90, 160, 186
Lorenz and Laura, 58, 59, 73-5, 78, 186
Louise, Agent, 45
Lownie, Andrew, 48, 187
Lucy, Agent, 46-50, 54, 66, 84, 85, 89, 90, 91, 98, 119, 120, 149, 160-6, 170, 171, 173, 175, *See also* Rössler, Rudolph
Luna Park Hotel, 94

Macintyre, 5, 33, 152
Maclean, Donald, 97, 107, 150, 181
Manhattan project, 151
Marriott, John, 105, 136
Masson, Brigadier Roger, 65, 77
Matthews, Owen, 152
Maude, *See* Hamel, Olga
Max, Agent, 21, 59, 147

May, Agent, 59, 61
MI5, 5
Miasnikov, 94, 121, 122
Molotov-Ribbentrop pact, 29, 115, 154, 155
Moral Rearmament, 143
Muggeridge, Malcolm, 2, 14, 187
  critique of *The Lucy Ring*, 64
  opinion of Foote, 7, 10, 182
  theory about the 'Lucy' source, 164-7, 170
Müller, Albert, *See* Foote, Alexander Allan
Müller, Anna, 78, 21, 22, 24
Murmansk convoys, 188
Muth, Olga 'Ollo', 33, 119

Nazi-Soviet pact, *See* Molotov-Ribbentrop pact
News Review, 143
Nicole, L, 34, 148
Nicole, Pierre, 78, 130, 148
Norwood, Melita, 35, 156, 158, 177
Novikov, Lieutenant Colonel, 90, 91

Obermanns, Franz, 25-7
  Service record, 26
OKW (Oberkommando der Wehrmacht), 37, 50, 64, 161
Olga, OKW source, 47, 64, 120
Operation Lucy, 6, 16, 109, 181, 183, 184, 185, 182, *See also* Read A. and Fisher D.
Order of Lenin, 85, 99
Order of the Red Banner, 127
Osborne S. Reggio-Browne, 136, 137
Ottawa debacle, 72, 125, 138

Paine, Joan, 109
Pakbo, 45, 71, 82, 83, 88, 89, 91, 98, 99
   See also Pünter, Otto
Pakbo group, The, 43, 45, 88, 90, 160, 171, 186
Parti du Travail, 34, 130, 148, 149
Pasche, Inspector, 86
Payot, Marc, 82, 86, 142, 145
Percy, Tony, 34, 170, 176
Peters, Hans, 81, 89
Philby, HAR (Kim), 105, 106, 107, 136, 137, 150, 155
Phillips, Bill, *See* Beurton, Len
Pincher, Chapman, 34, 150, 151-4
Pollitt, Harry, 113
Powell, Margaret, Sister, 3, 4, 10, 23, 130, 131, 135, 137, 168, 169, 183, 185
   Concern for Agnes Zimmerman, 23-4
Pünter, Otto, 43, 45, 61, 82, 168, 186, 187

Radó, Hélène, 35, 36, 53, 85
   as Maria Arnold, 35
Radó, Sándor, 37-9, 40, 42, 46, 47, 48, 55, 60, 67, 73, 77, 81, 88, 113, 119, 127, 147, 163, 170, 176
   and the Red Orchestra, 38, 39
   arrest attempt, 83
   autobiography, 45, 145, 185
   background, 36, 37-8
   Codename Dora, 66, 83, 160, 168, 170, 187
   contact with Lucy, 46-8, 50, 52, 164, 165, 168

contact with the British, 83, 84, 102, 114, 173, 192
critique of *Handbook for Spies*, 145, 186
disappearence in Cairo, 94-6, 116, 125, 174
financial accounts, 68-71, 117, 124
first contact with Sonya, 34, 40, 156
gone underground, 85, 149, 153
Paris, 90-3, 123
on Foote's politics, 18, 19, 29
opinion of Foote, 8, 58, 63
Order of Lenin, 103
security concerns, 78, 80, 82, 94, 96
soviet mistrust of Lucy material, 48, 120, 161, 162, 170
trial and sentence, Soviet, 99, 102, 174, 188
trial and sentence, Swiss, 89
See also Dora, Agent and Albert, Agent
RAF, 12, 17, 106, 111, 113, 124, 128, 169, 189
Rathbone, Eleanor, 41, 119
Read A and Fisher D, 3, 4, 13, 14, 15, 28, 109, 110, 120, 130, 167, 169, 170, 171, 182, 187
Red Joan, 158
Red Orchestra, The, 38, 39, 43, 51, 95, 177, 188
Red Orchestra (book), 7, 170, 184
   See aslo Tarrant V.E.
Reiss, Ignatz, 127
Richardson, Maurice, 151
Rimm, Karl, 152
Rimm, Luisa, 152
Robert Hale, publishers, 133, 140, 141

Romeo, Agent *See* Peters, Hans
Romilly, Giles, 113
Rössler, Rudolph, 37, 38, 46-8, 50, 54, 72, 110, *See also* Lucy, Agent
   remuneration, 68
   links with Swiss intelligence, 47, 64, 66
   meeting with Foote, 89
   volume of material, 48, 160-6
Rosy, Agent, 50, 88, 89, 117, 146, 147
   arrest, 80, 81
   and Abwehr agent Romeo, 80
   courier for Foote, 53
   recruitment, 42
Rote Drei, 38, 40, 42-6, 53, 67, 76, 82, 110, 120, 130, 138, 155, 160, 166, 177
Rote Kapelle, *See* Red Orchestra, The
Rugby Mansions, 128

Salter, Agent, 83, 84, 99
Saville, Mr, 114, 135, 140, *See also* Serpell, Michael
Schellenberg, SS Brigadegeneral Walter, 77
Schneider, Christian, 46, 48, 66, 68, 120, *See also* Taylor, Agent
Schnieper, friend of Rudolph Rössler, 164
Scott, Winston M., 105, 131
Serpell, Michael, 105, 109, 110, 111, 113-26, 128, 130-41, 155, 157, 159, *See also* Saville, Mr and Sonya, Agent
   on Foote's politics, 9, 114
   opinion of Foote, 109
Shanghai, 25, 151, 152, 154

Shanghai Post, 151
Shillito, Hugh, 96
Sissy, Agent, 9, 38, 60, 66, 71, 72, 78, 88, 89, 102, 125, 126, 138, 171 *See also* Dübendorfer, Rachel
Skardon, Jim, 159
Smedley, Agnes, 151, 152
Sokulov, Victor, 39, *See also* Kent, Agent
Sonya, Agent, 30, 38, 39, 40, 115, 117, 185, 186
   and Franz Obermanns arrest, 26, 27
   at La Taupinière, 29
   autobiography, 9, 155
   career in espionage, 25
   evacuation from Switzerland, 32-4
   Finnish war, 159
   Hamburger by marriage, 20, 30
   Hollis controversy, 106, 150-60
   meets Len Beurton, 27-30
   marriage of convenience, 119, 30-2
   on Foote's politics, 9, 18, 20
   opinion of Foote, 6, 144
   reaction to Molotov-Ribbentrop pact, 30
   recruitment of Foote, 18
   resumes career in Oxfordshire, 41, 139, 177-80
Sonya's Report, 69, 144, 154
Sorge, Richard, 25, 60, 151, 152
Spanish Civil War, 2, 12, 33, 124
Springhall, Dave, 14, 17, 113, 114
Spycatcher, 106, *See also* Wright, Peter
Stalin, Josef, 14, 55, 60, 99, 112, 122, 158, 171, 186, 188
Stalingrad, Battle of, 1, 48, 50, 54, 61, 66, 77, 170

Staples, Captain Anthony, 152
Stiassny, Anne, Sister, 131, 134
Sunday Sun, 144
Sviattsky, Herzel, 129, 132
Swiss Socialist Party, 43

Tarrant, V.E., 7, 163, 170, 171
Taylor, Agent, 38, 46, 48, 66, 68, 120
Teddy, OKW source, 47, 64, 120
Thaëlmann, Ernst, 32
The Enigma Spy: The Story of the Man Who Changed the Course of World War Two, 171, 186, See also Cairncross, John
The Lucy Ring, 63, 77, See also Accoce P and Quet P
The Observer, 64, 164, 170
The Red Orchestra, 7, 170, 184, See also Tarrant, V.E.
The Wake Arms, 34, 157
Their Trade is Treachery, 150, See also Pincher, Chapman
Thistlethaite, R, 142
Thorez, Maurice, 94
Too Secret Too Long, 157 See also Pincher, Chapman
Trepper, Leopold, 121, 188
Tribune de Genève, 81
Trotsky, Leon, 94
Tube Alloys, 158

Uhlman, Fred, 17
Ultra, 166, 167, 170, 171, 172

Unreliable Witness: Espionage Myths of the Second World War, 161, See also West, Nigel

Vera, Major, 71, 96, 102, 103, 117, 121, 124, 125, 173, 174
Vesey, D, 133, 138, 140-3, 149, 176, See also Robert Hale, publishers
Vigier, Jean Pierre, 138
Villa Stutz, 64, See also Buro Ha
Vivian, Colonel, 155
Vladimir, 129
VYRDO messages, 49, 50, 54

Weber, Frau, 104, 122, 123
Werner, Ruth, See Sonya, Agent
Werther, OKW source, 47, 62, 64, 120
West London Observer, 181
West, Nigel, 50, 161, 163
Williams, Archie Campbell, 12
Willis, Bernard, 142, See also Young, Courtenay
Wintringham, Tom, 113
Wright, Peter, 106, 107

Young, Courtenay, 92, 137, 142, 175

Z Organisation, 168, 169, 172
Zimmerman, Agnes, 21-4, 117, 122, 123, 127, 137, 172
　Inge, Agent 23-4
　Marianne, Agnes' sister, 23
　Mikki, Agent, 21, 22, 122